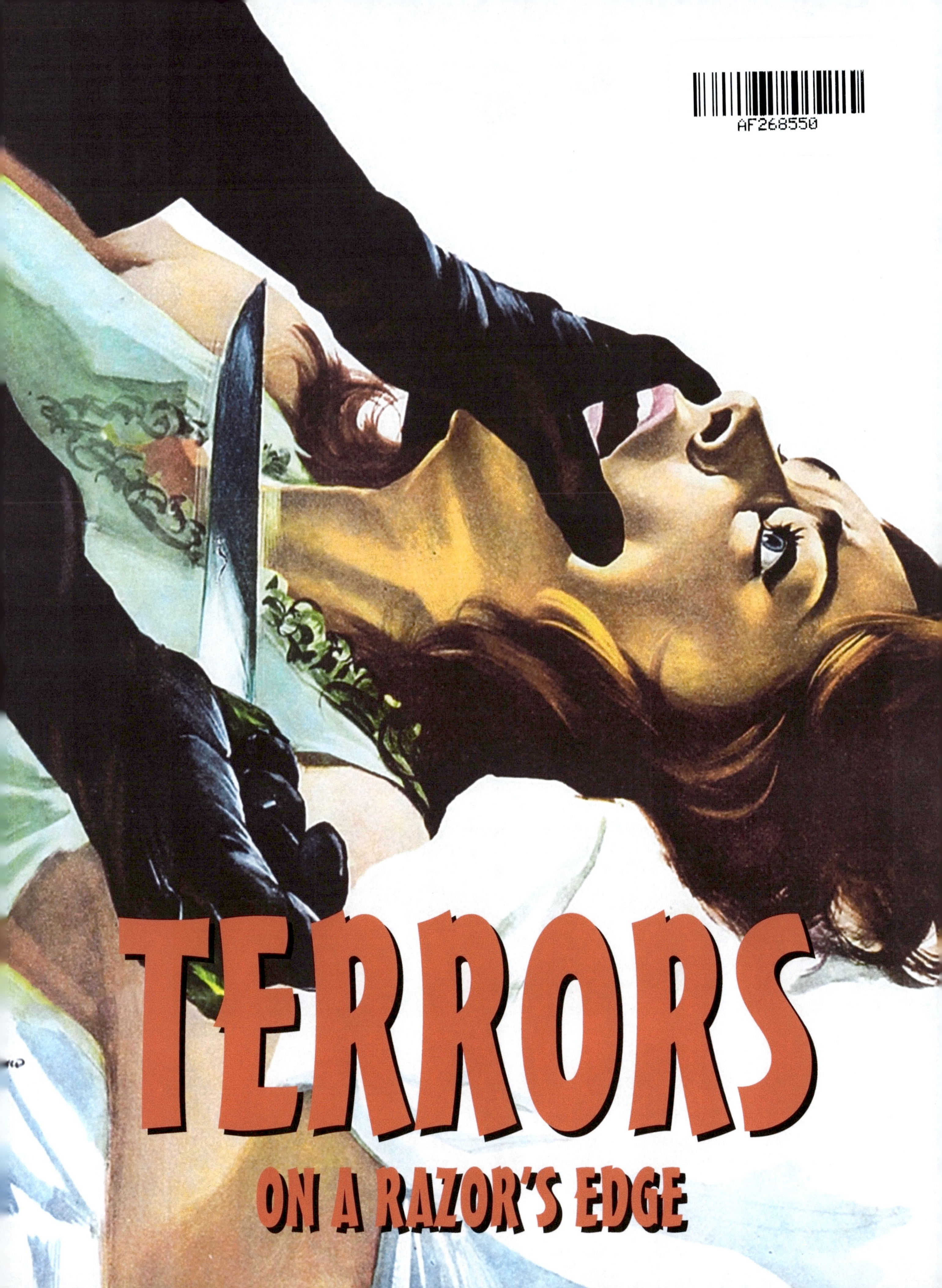
AF268550
TERRORS
ON A RAZOR'S EDGE

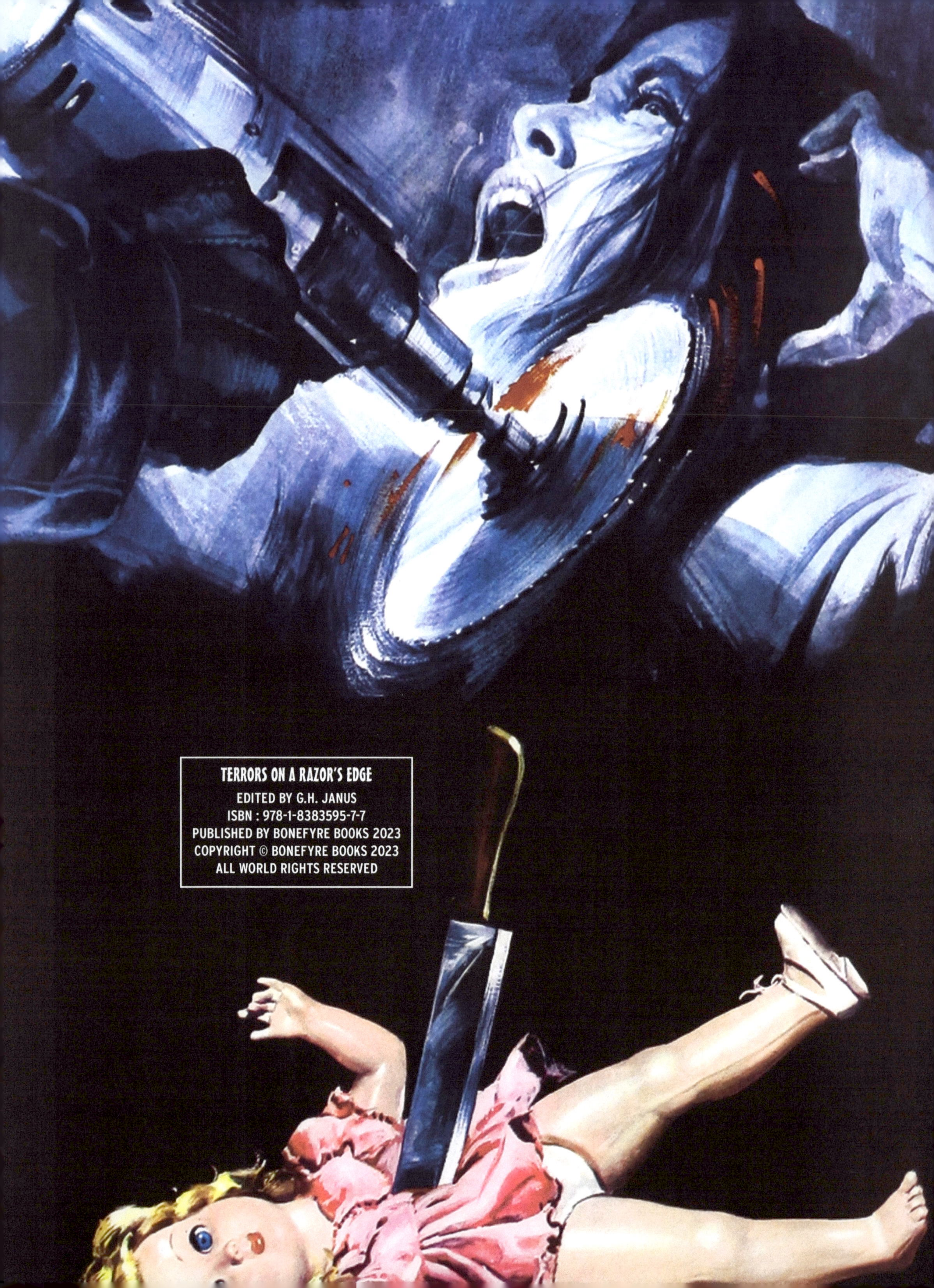
TERRORS ON A RAZOR'S EDGE
EDITED BY G.H. JANUS
ISBN : 978-1-8383595-7-7
PUBLISHED BY BONEFYRE BOOKS 2023
COPYRIGHT © BONEFYRE BOOKS 2023
ALL WORLD RIGHTS RESERVED

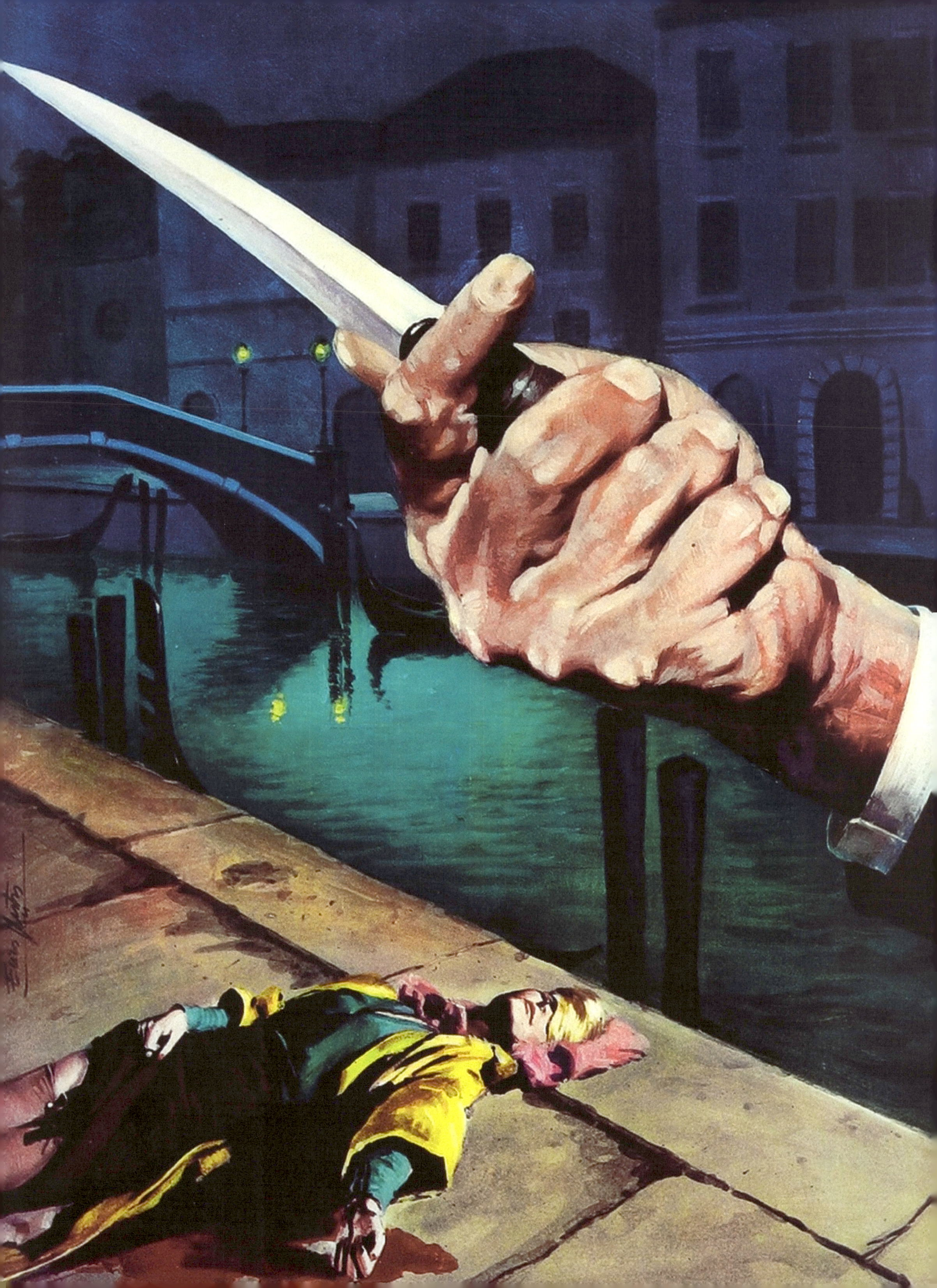

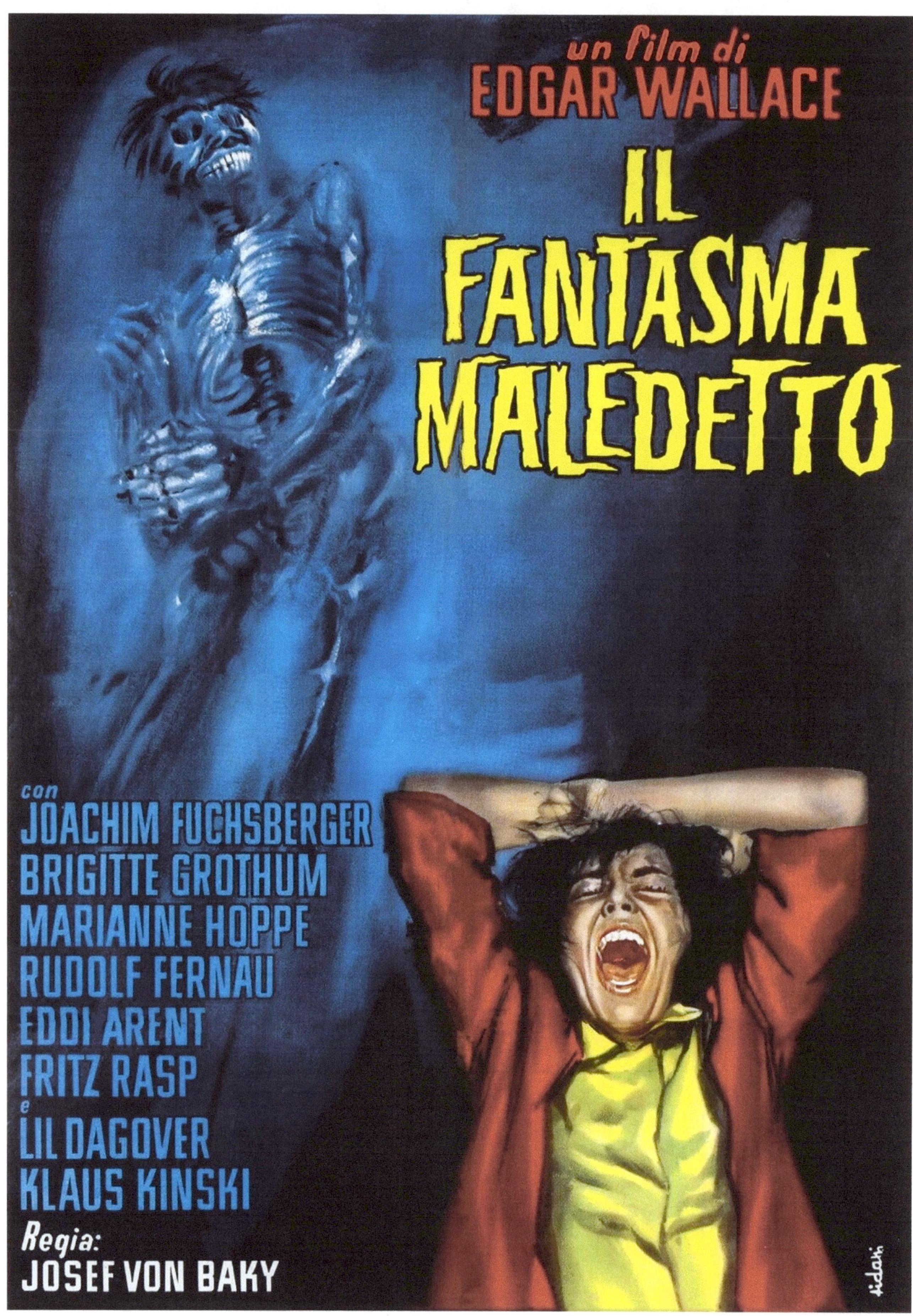

IL FANTASMA MALEDETTO

("The Accursed Phantom"; Germany, 1961). Artist: Fidani. Original Title: **Die Seltsame Gräfin.**

6

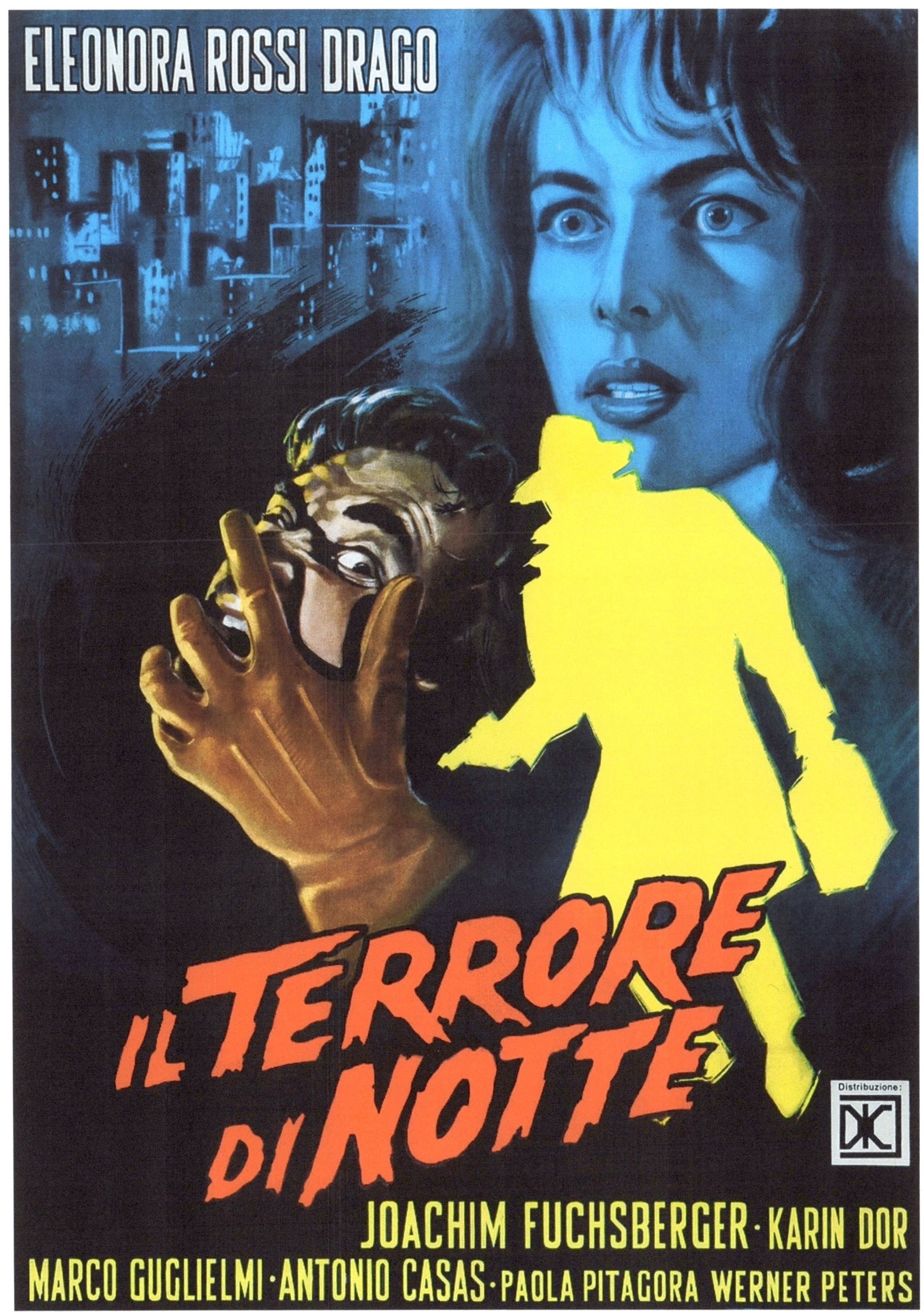

("The Night Terror"; Germany/Spain/Italy, 1962). Artist: unsigned. Original Title: **Der Teppich Des Grauens.**

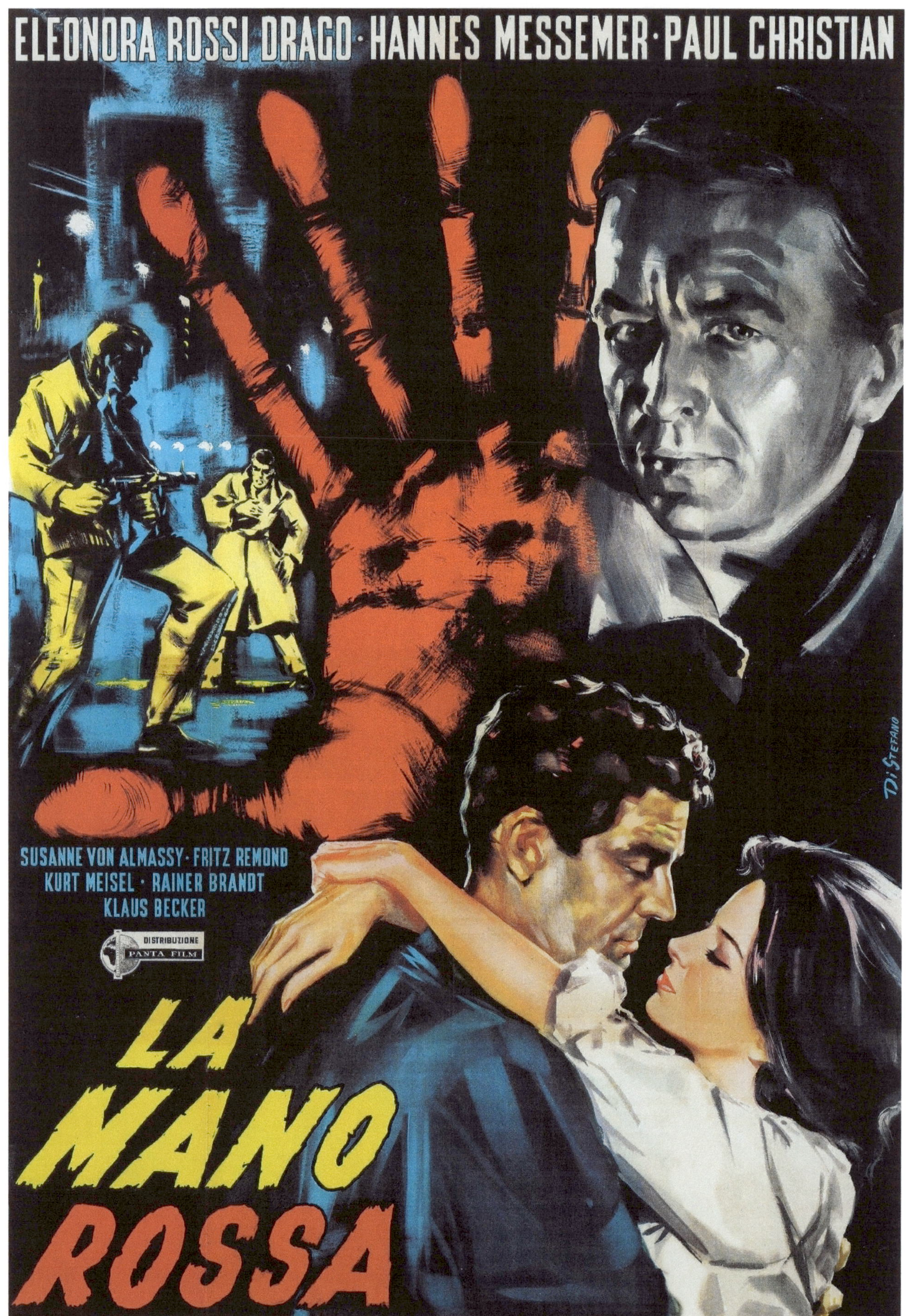

LA MANO ROSSA

("The Red Hand"; Italy/Germany, 1960). Artist: Giovanni Di Stefano. Original Title: **Die Rote Hand.**

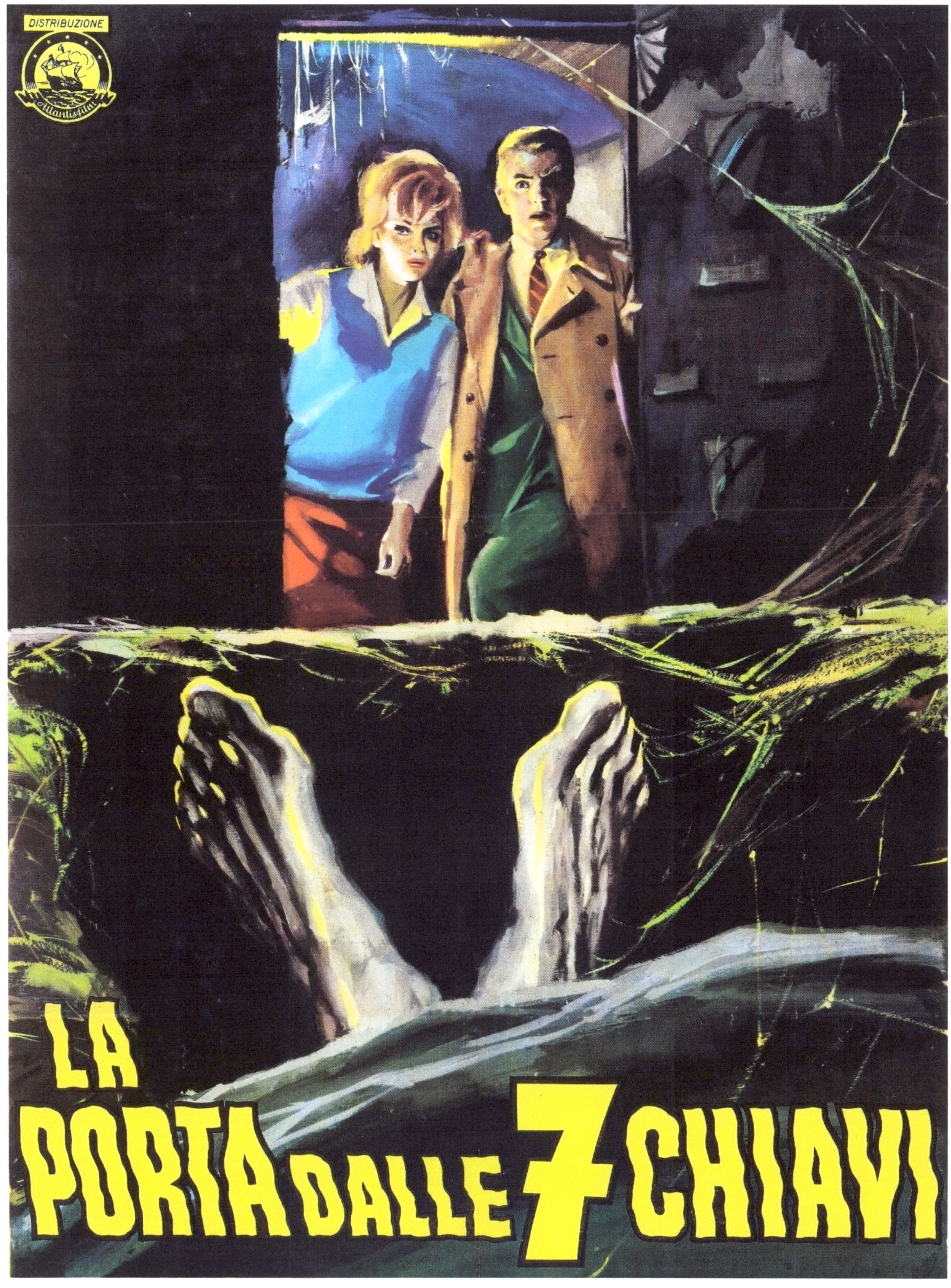

LA PORTA DALLE 7 CHIAVI
("The Door With 7 Keys"; Germany/France, 1962). Artist: unsigned. Original Title: **Die Tür Mit Den 7 Schlössern.**

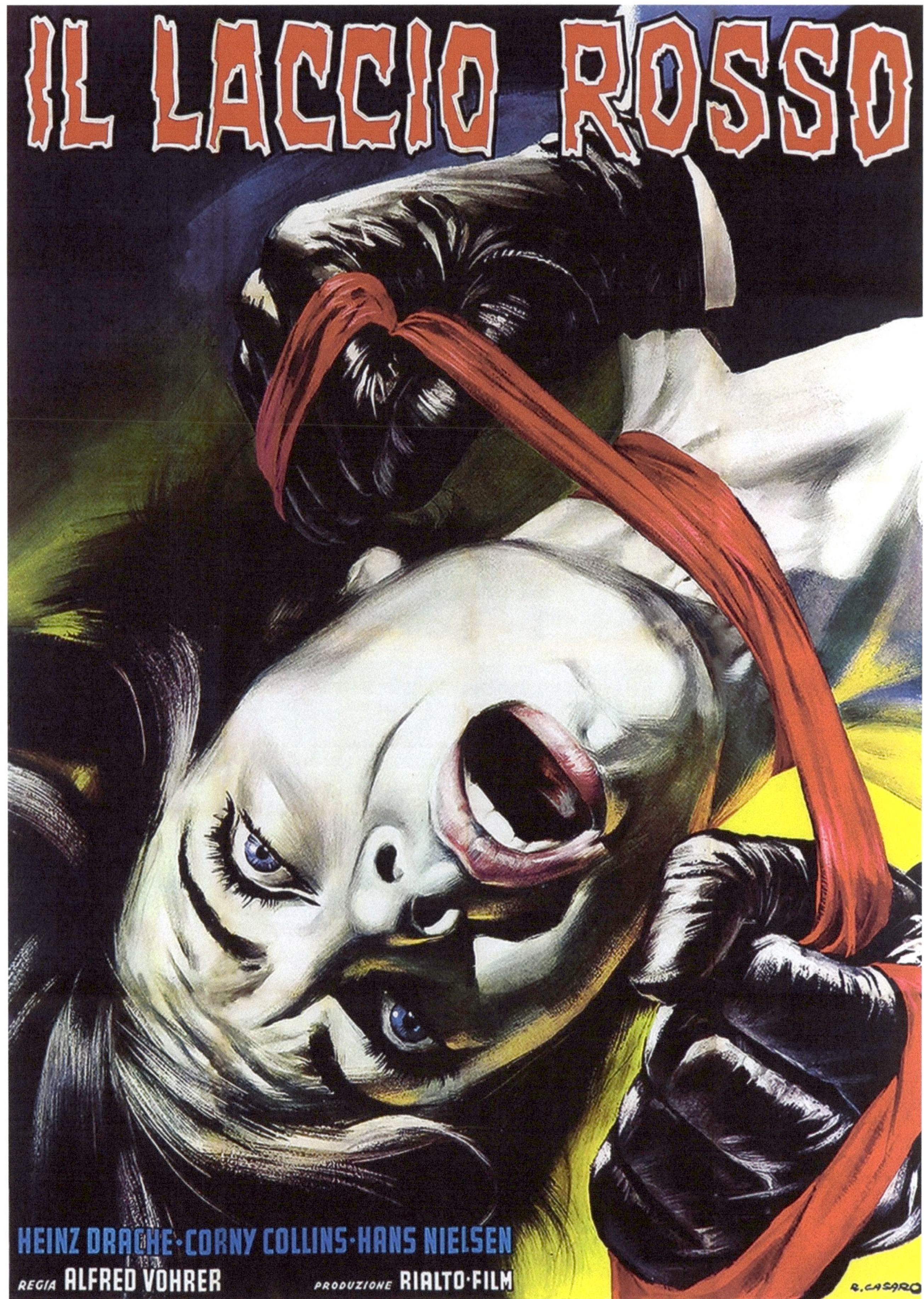

IL LACCIO ROSSO

(''The Red Snare''; Germany, 1963). Artist: Renato Casaro. Original Title: **Das Indische Tuch.**

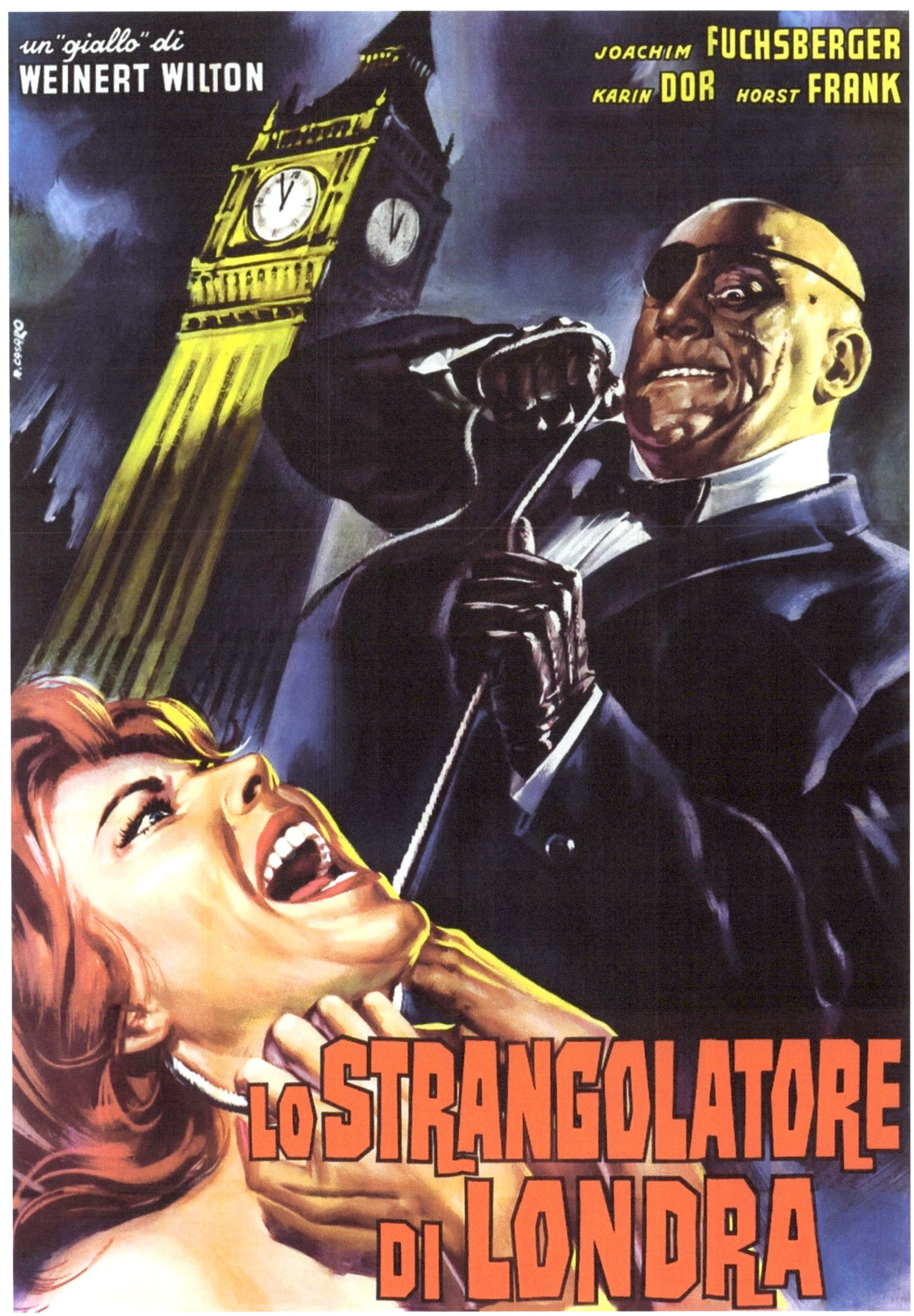

LO STRANGOLATORE DI LONDRA

("The London Strangler"; Germany, 1963). Artist: Renato Casaro. Original Title: **Die Weiße Spinne.**

11

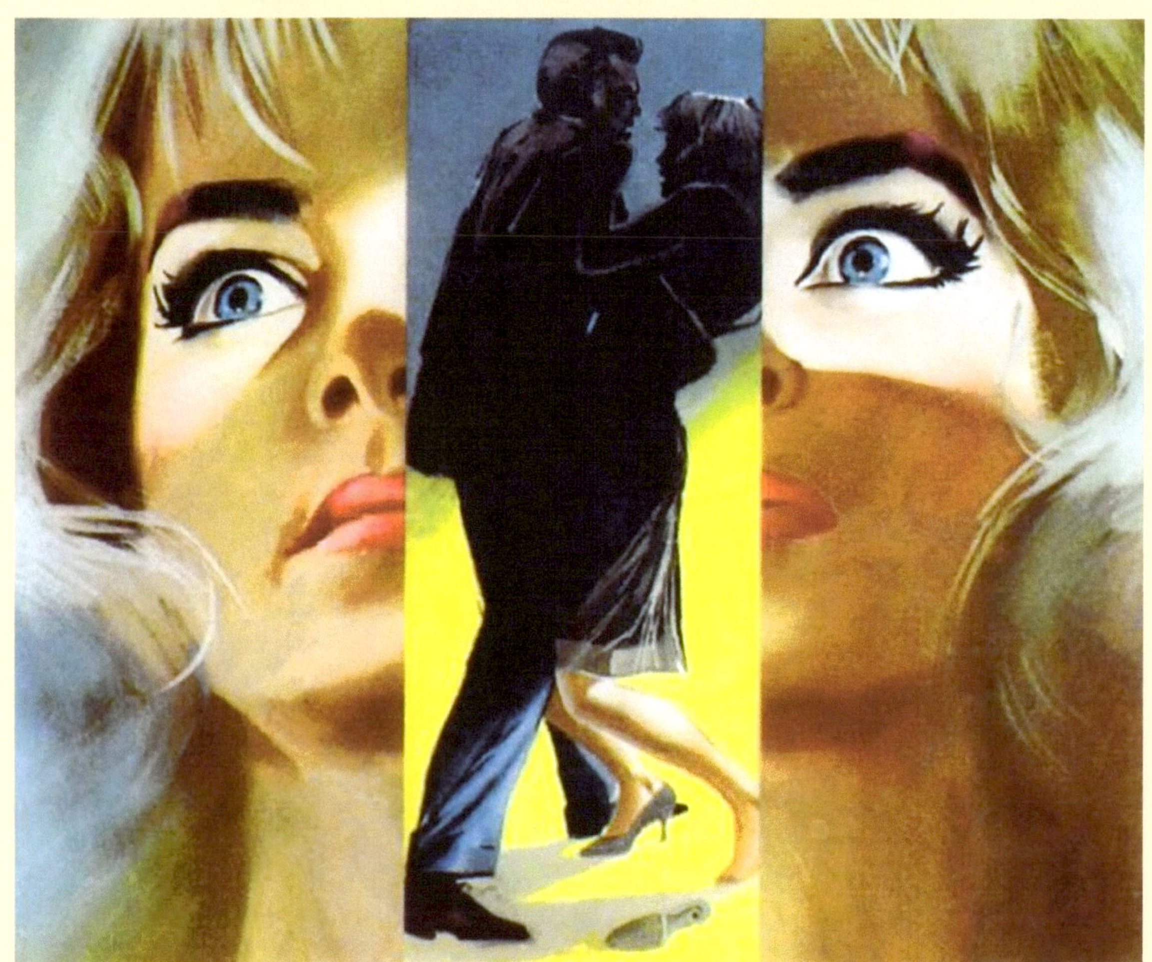

LA RAGAZZA CHE SAPEVA TROPPO

("The Girl Who Knew Too Much"; Italy, 1963). Artist: unsigned.

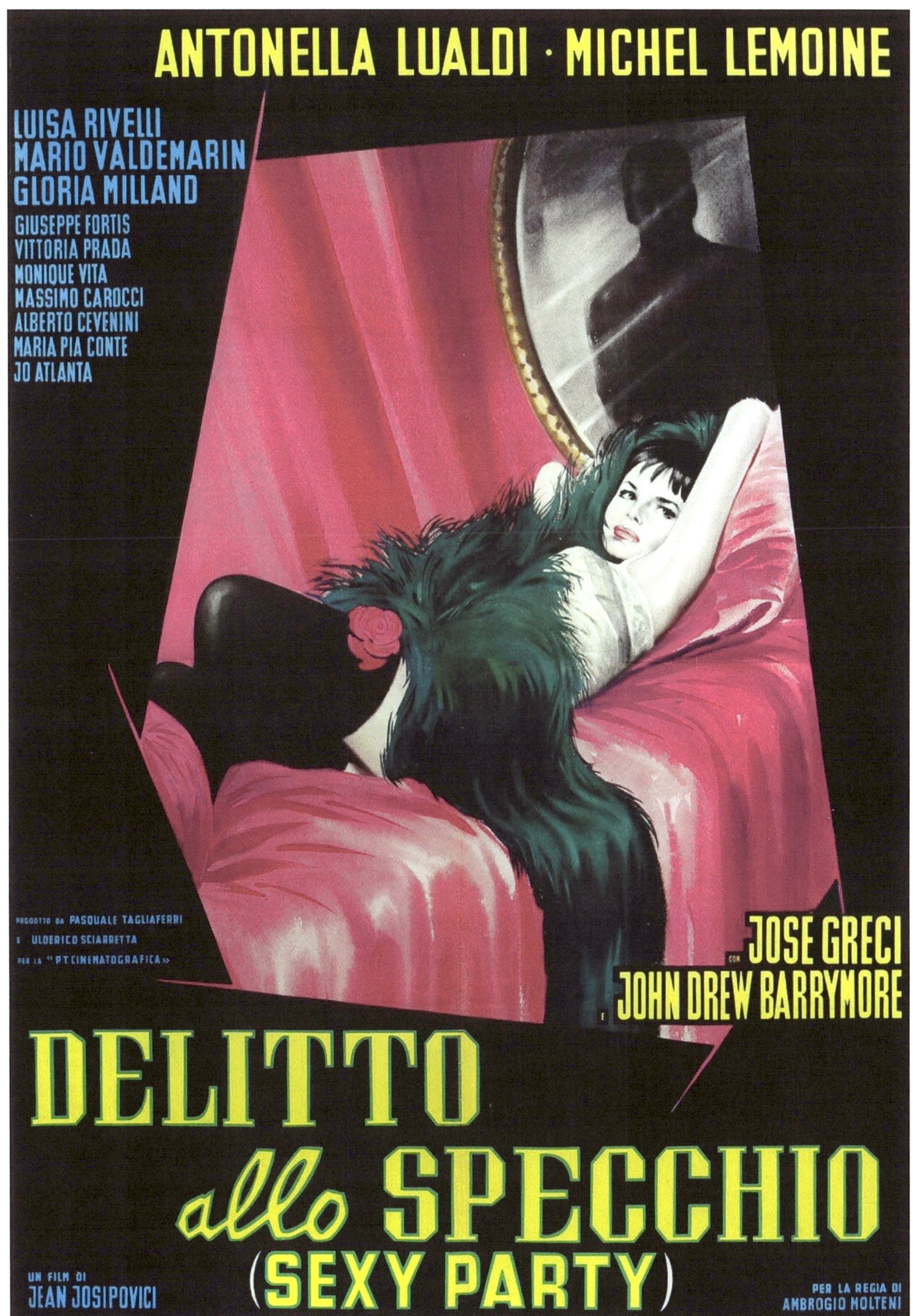

DELITTO ALLO SPECCHIO

("Crime In The Mirror"; Italy/France, 1964). Artist: unsigned.

13

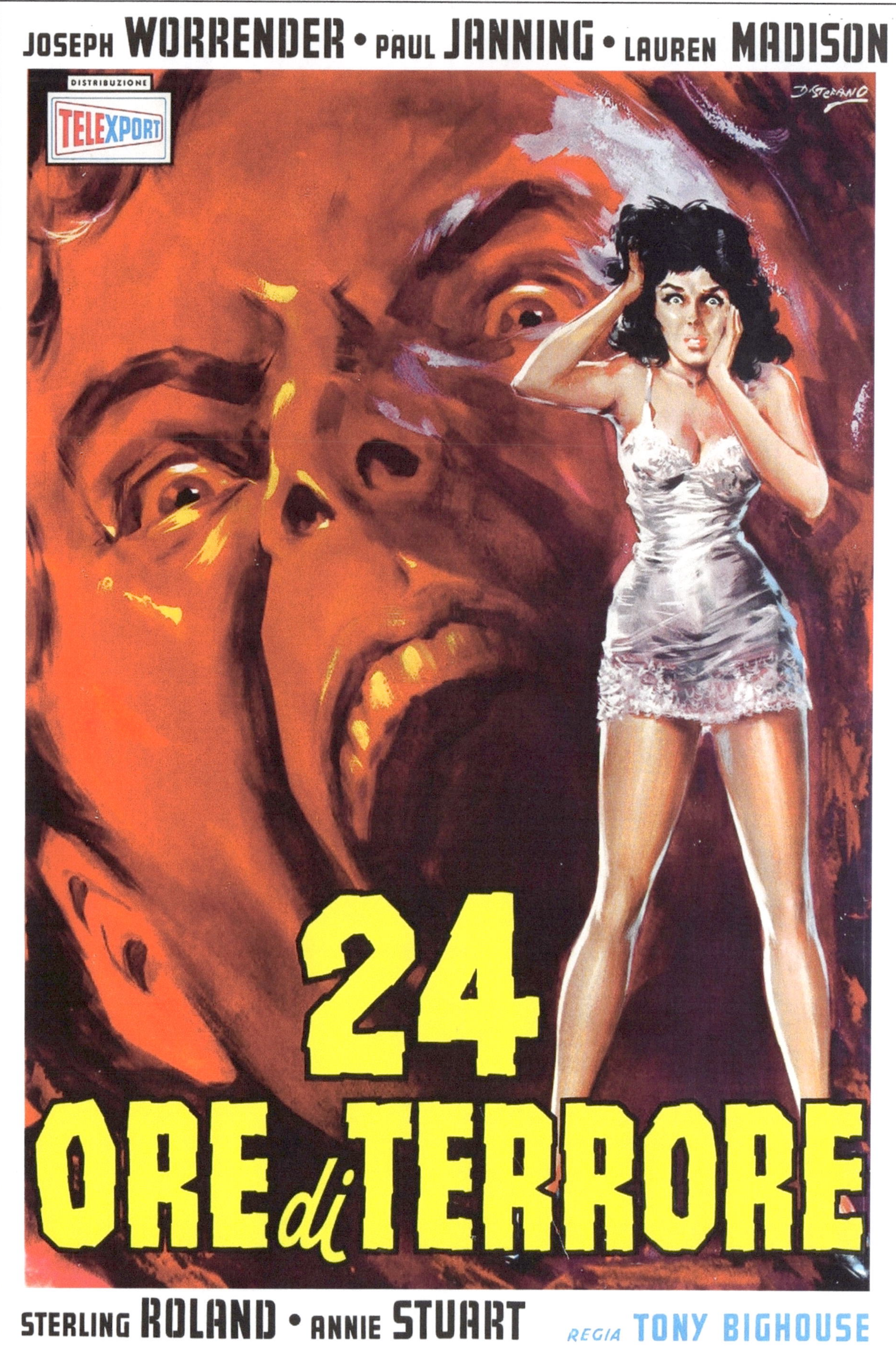

24 ORE DI TERRORE

("24 Hours Of Terror"; Italy, 1964). Artist: Giovanni Di Stefano.

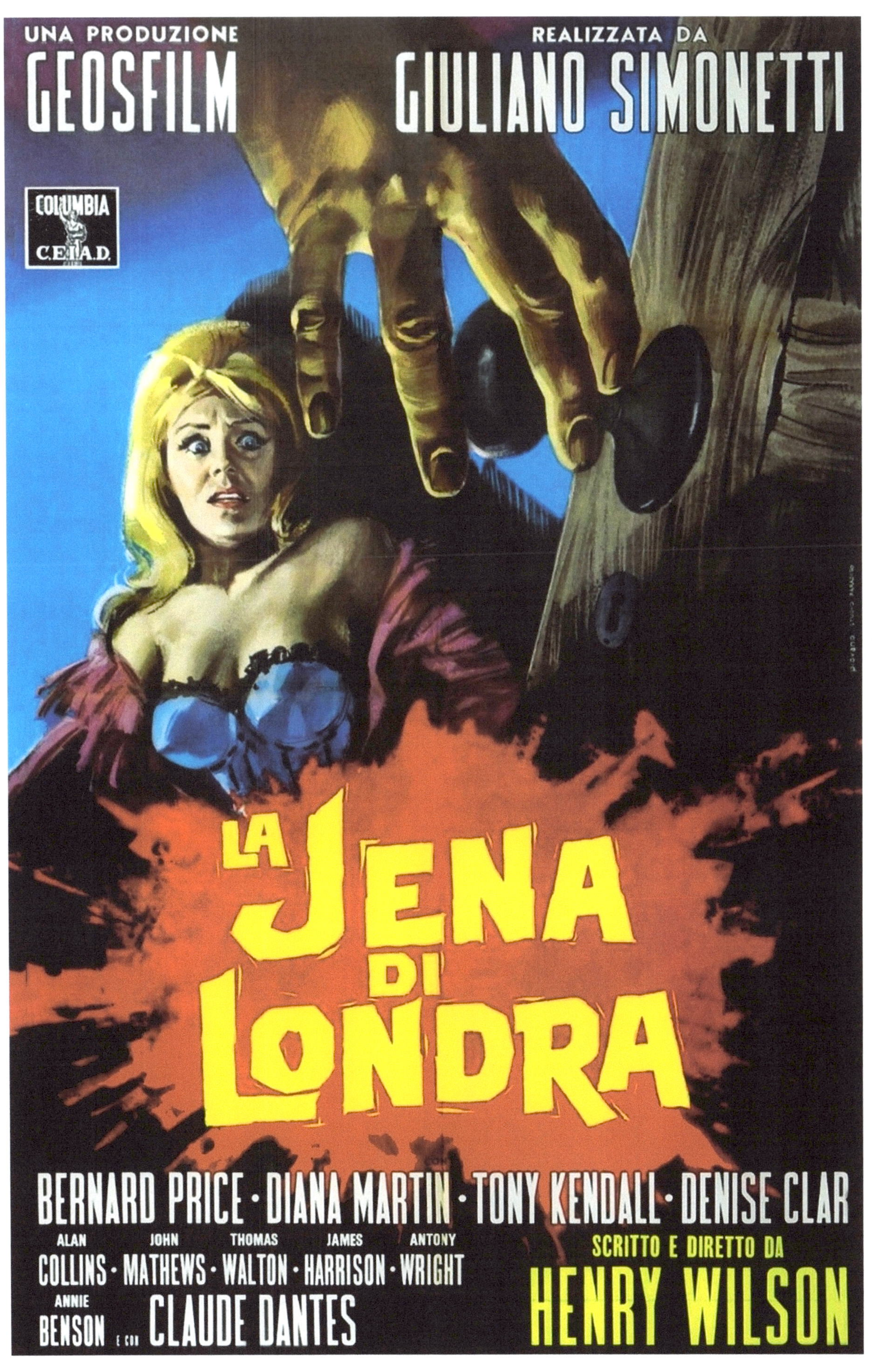

LA JENA DI LONDRA

("The Beast Of London"; Italy, 1964). Artist: Mario Piovano.

15

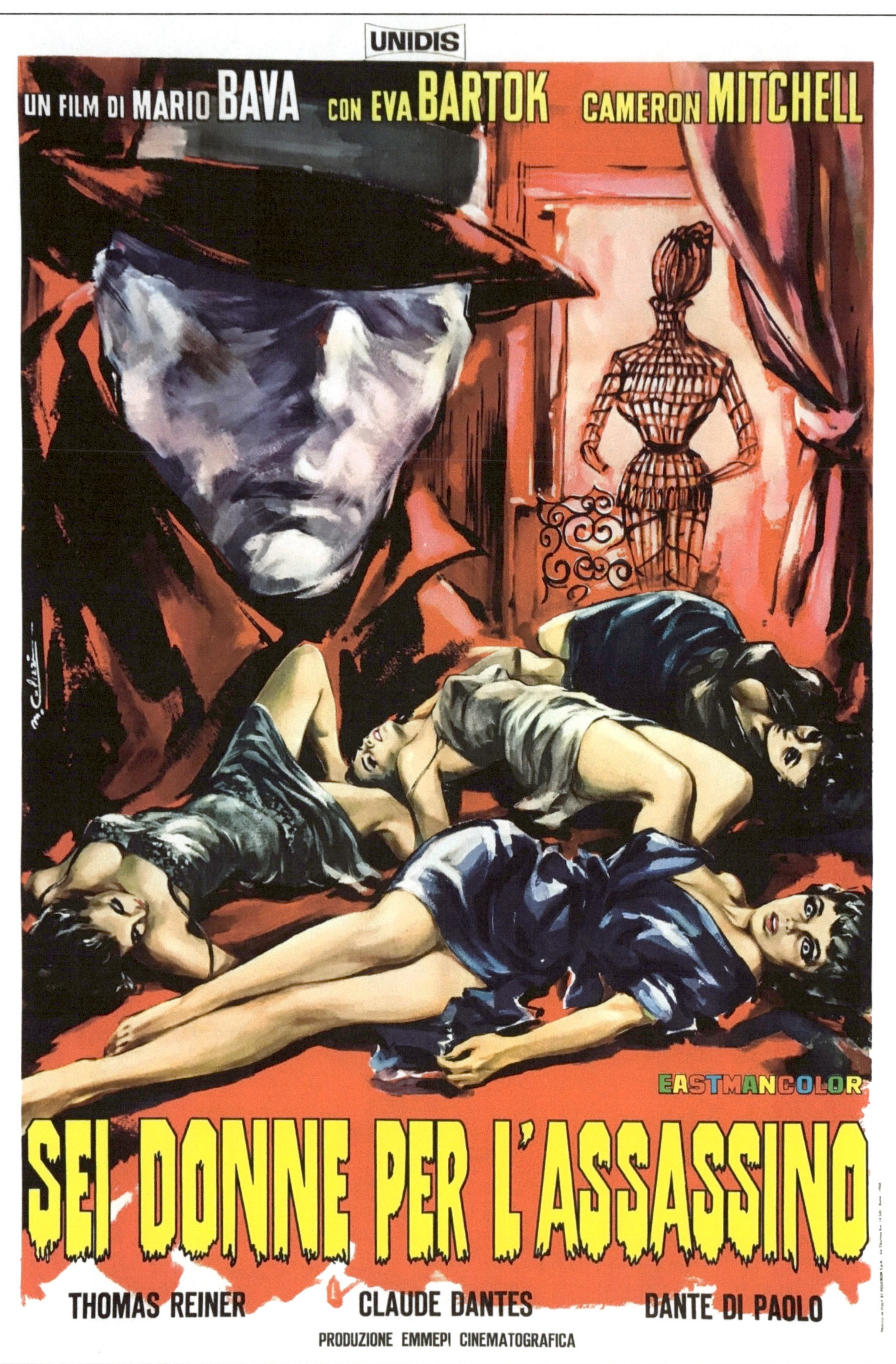

SEI DONNE PER L'ASSASSINO

("Six Women For The Killer"; Italy, 1964). Artist: Mauro Colizzi.

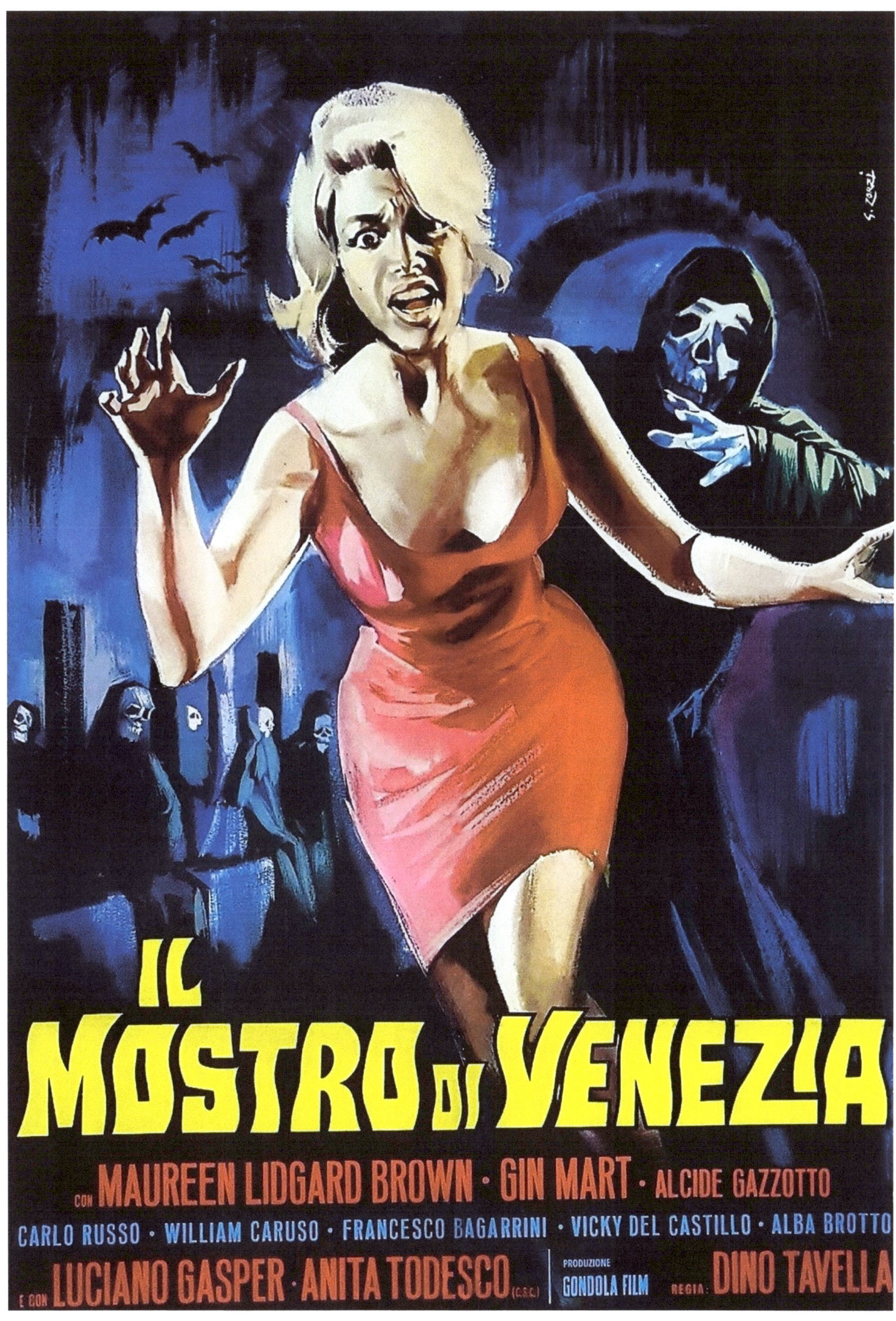

("The Monster Of Venice"; Italy, 1964-67). Artist: Francesco Zorzi.

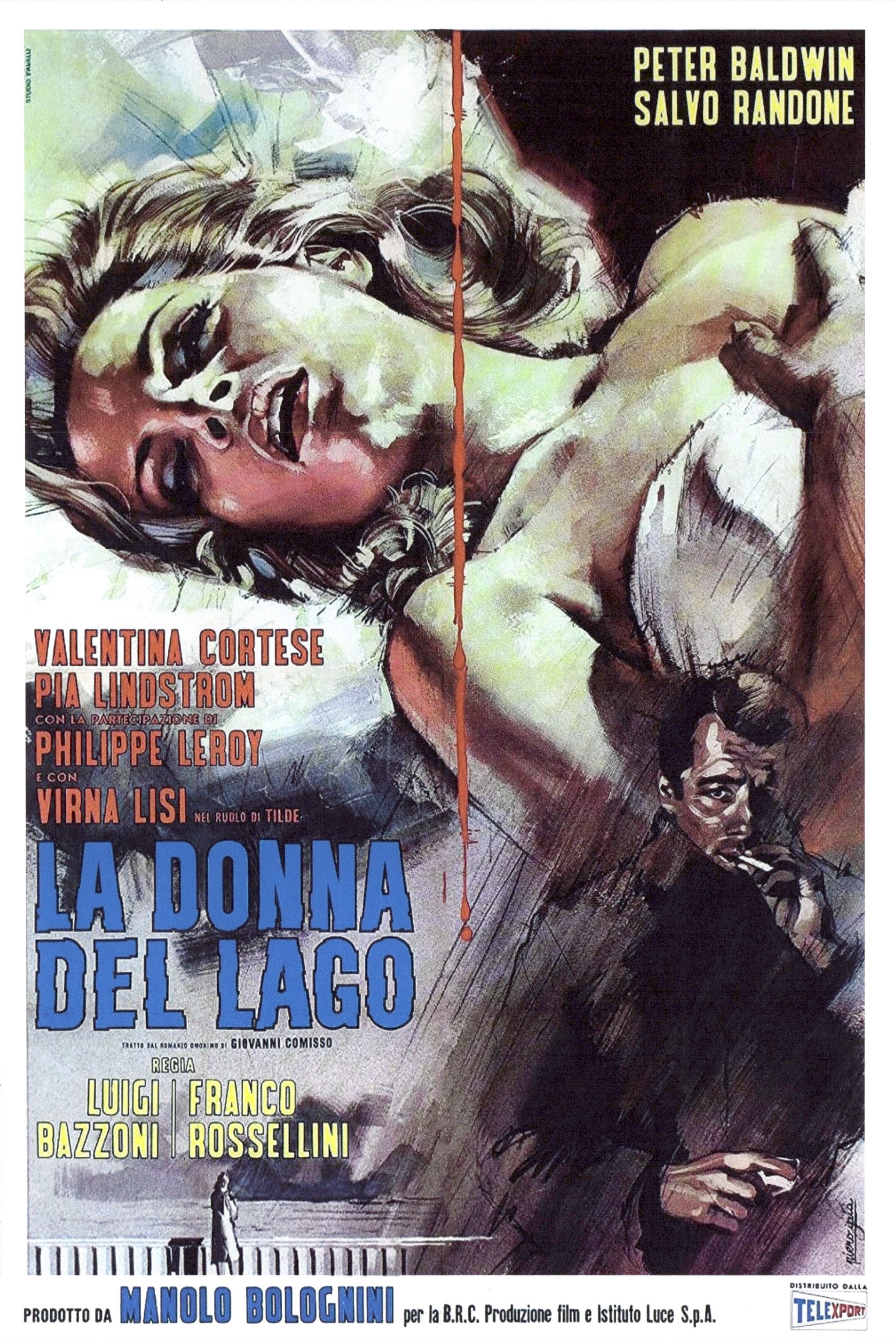

LA DONNA DEL LAGO

("The Lady Of The Lake"; Italy, 1965). Artist: Piero Iaia.

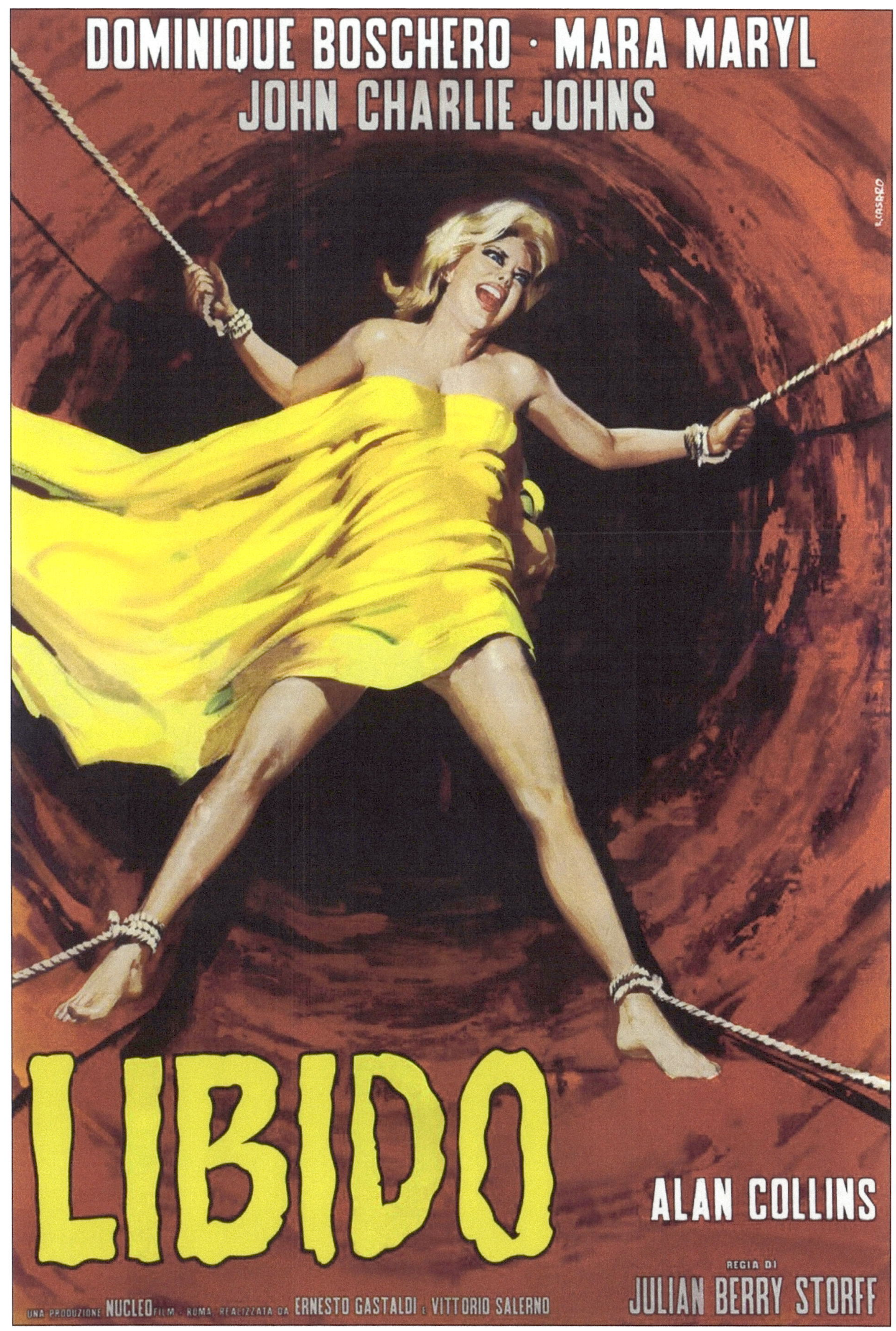

LIBIDO

("Libido"; Italy, 1965). Artist: Renato Casaro.

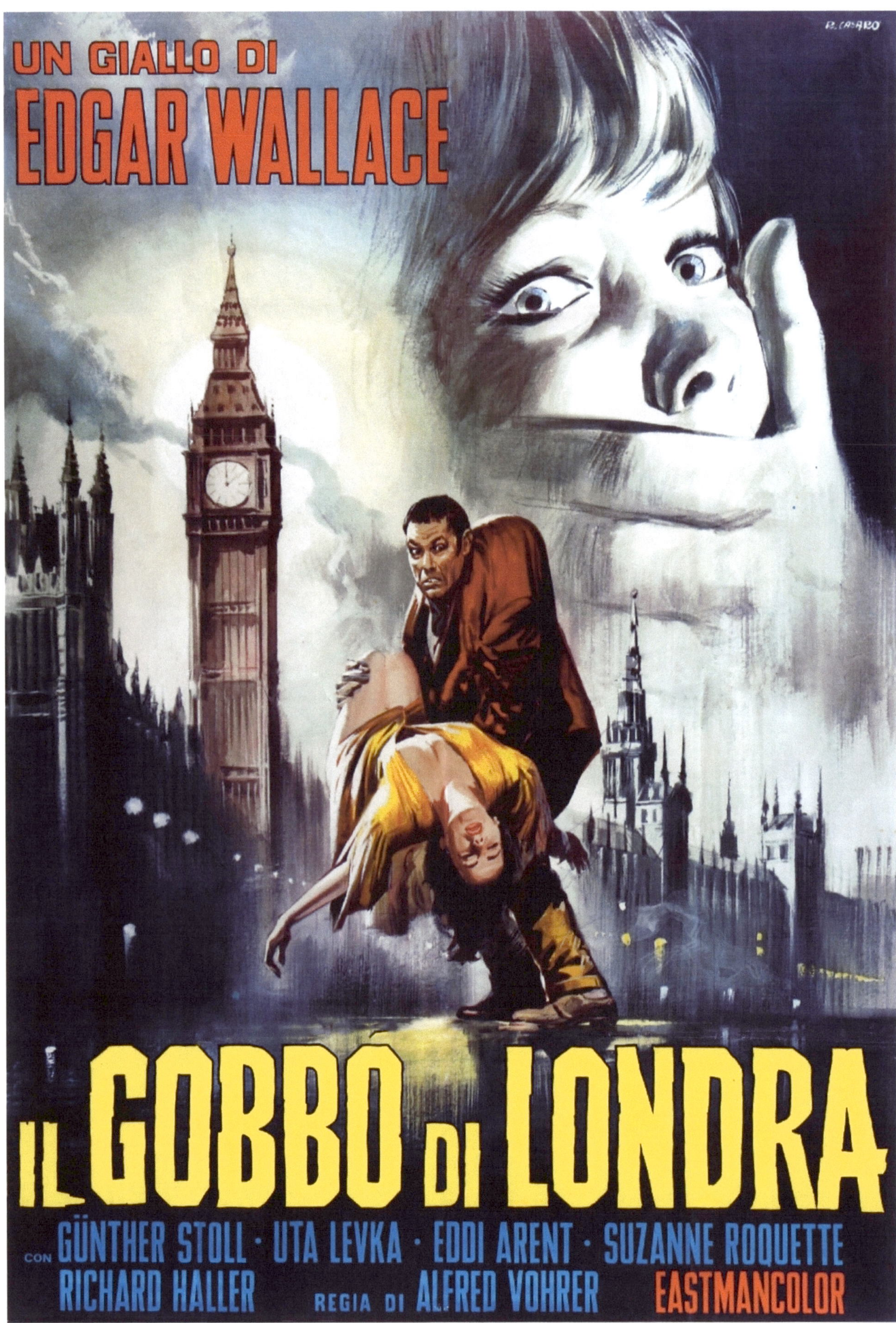

IL GOBBO DI LONDRA

("The Hunchback Of London"; Germany, 1966). Artist: Renato Casaro. Original Title: **Der Bucklige Von Soho.**

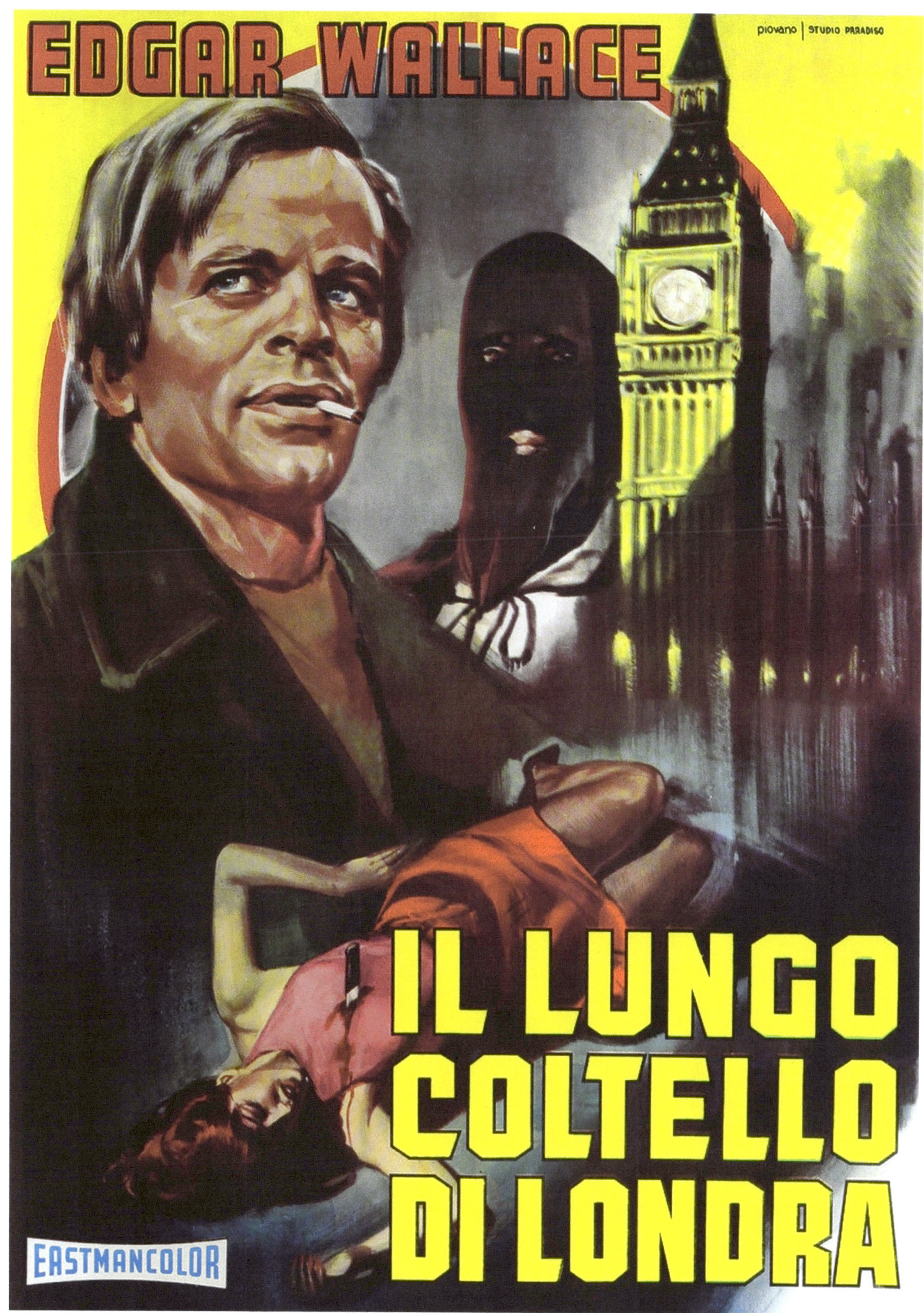

(''The Long Blade Of London''; Germany/UK, 1966). Artist: Mario Piovano. Original Title: **Das Rätsel Des Silbernen Dreieck.**

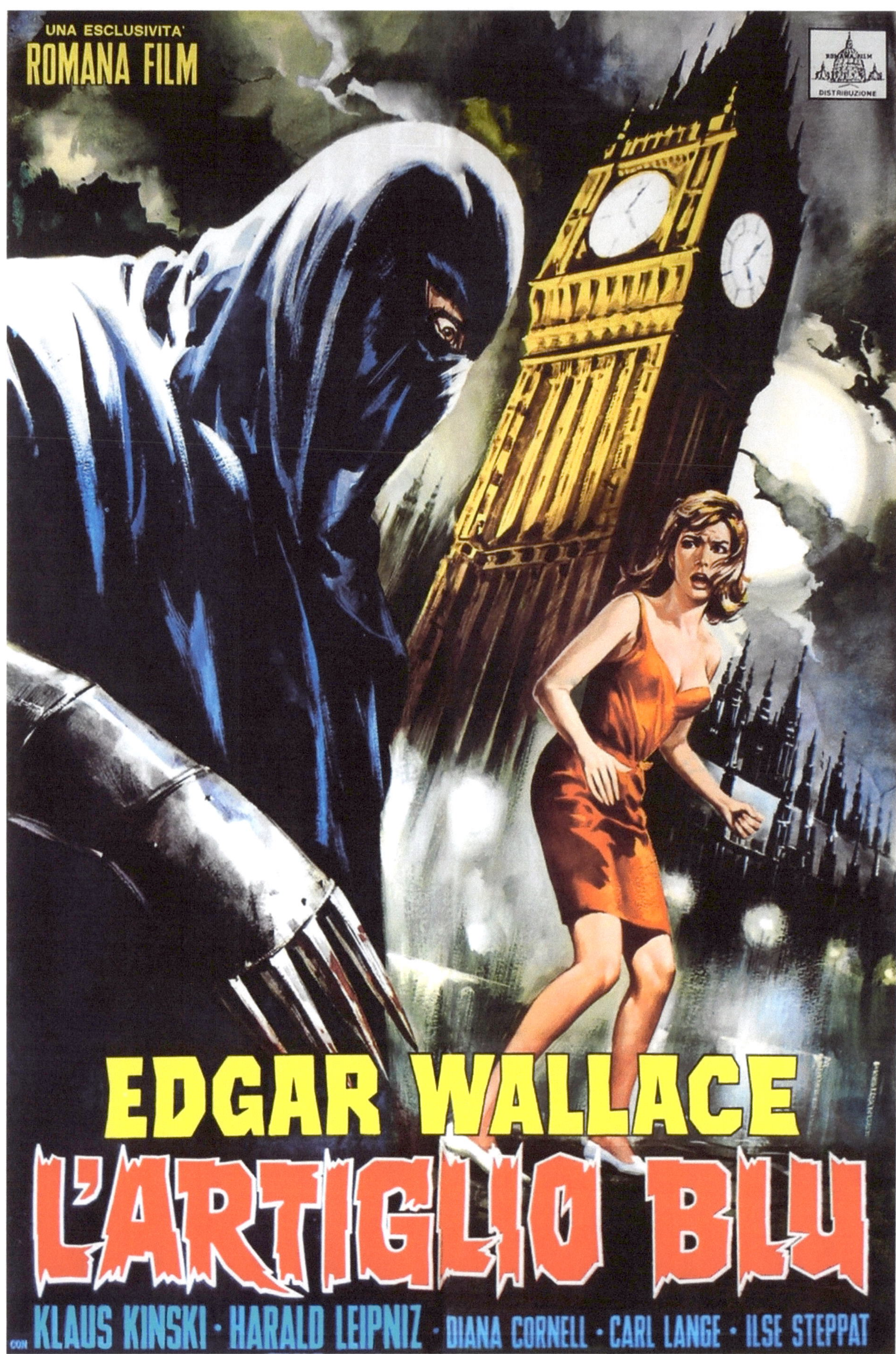

L'ARTIGLIO BLU

("The Blue Claw"; Germany, 1967). Artist: unsigned. Original Title: **Die Blaue Hand.**

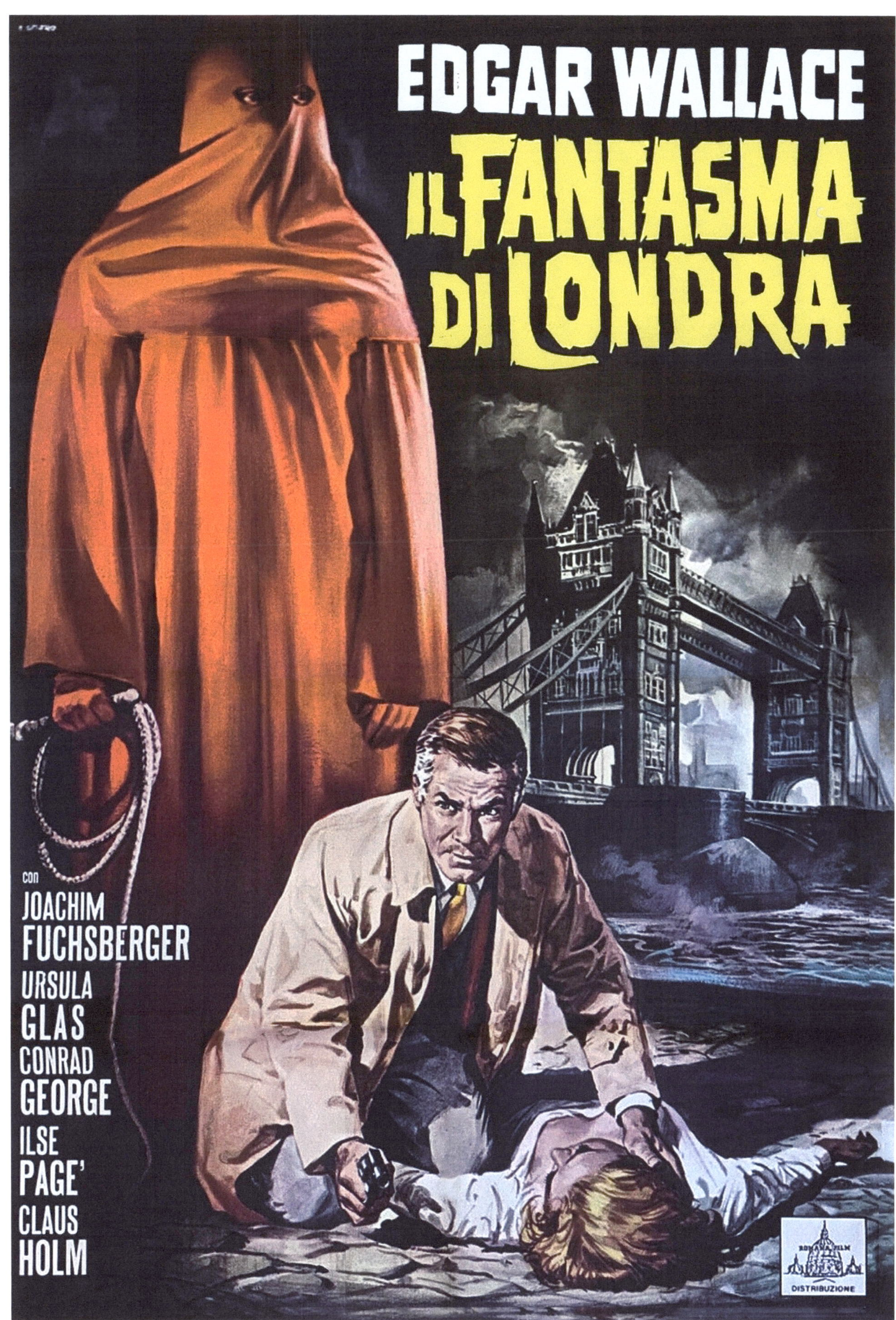

("The Phantom Of London"; Germany, 1967). Artist: Renato Casaro. Original Title: **Der Mönch Mit Der Peitsche.**

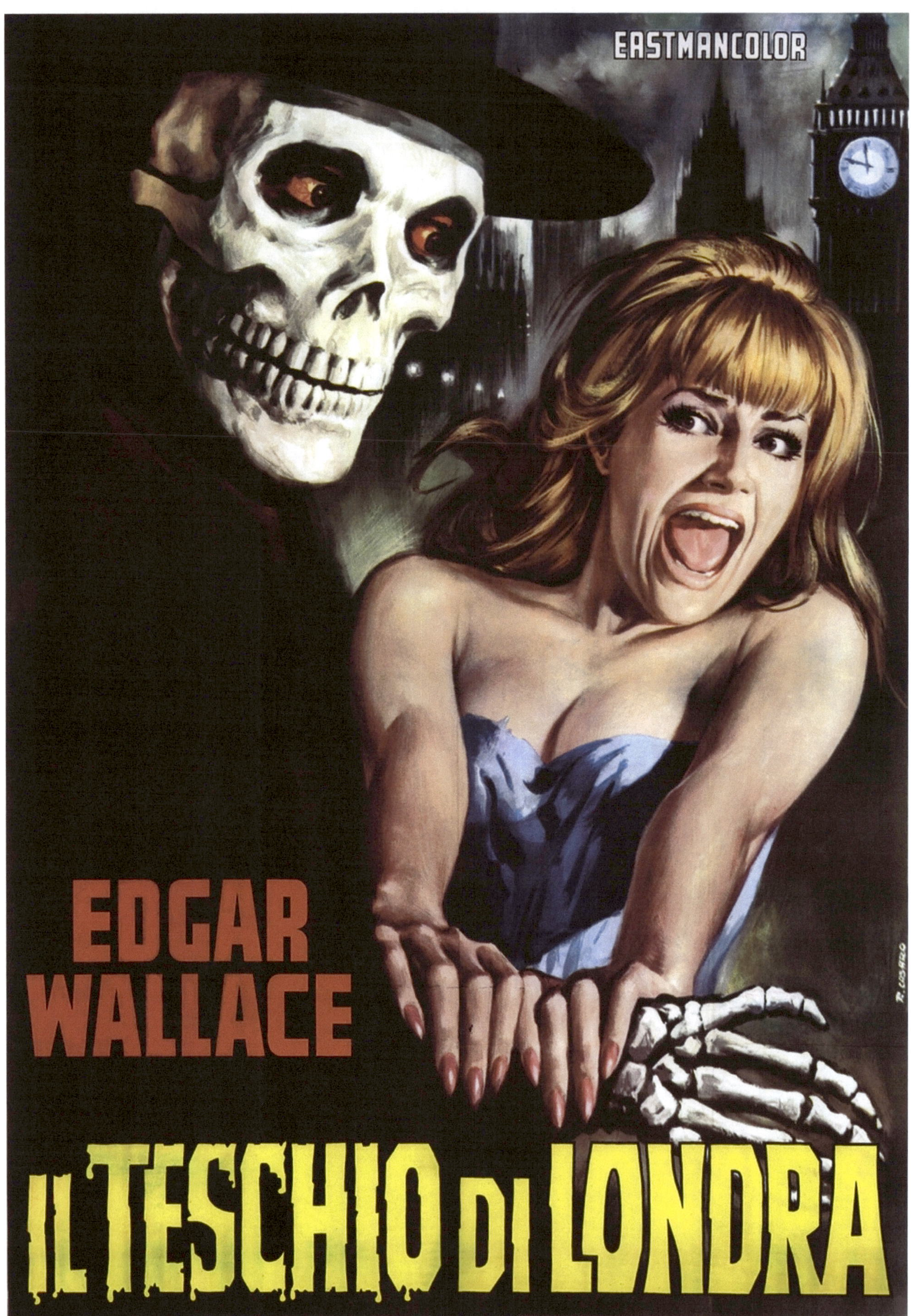

IL TESCHIO DI LONDRA

("The London Skull"; Germany, 1968). Artist: Renato Casaro. Original Title: **Im Banne Des Unheimlichen**.

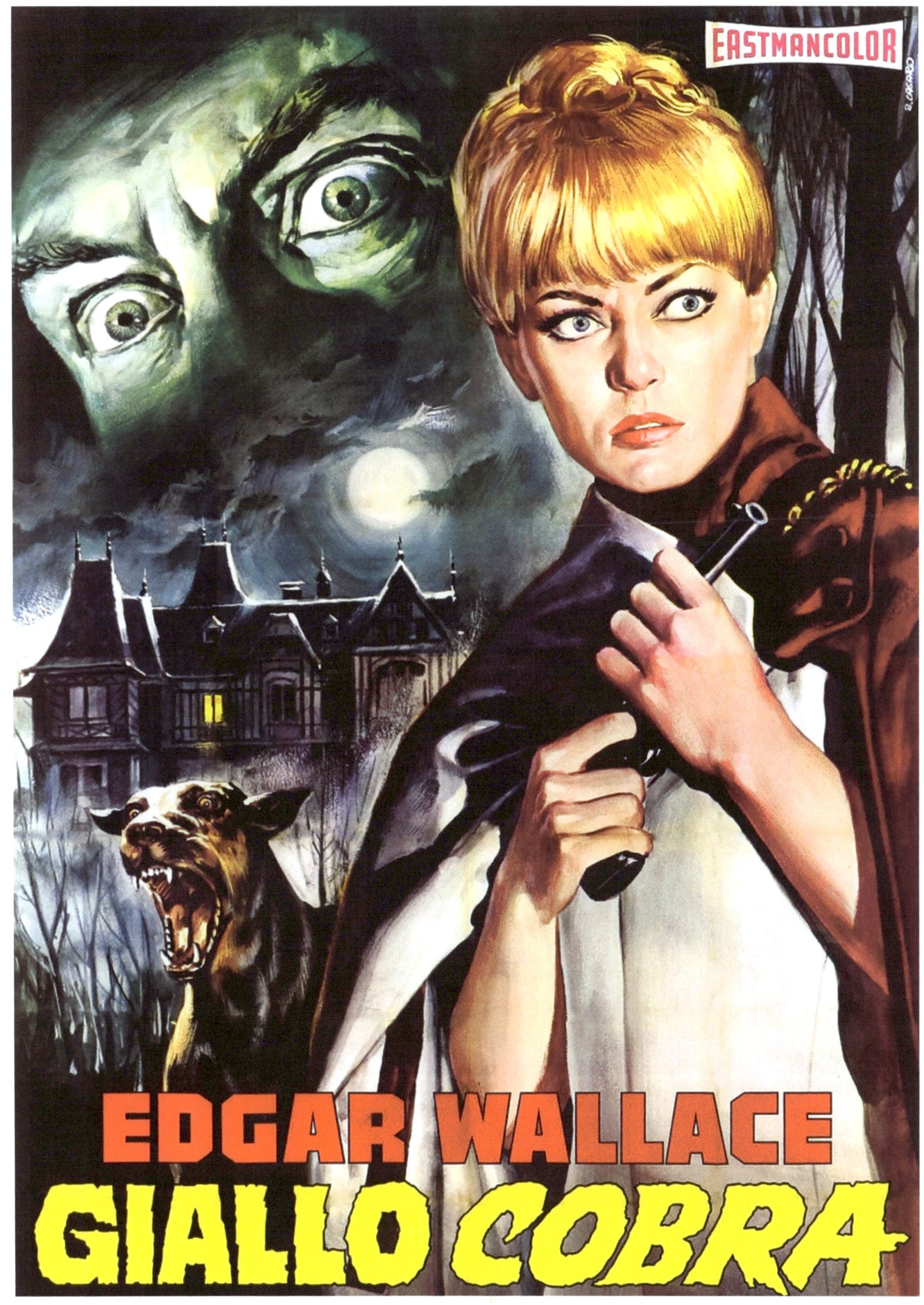

("Yellow Cobra"; Germany, 1968). Artist: Renato Casaro. Original Title: **Der Hund Von Blackwood Castle.**

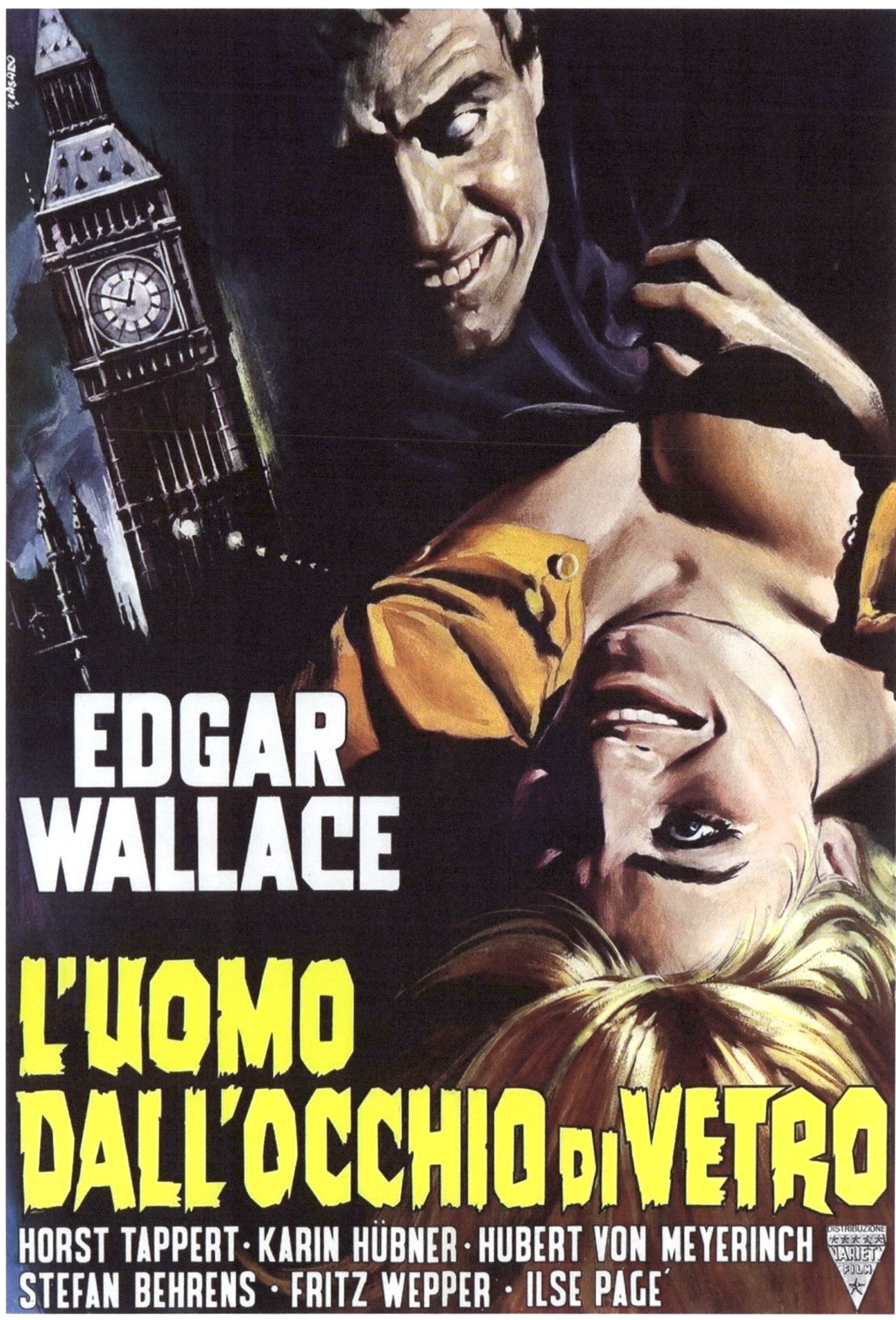

L'UOMO DALL'OCCHIO DI VETRO

("The Man With The Glass Eye"; Germany, 1969). Artist: Renato Casaro. Original Title: **Der Mann Mit Dem Glasauge.**

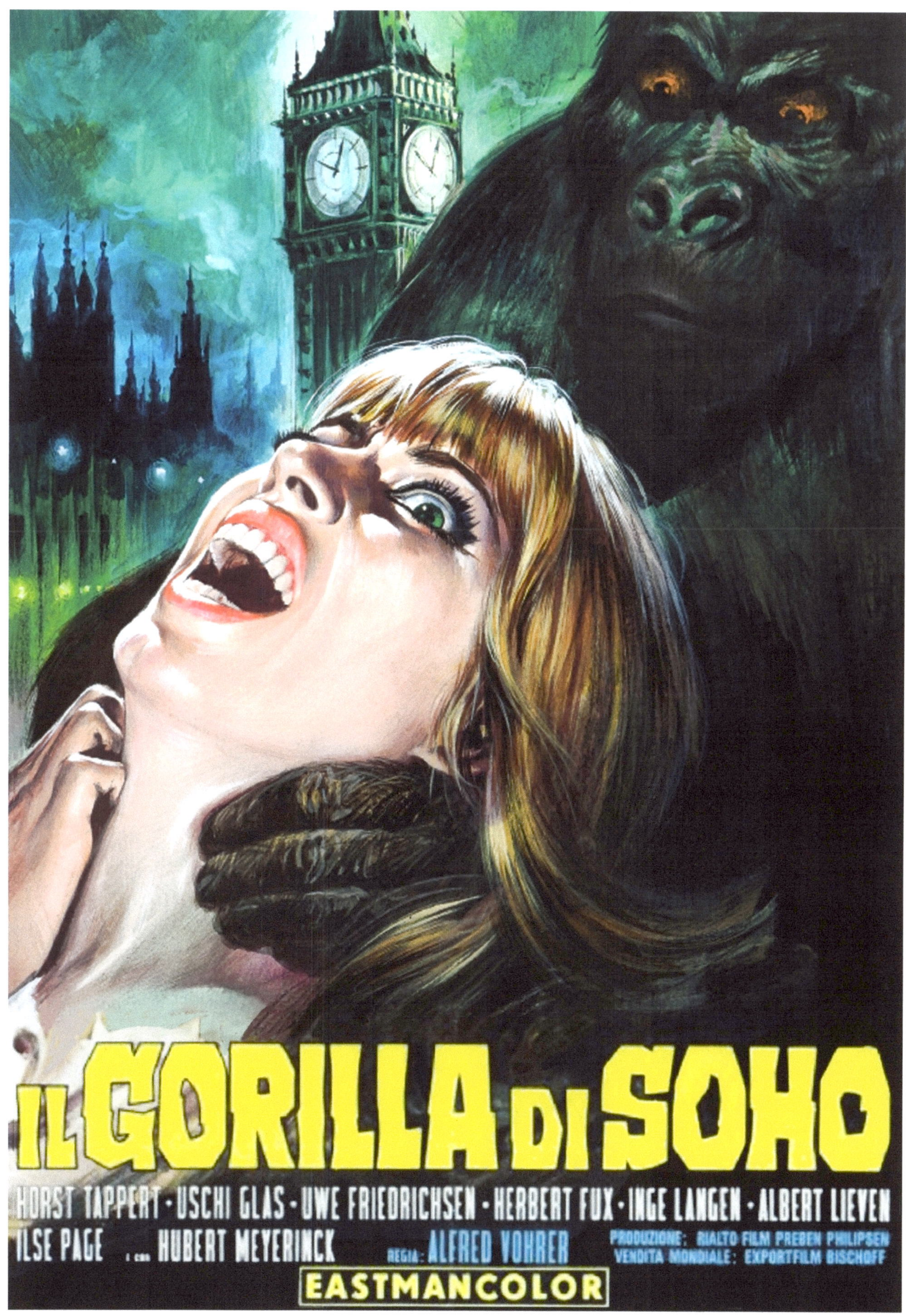

("The Gorilla Of Soho"; Germany, 1968). Artist: Renato Casaro. Original Title: **Der Gorilla Von Soho.**

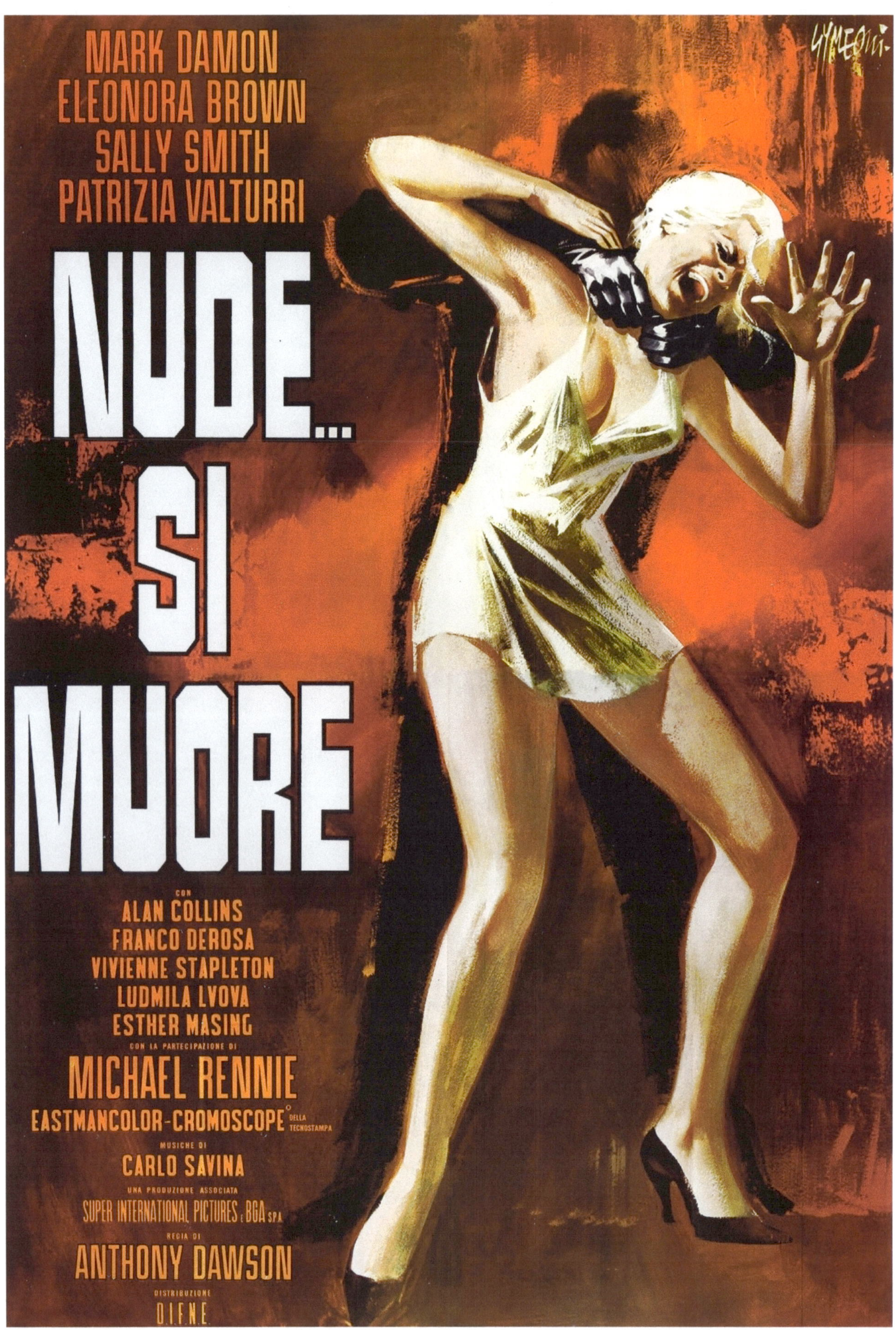

NUDE... SI MUORE

("Naked... You Die"; Italy, 1968). Artist: Sandro Symeoni.

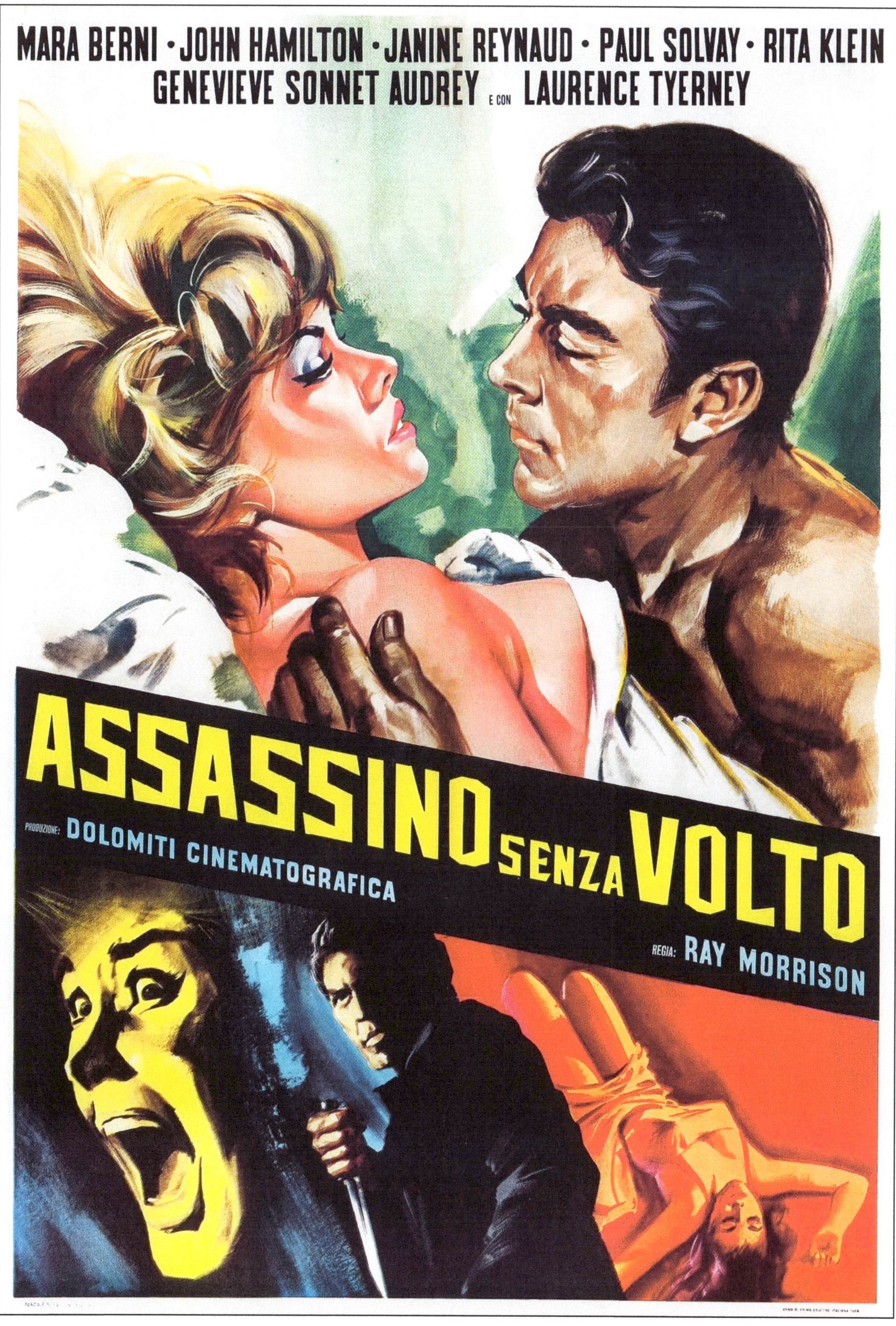

("Killer Without A Face"; Italy, 1968). Artist: unsigned.

29

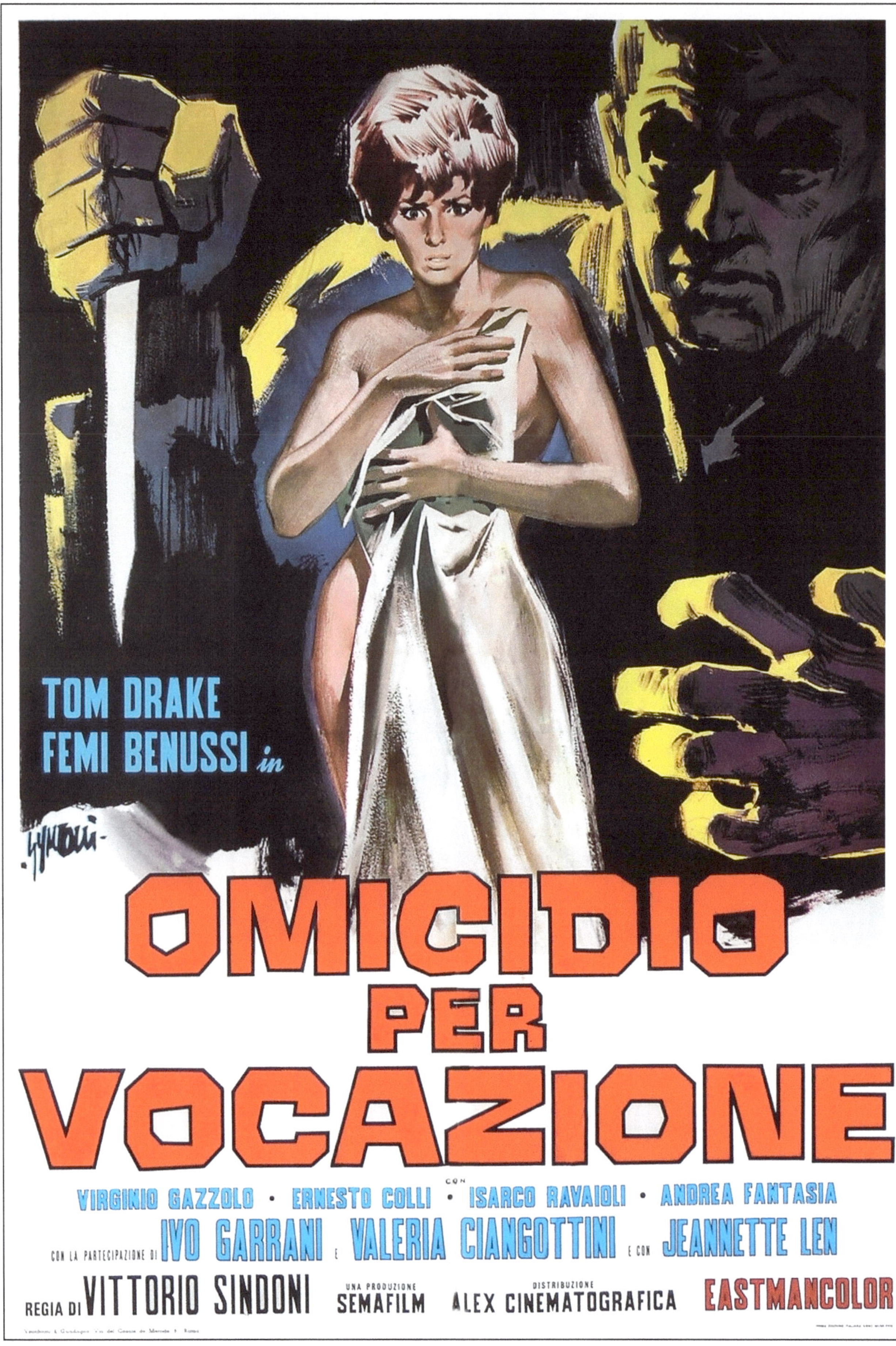

OMICIDIO PER VOCAZIONE

("Homicide By Profession"; Italy, 1968). Artist: Sandro Symeoni.

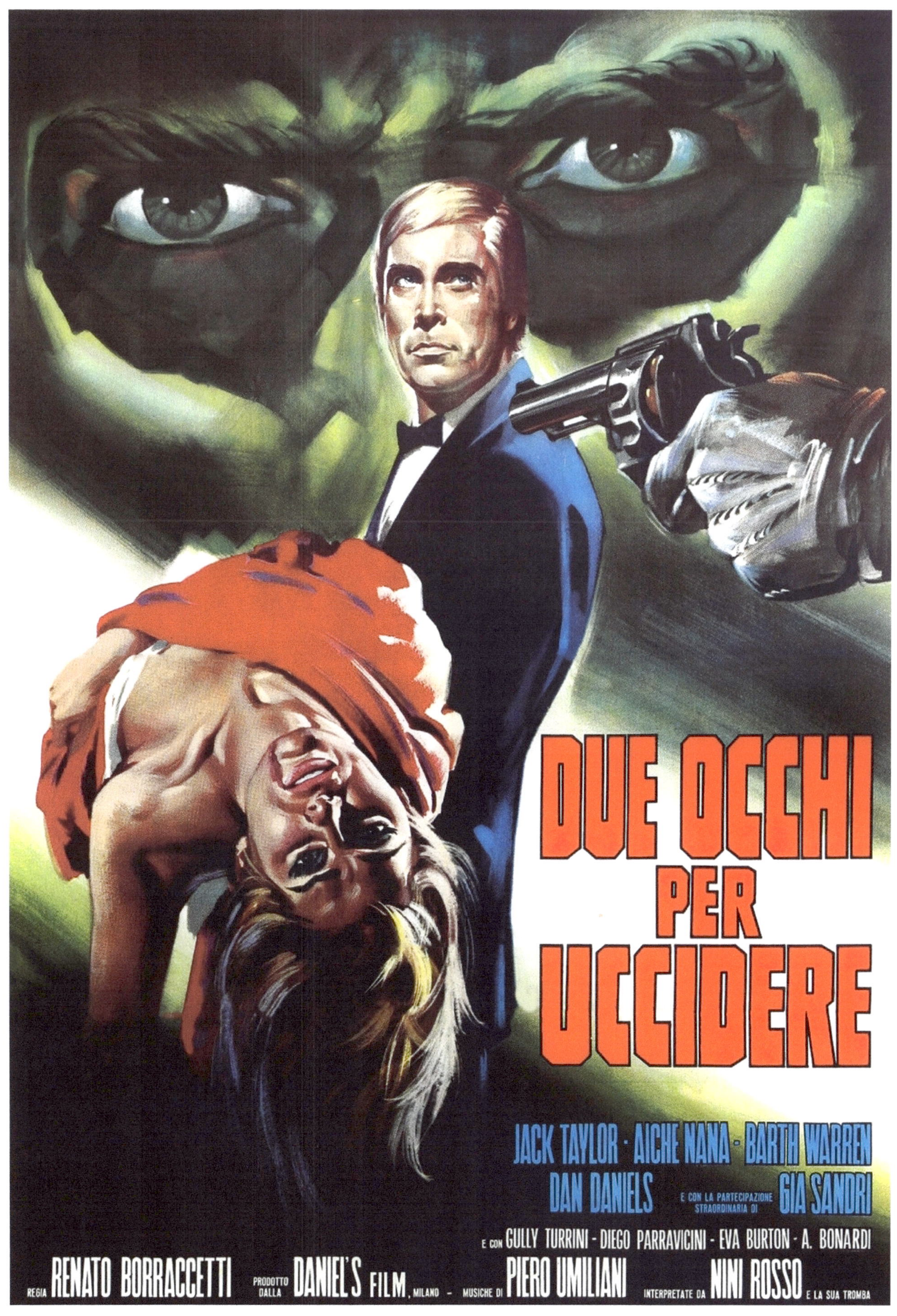

DUE OCCHI PER UCCIDERE
("Two Eyes To Kill"; Italy, 1968). Artist: unsigned.

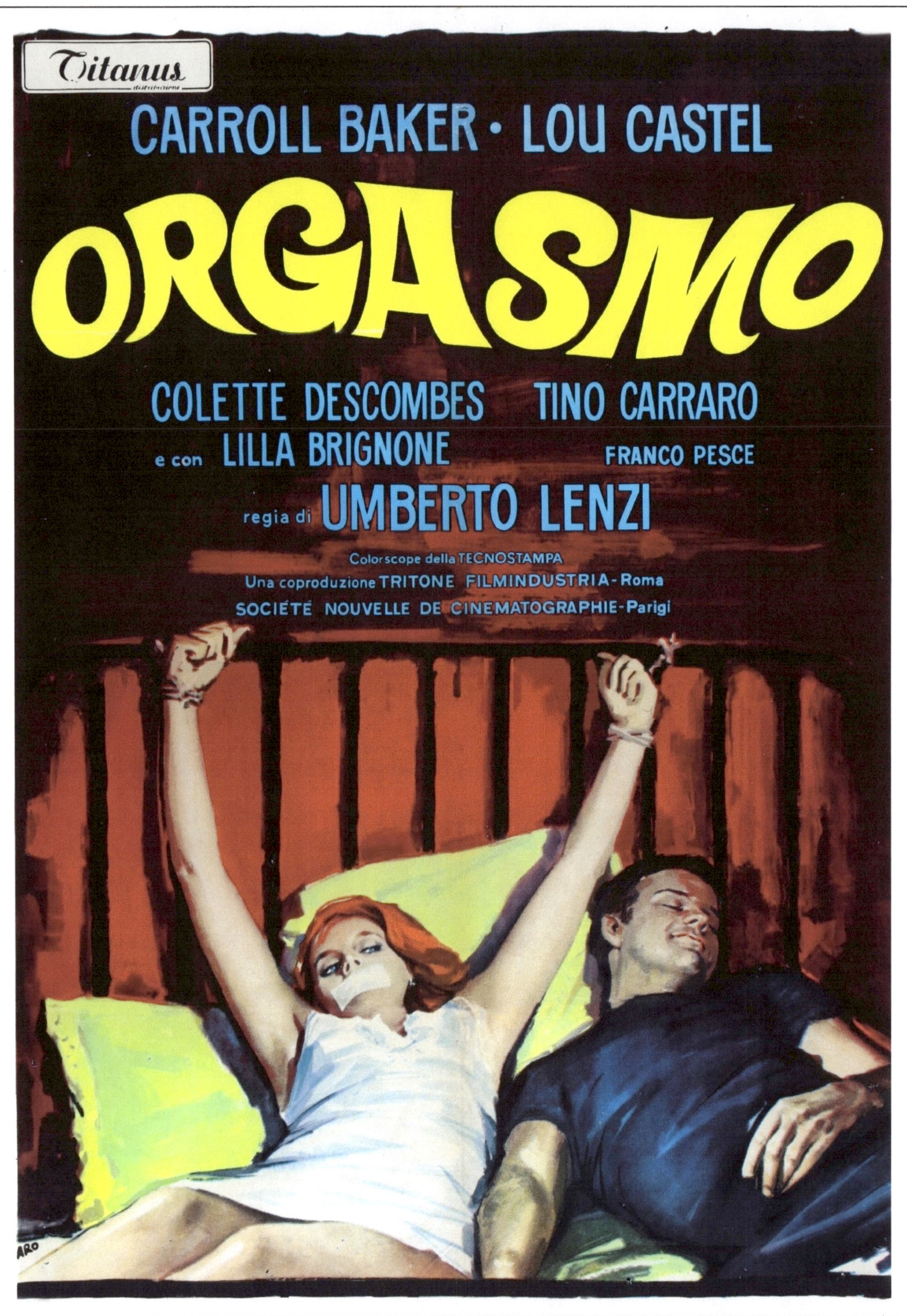

ORGASMO

("Orgasmo"; Italy/France, 1968). Artist: Aro.

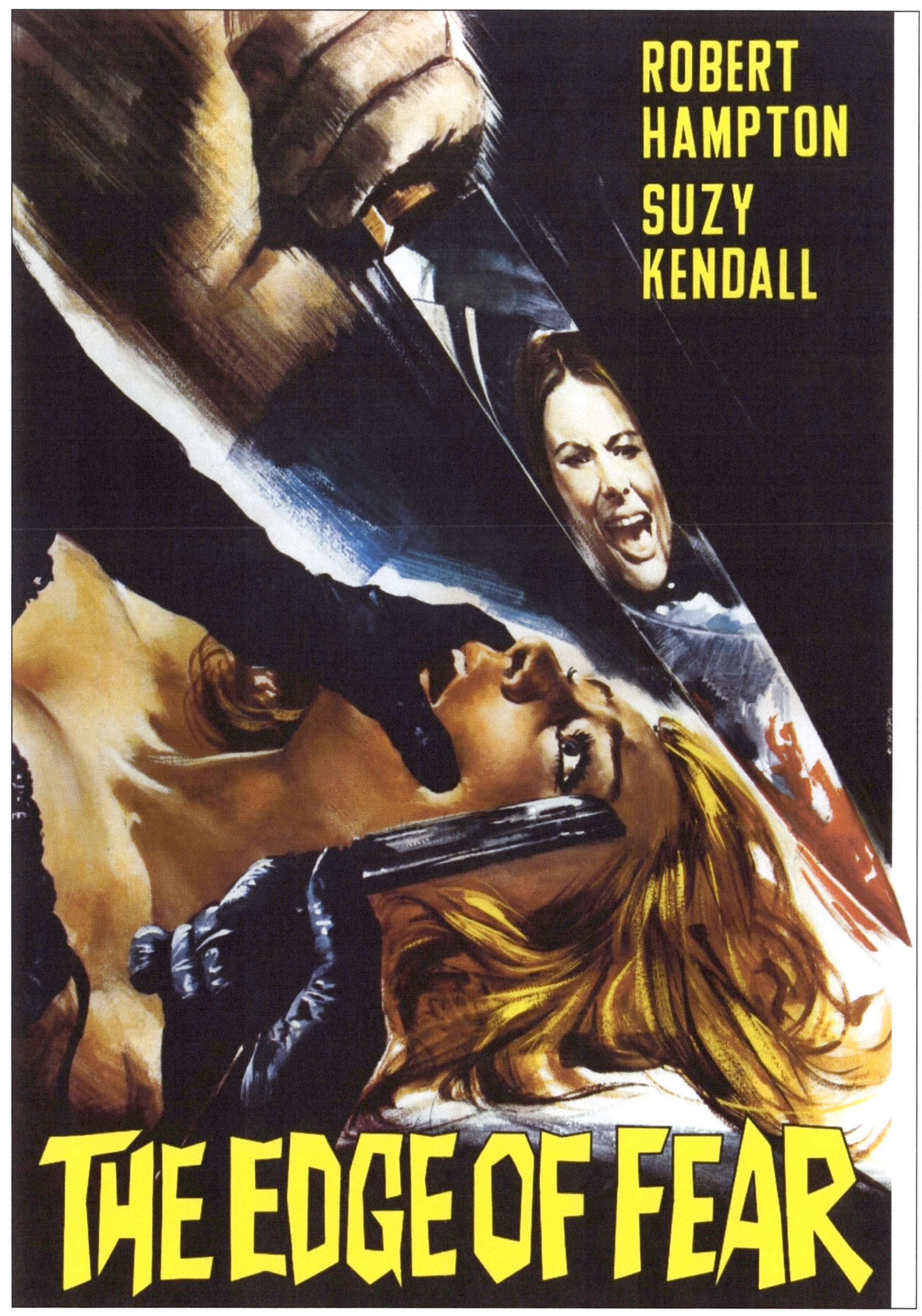

THE EDGE OF FEAR

("The Edge Of Fear"; Italy, c.1969). Artist: Renato Casaro.

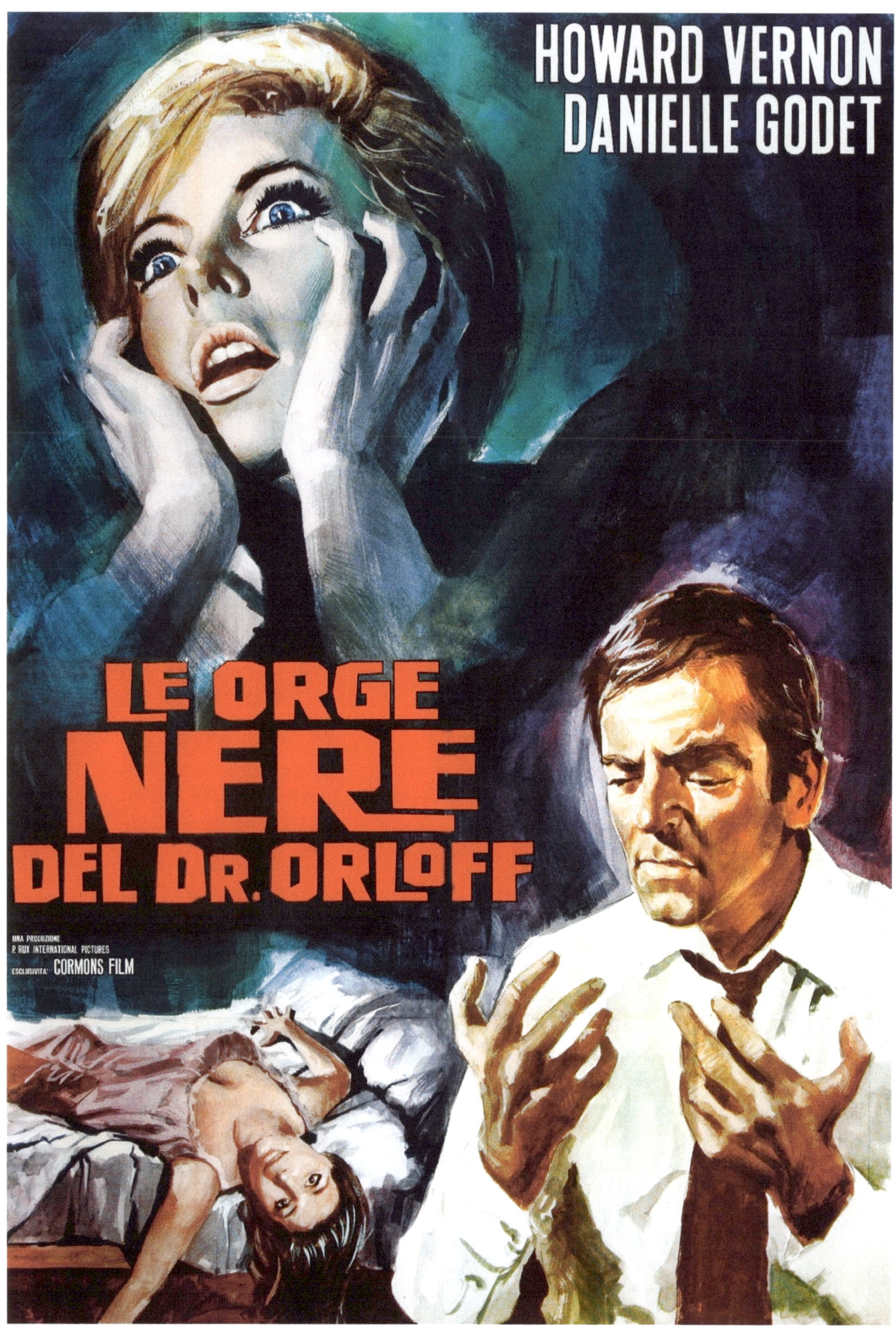

LE ORGE NERE DEL DR. ORLOFF

("Dr. Orloff's Black Orgy"; Spain, 1967). Artist: unsigned. Original Title: "El Enigma Del Ataúd".

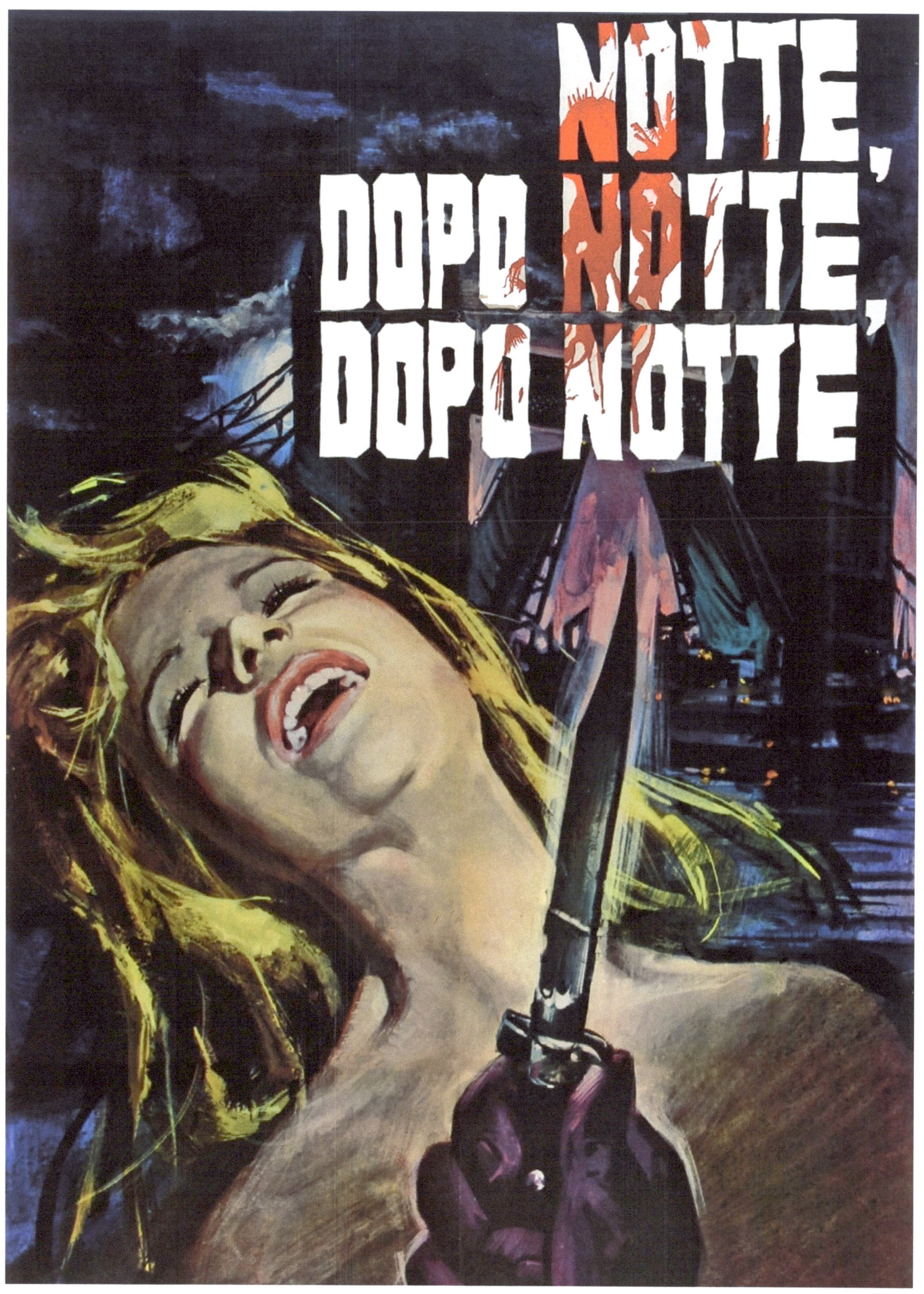

NOTTE, DOPO NOTTE, DOPO NOTTE
(''Night, After Night, After Night''; UK, 1969). Artist: Rodolfo Gasparri. Original Title: ''Night After Night After Night''.

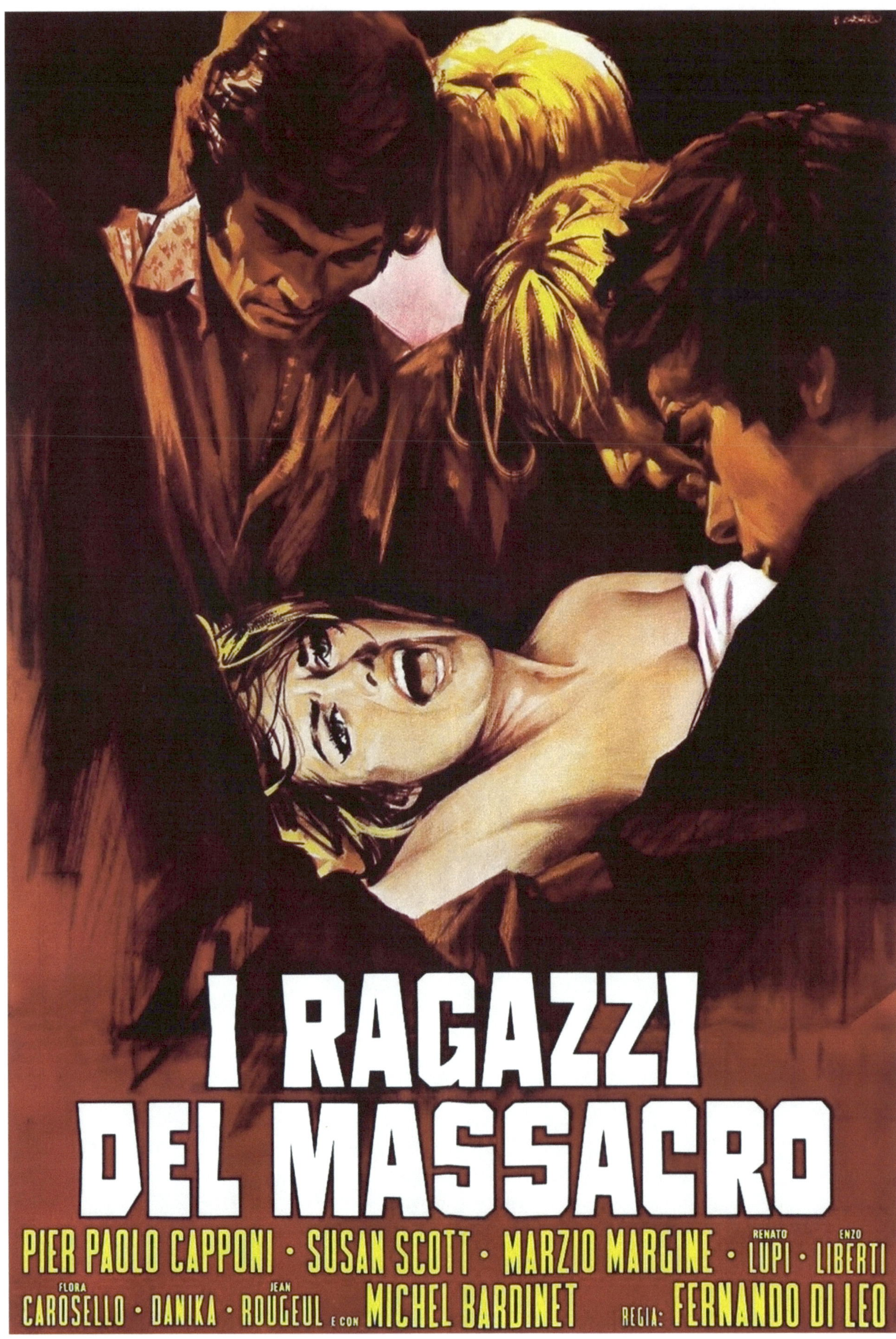

I RAGAZZI DEL MASSACRO

(''THe Massacre Boys''; Italy, 1969). Artist: Renato Casaro.

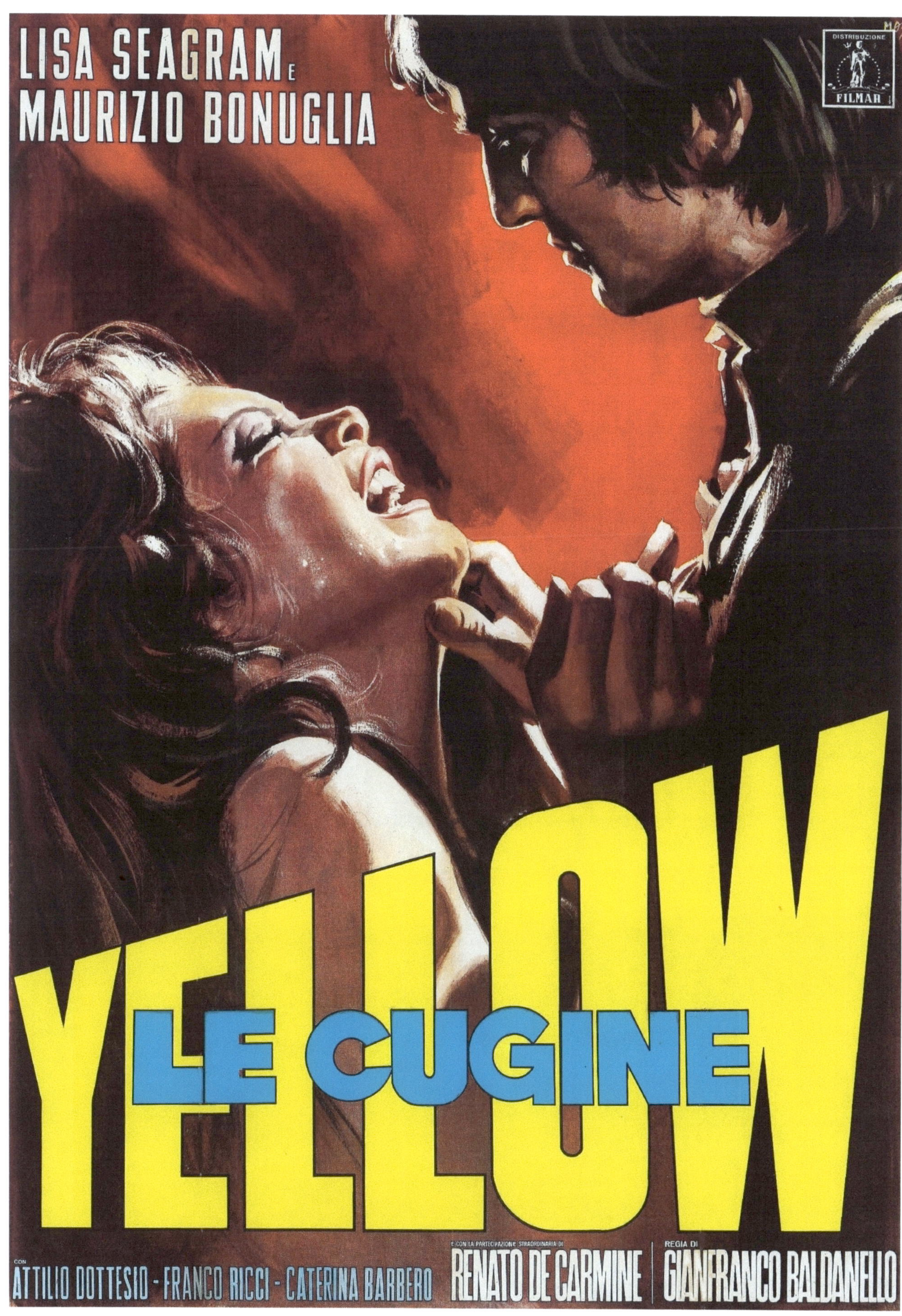

YELLOW: LE CUGINE

("Yellow: The Cousins"; Italy, 1969). Artist: Moz.

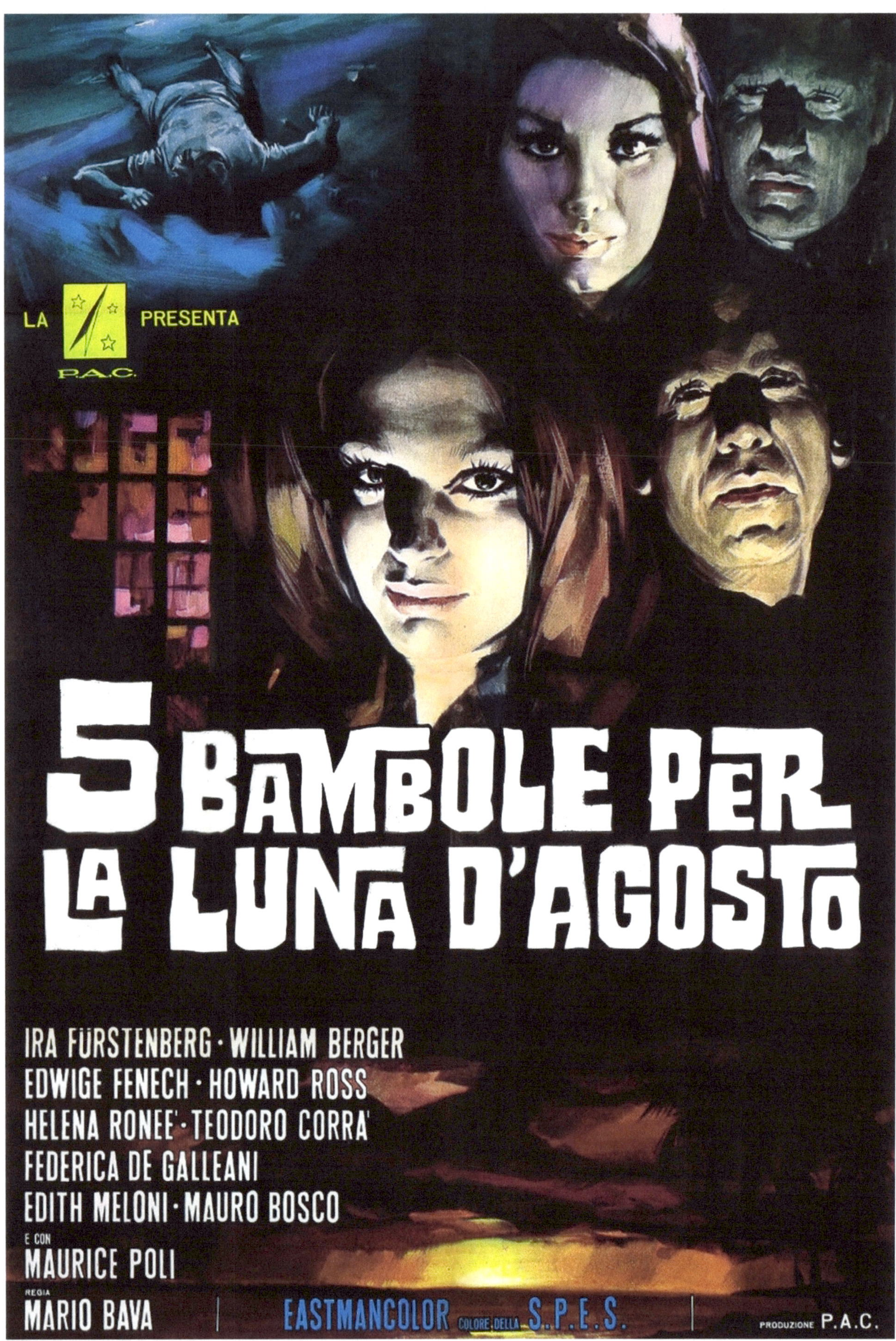

5 BAMBOLE PER LA LUNA D'AGOSTO

("5 Dolls For The August Moon"; Italy, 1970). Artist: unsigned.

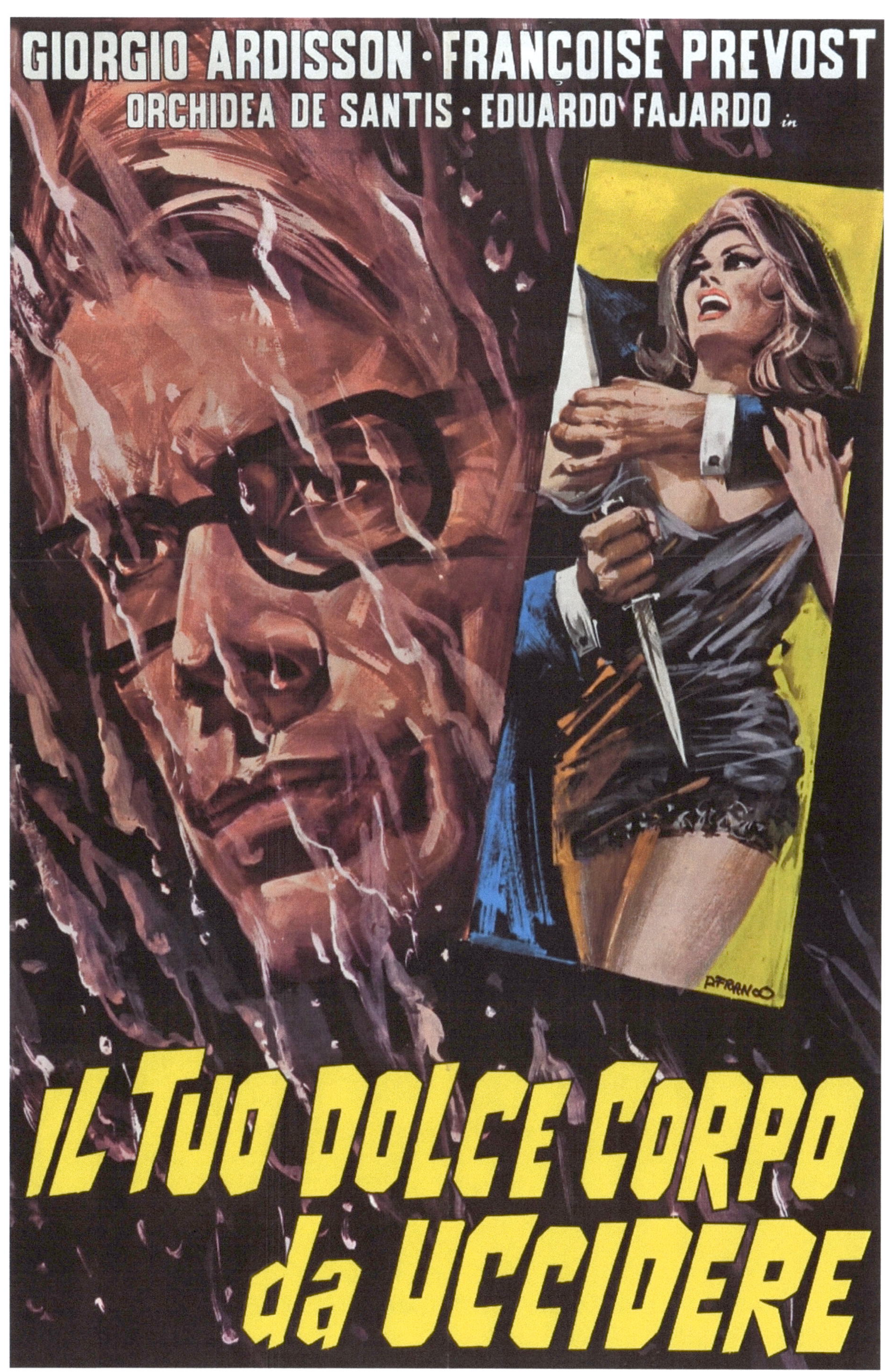

IL TUO DOLCE CORPO DA UCCIDERE

("Your Sweet Body To Kill"; Italy/Spain, 1970). Artist: P. Franco.

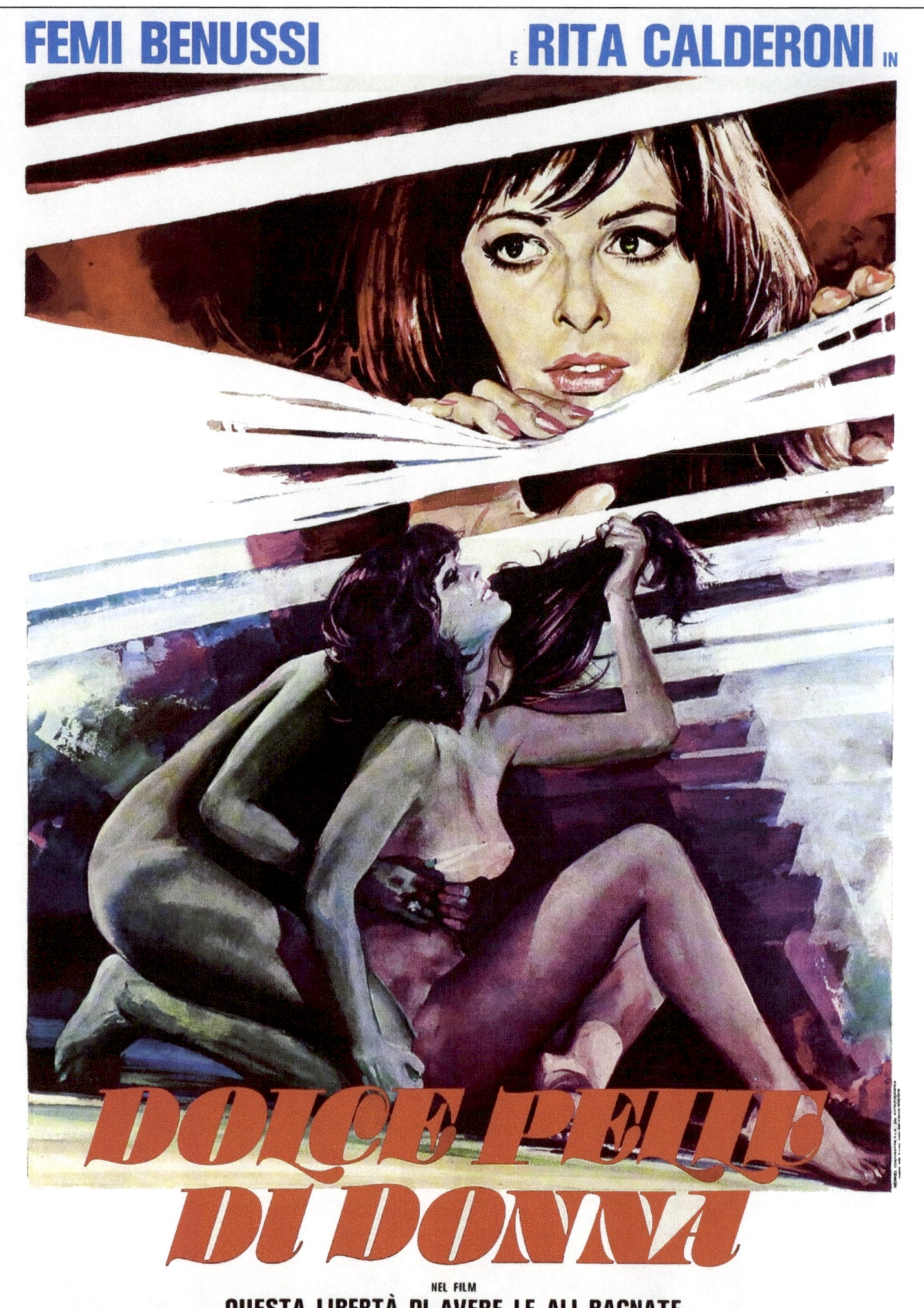

DOLCE PELLE DI DONNA

("Sweet Female Skin"; Italy, 1971). Artist: unsigned.

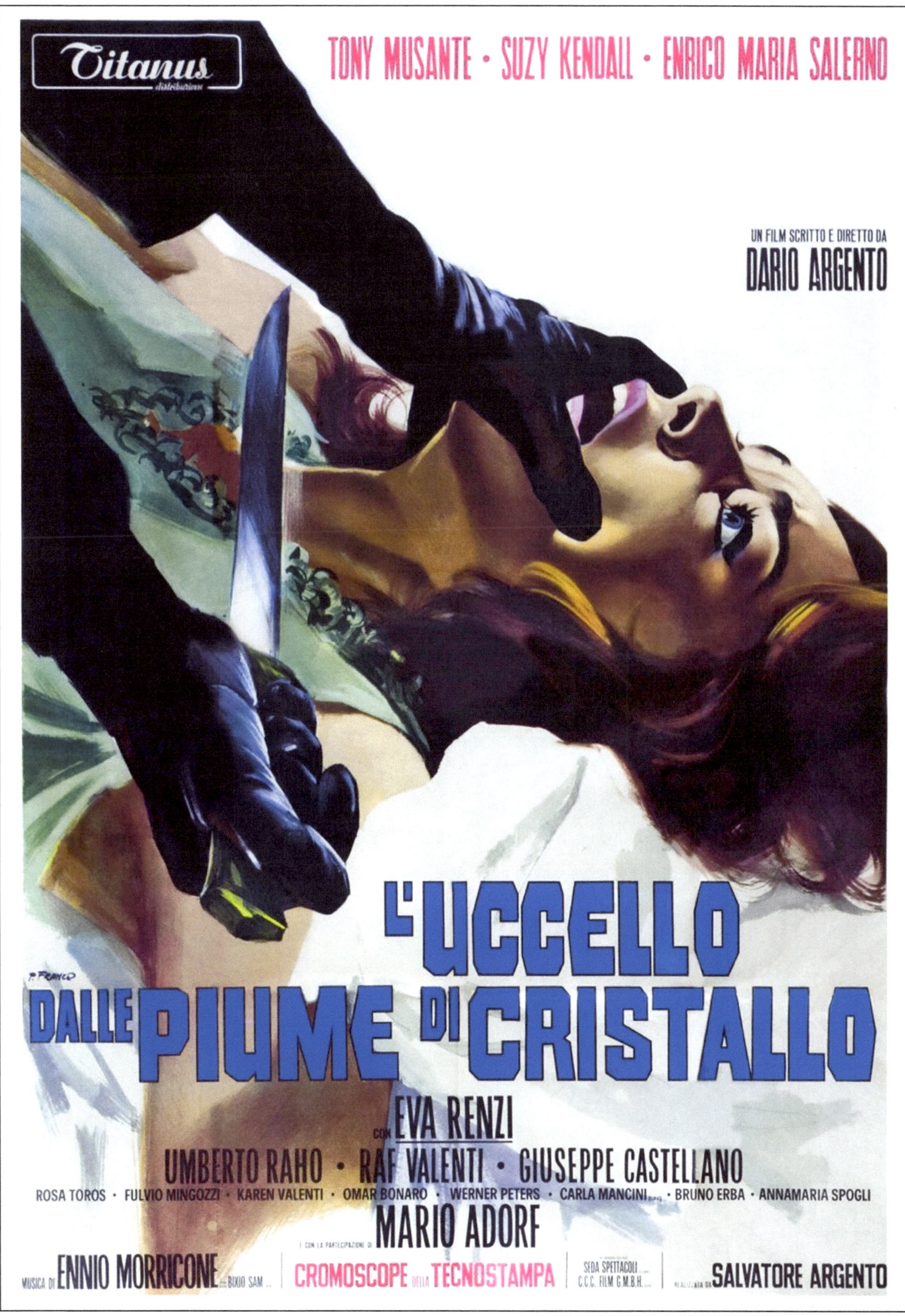

L'UCCELLO DALLE PIUME DI CRISTALLO

(''The Bird With Crystal Plumage''; Italy/Germany, 1970). Artist: P. Franco.

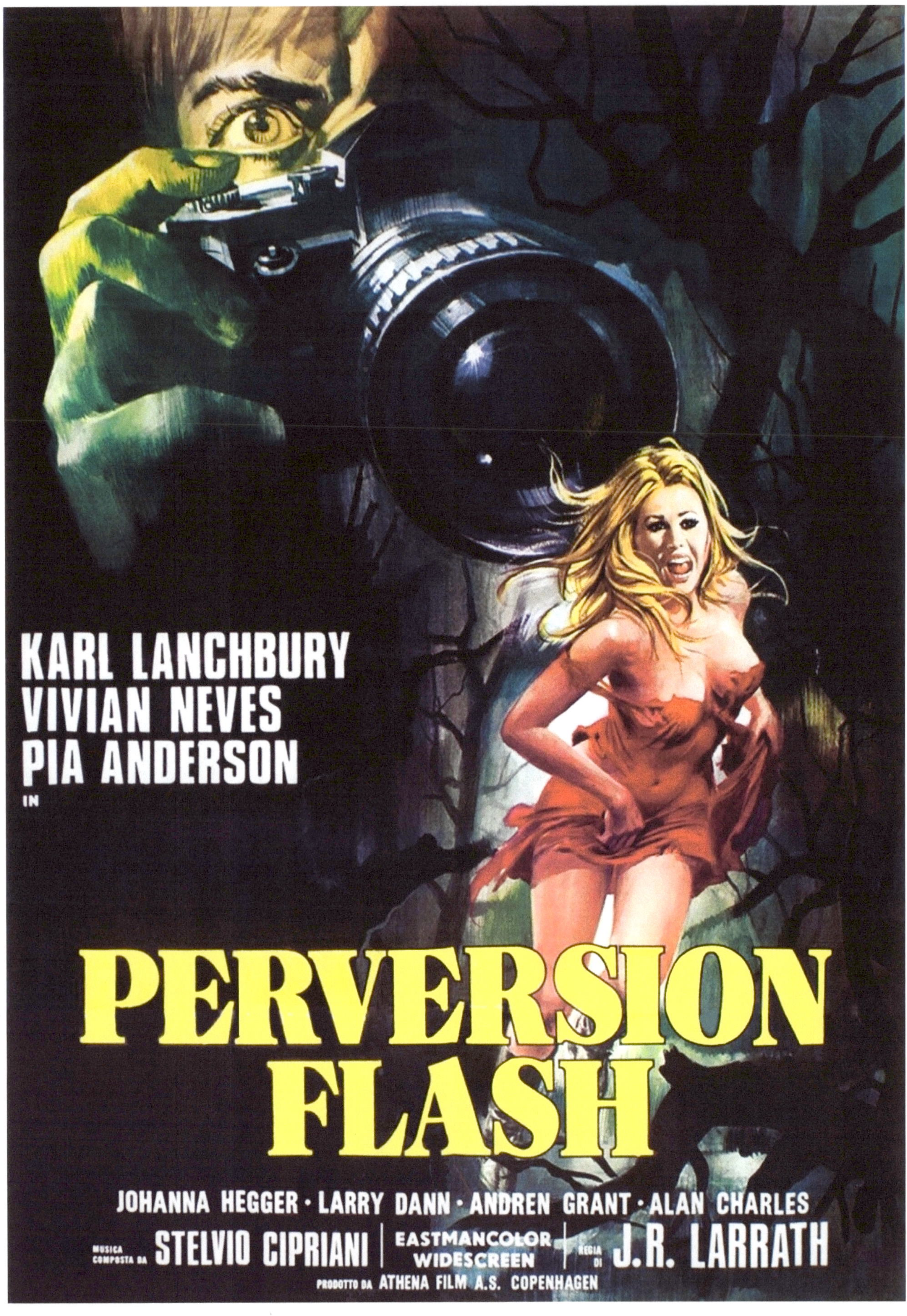

PERVERSION FLASH

("Perversion Flash"; UK/Denmark, 1970). Artist: unsigned. Original Title: **Whirlpool**.

42

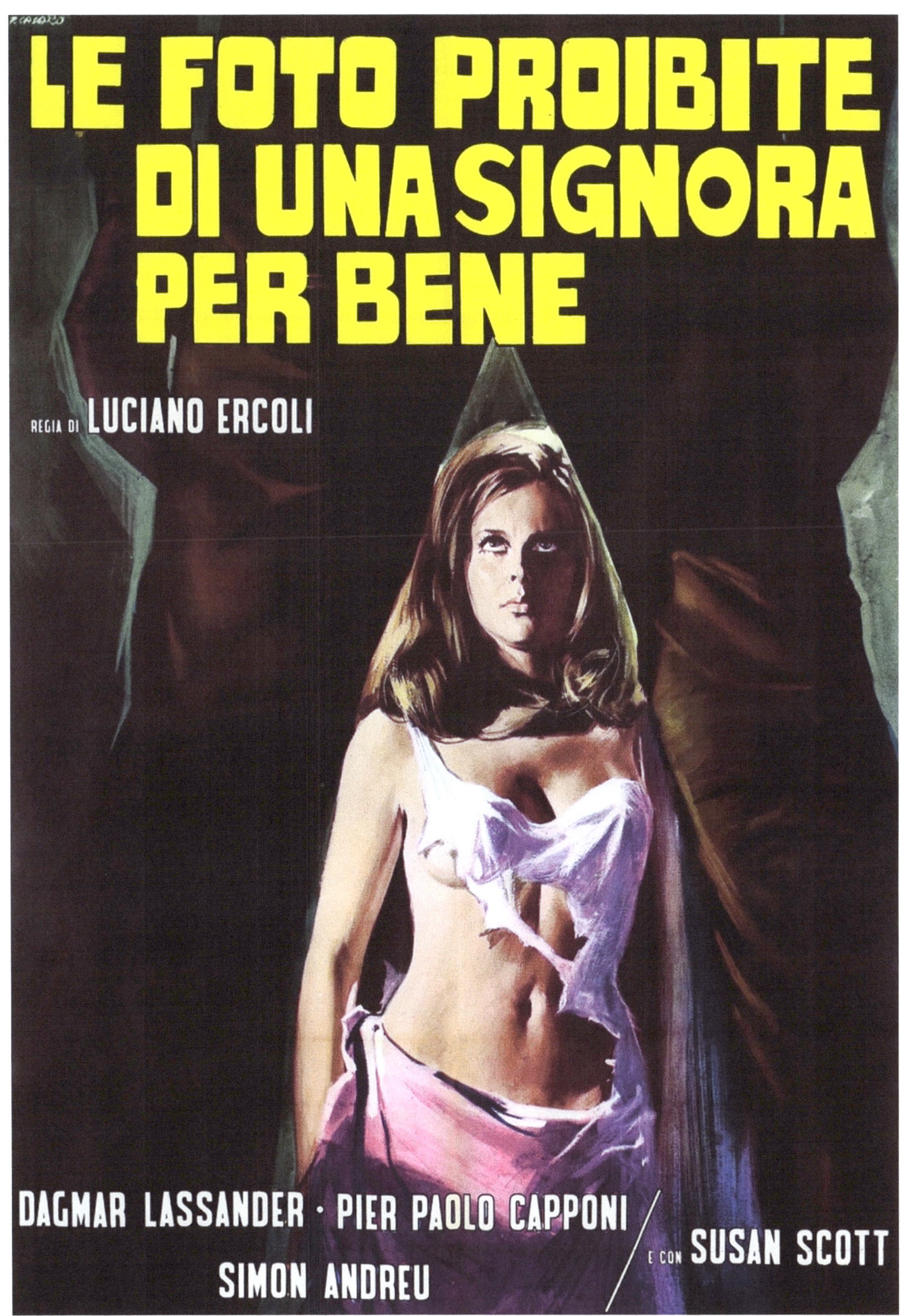

LE FOTO PROIBITE DI UNA SIGNORA PERBENE

("Forbidden Photos Of A Respectable Lady"; Italy/Spain, 1970). Artist: Renato Casaro.

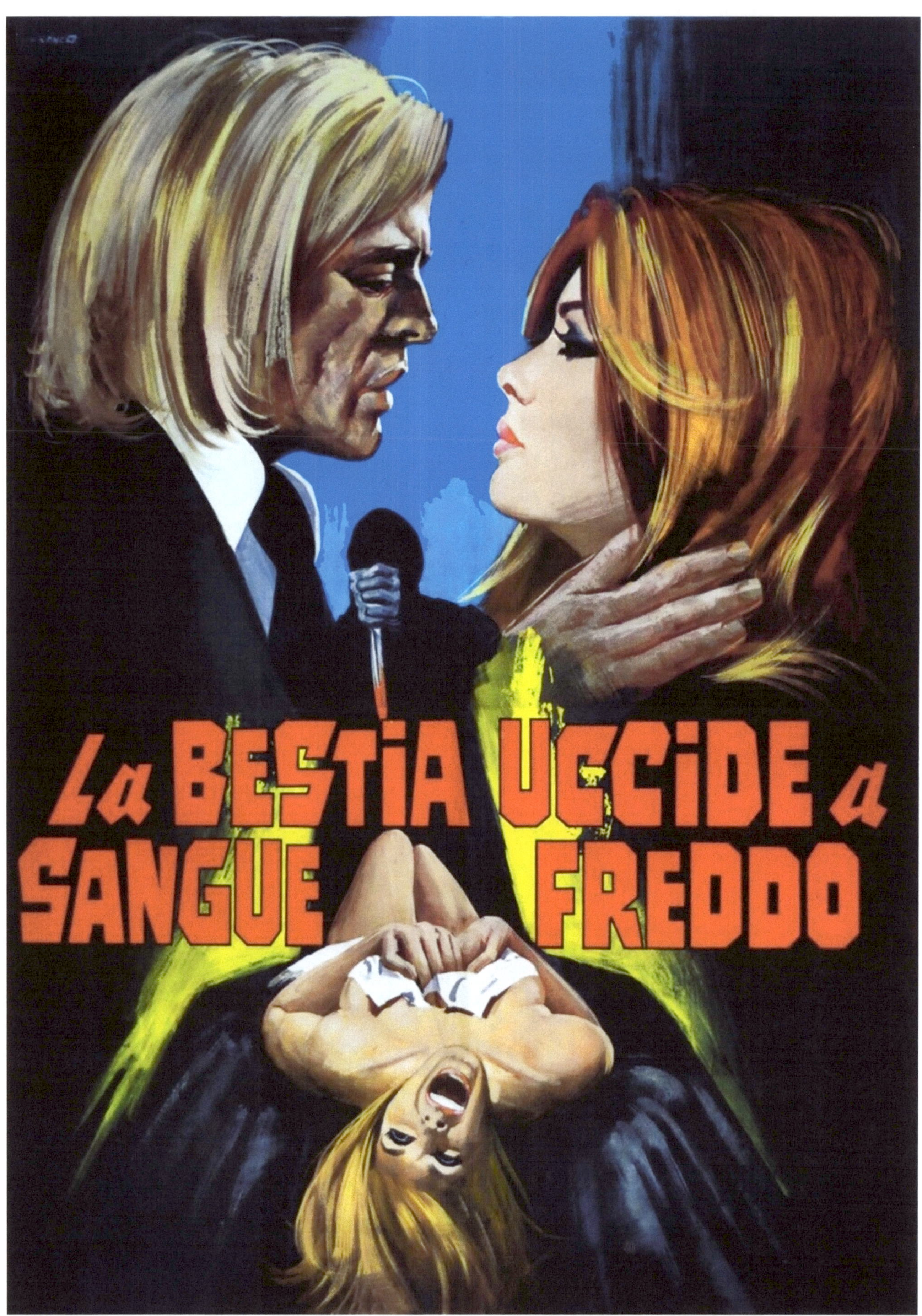

LA BESTIA UCCIDE A SANGUE FREDDO

("The Beast Kills In Cold Blood"; Italy, 1971). Artist: P. Franco.

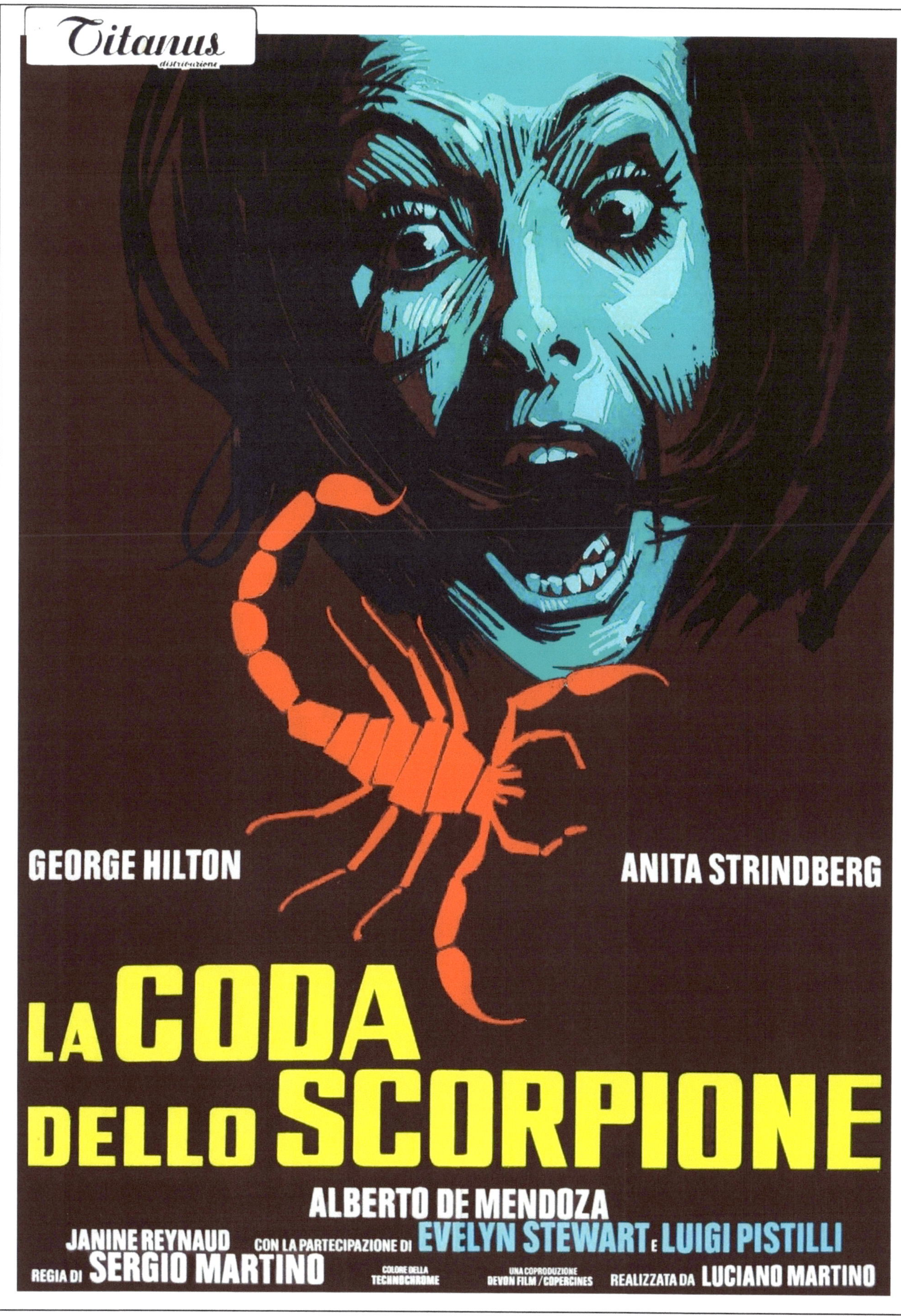

LA CODA DELLO SCORPIONE

(''The Scorpion's Tail''; Italy/Spain, 1971). Artist: unsigned.

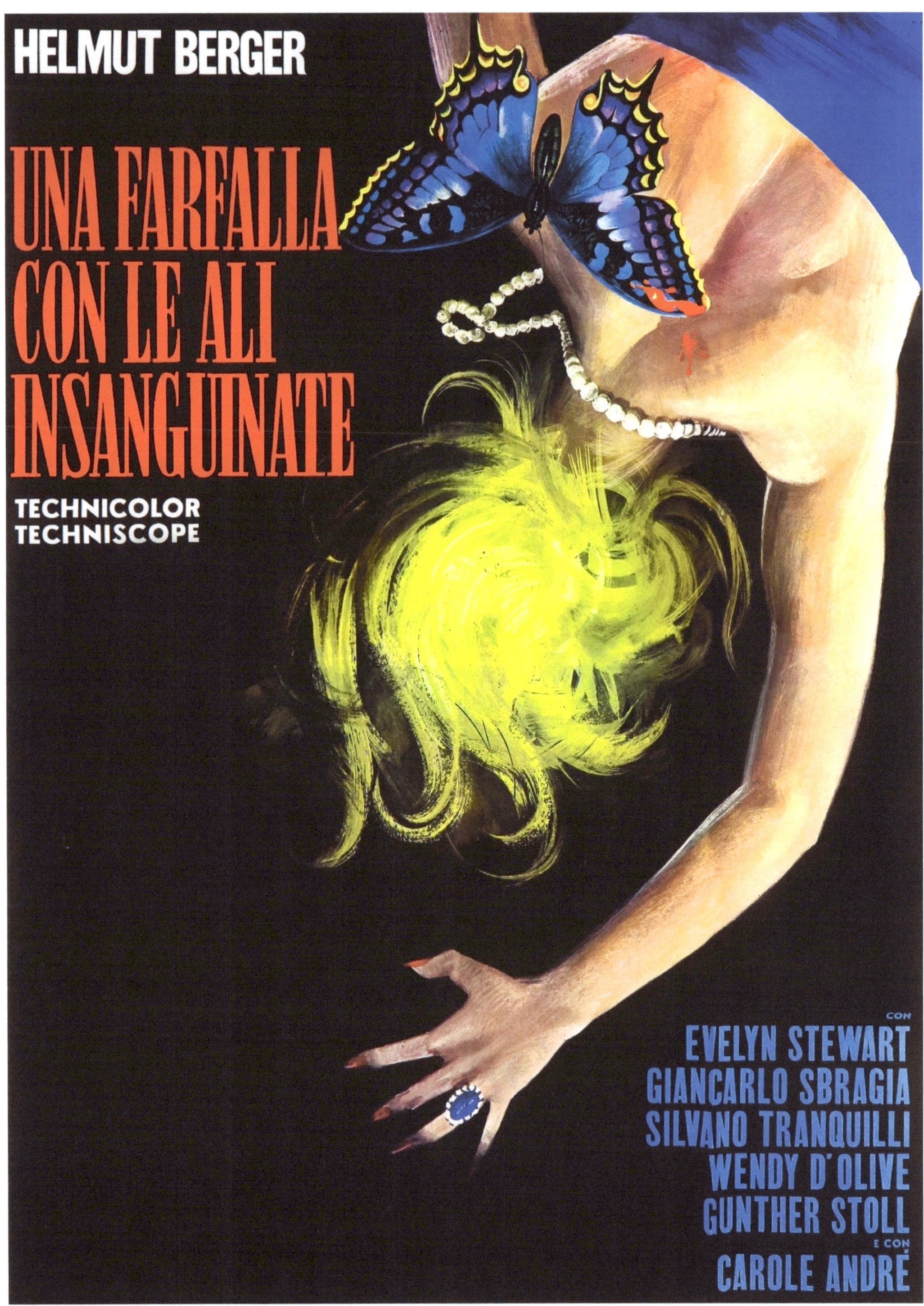

UNA FARFALLA CON LE ALI INSANGUINATE

(''A Butterfly With Bloody Wings''; Italy, 1971). Artist: unsigned.

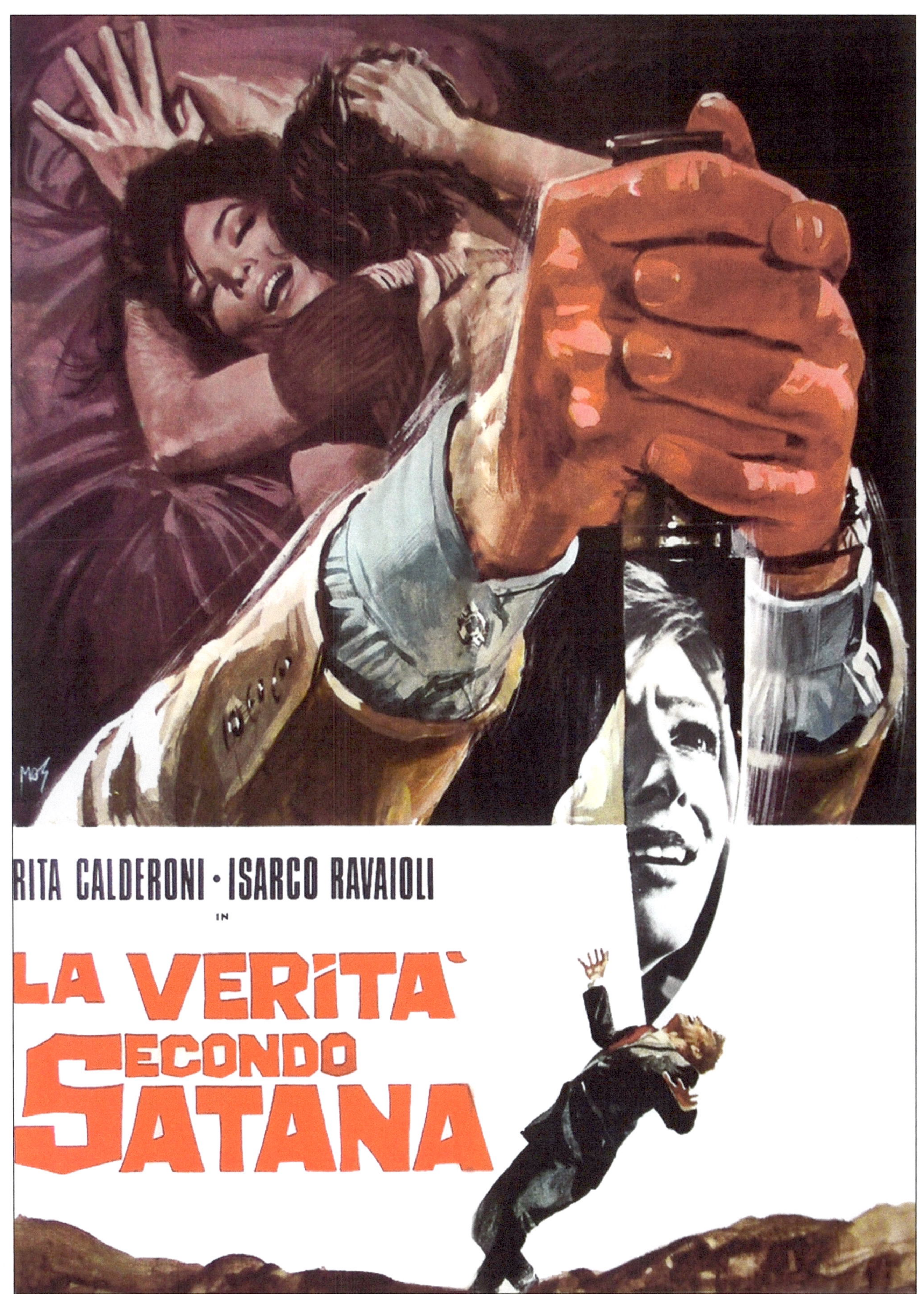

LA VERITÀ SECONDO SATANA

("The Truth According To Satan"; Italy, 1971). Artist: Moz.

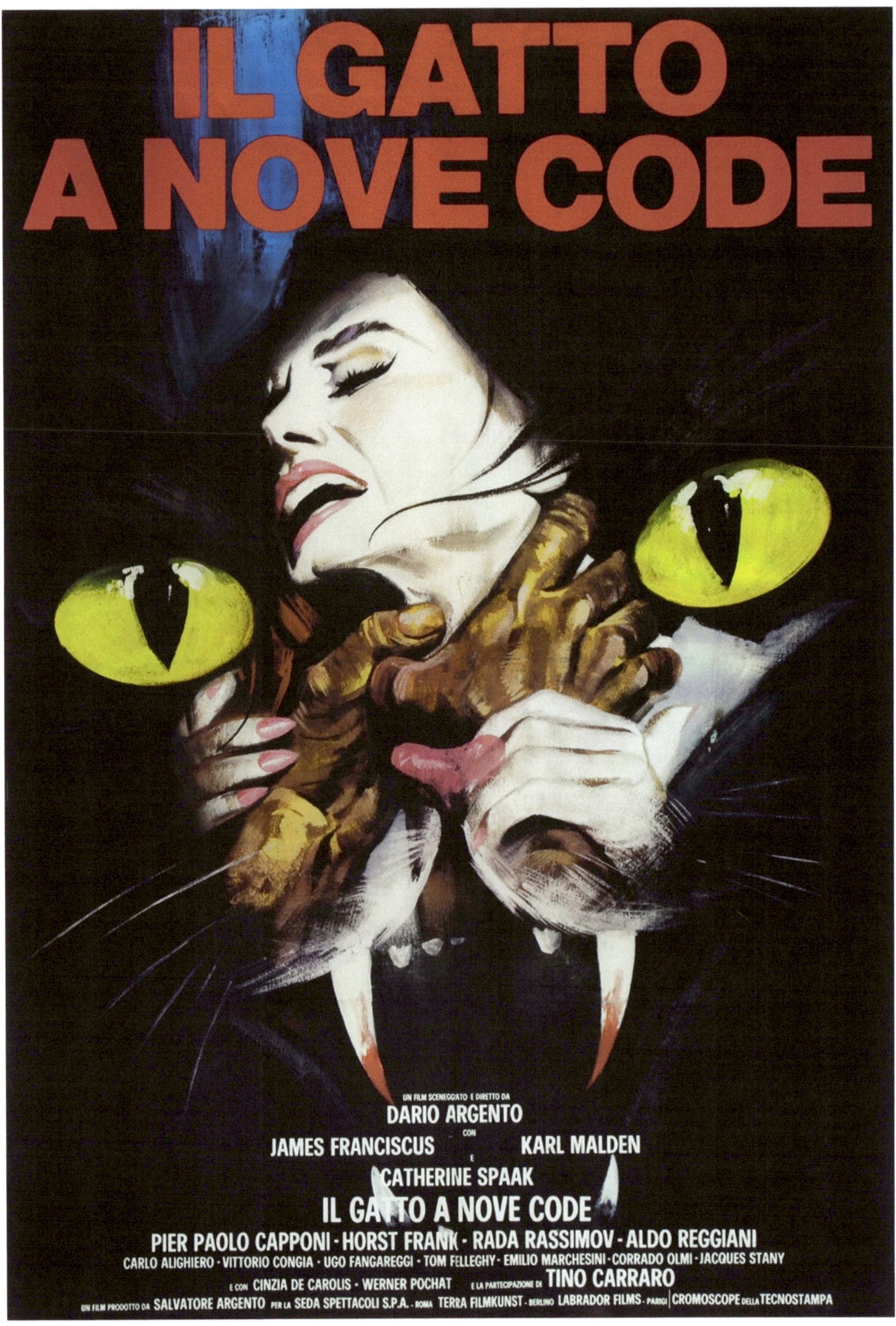

IL GATTO A NOVE CODE

(''The Nine-Tailed Cat''; Italy/Germany/France, 1971). Artist: P. Franco.

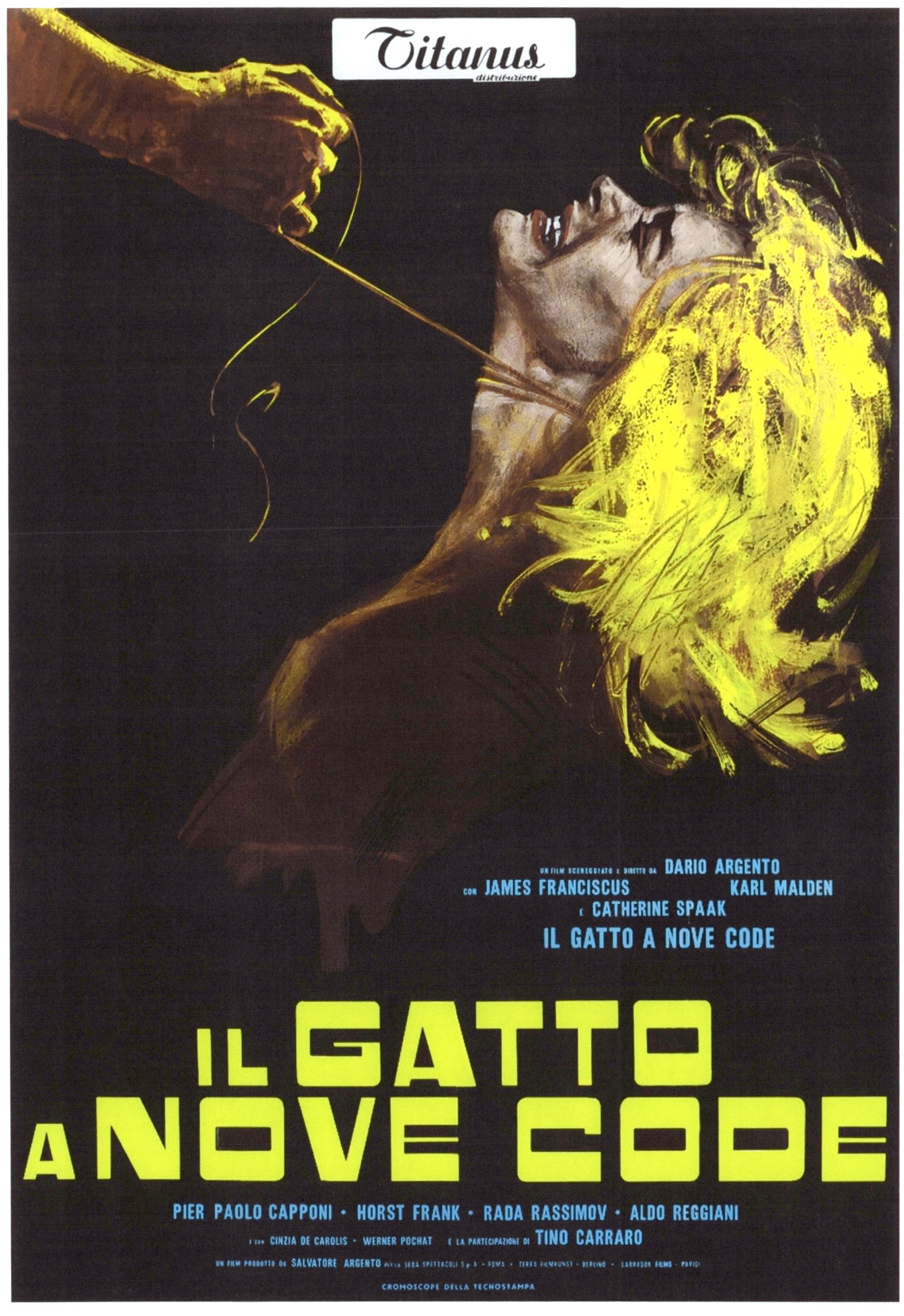

IL GATTO A NOVE CODE

("The Nine-Tailed Cat"; Italy/Germany/France, 1971). Artist: unsigned.

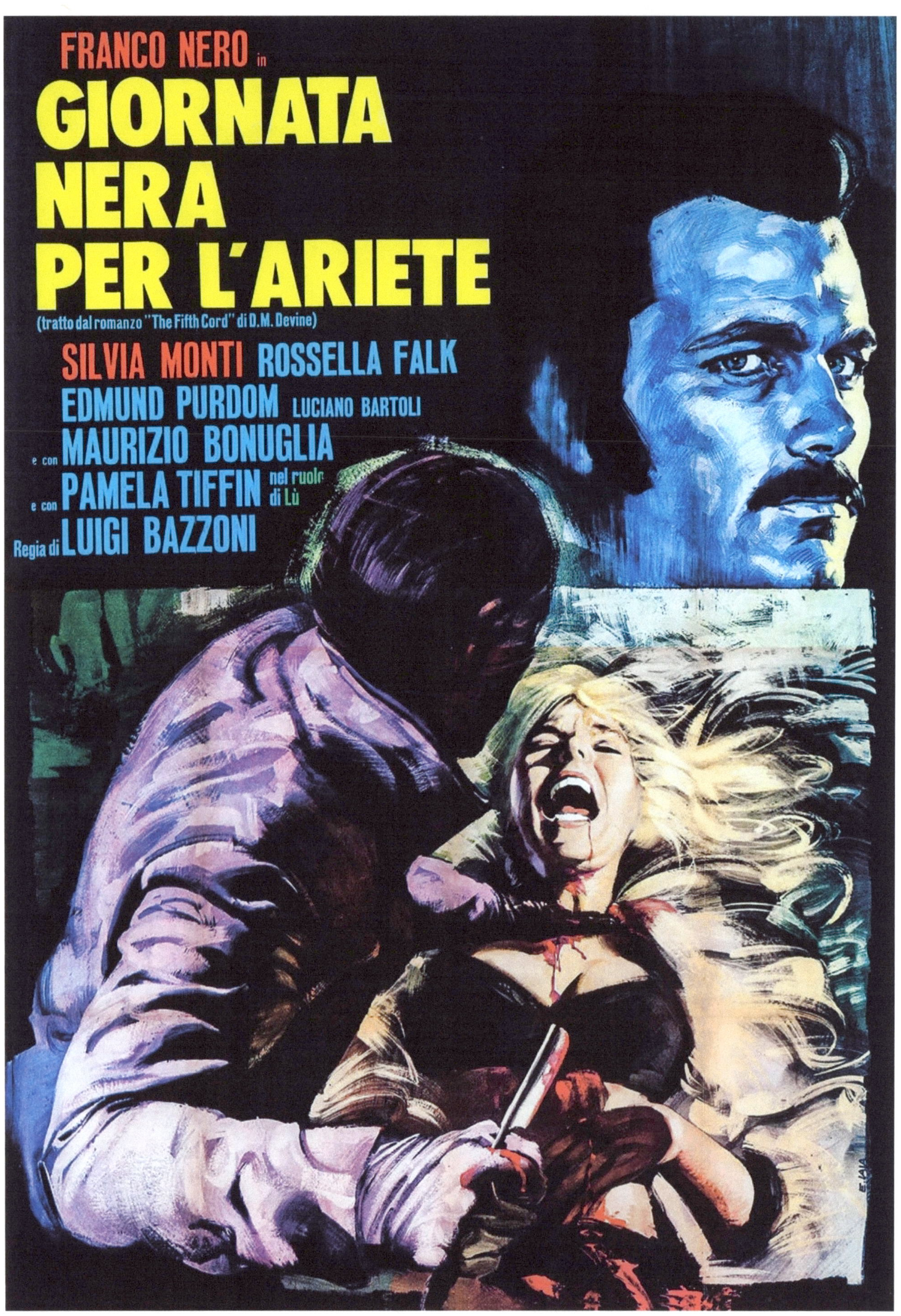

GIORNATA NERA PER L'ARIETE

("Black Day For Ariete"; Italy, 1971). Artist: unsigned.

50

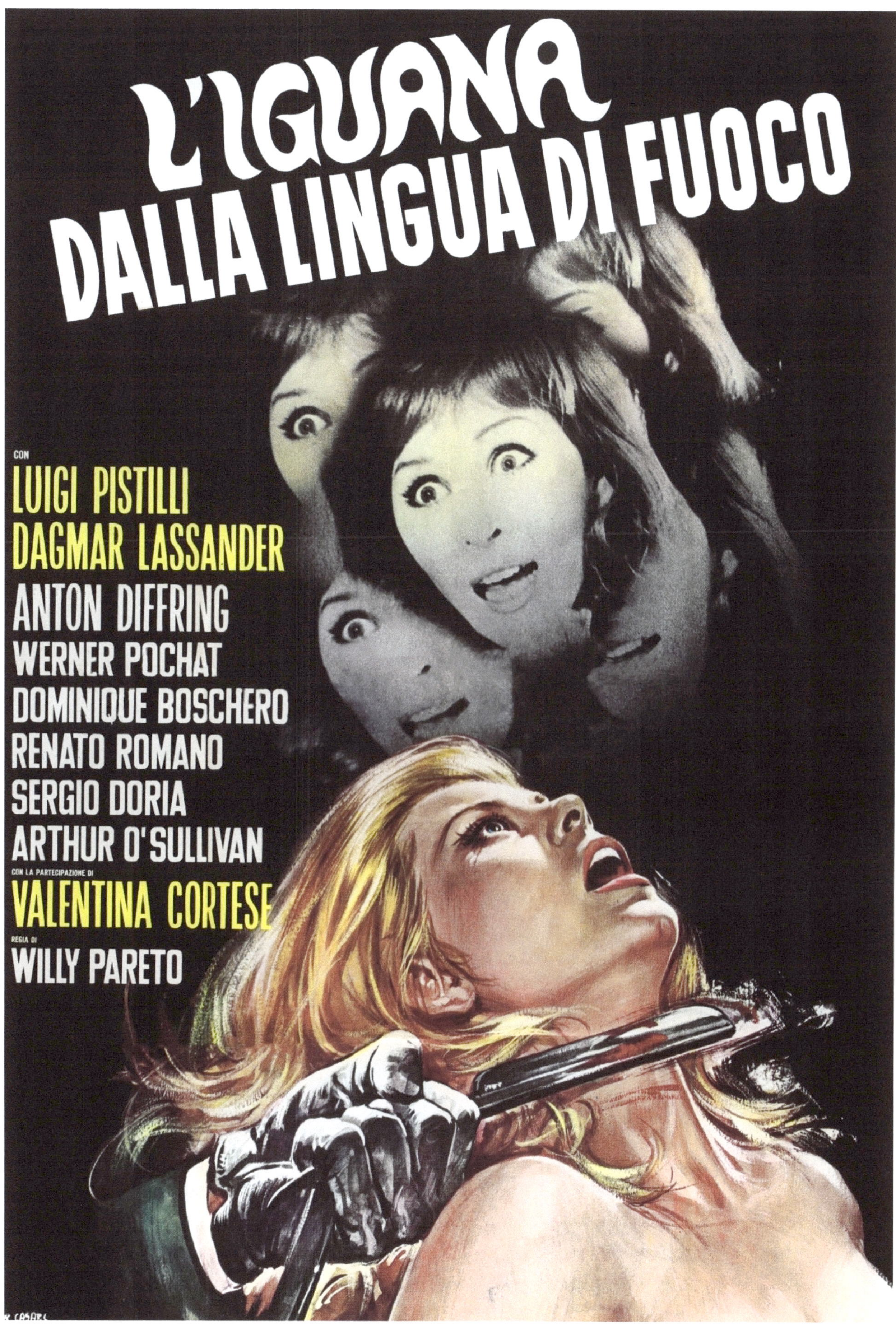

("The Lizard With A Tongue Of Fire"; Italy/Germany/France, 1971). Artist: Renato Casaro.

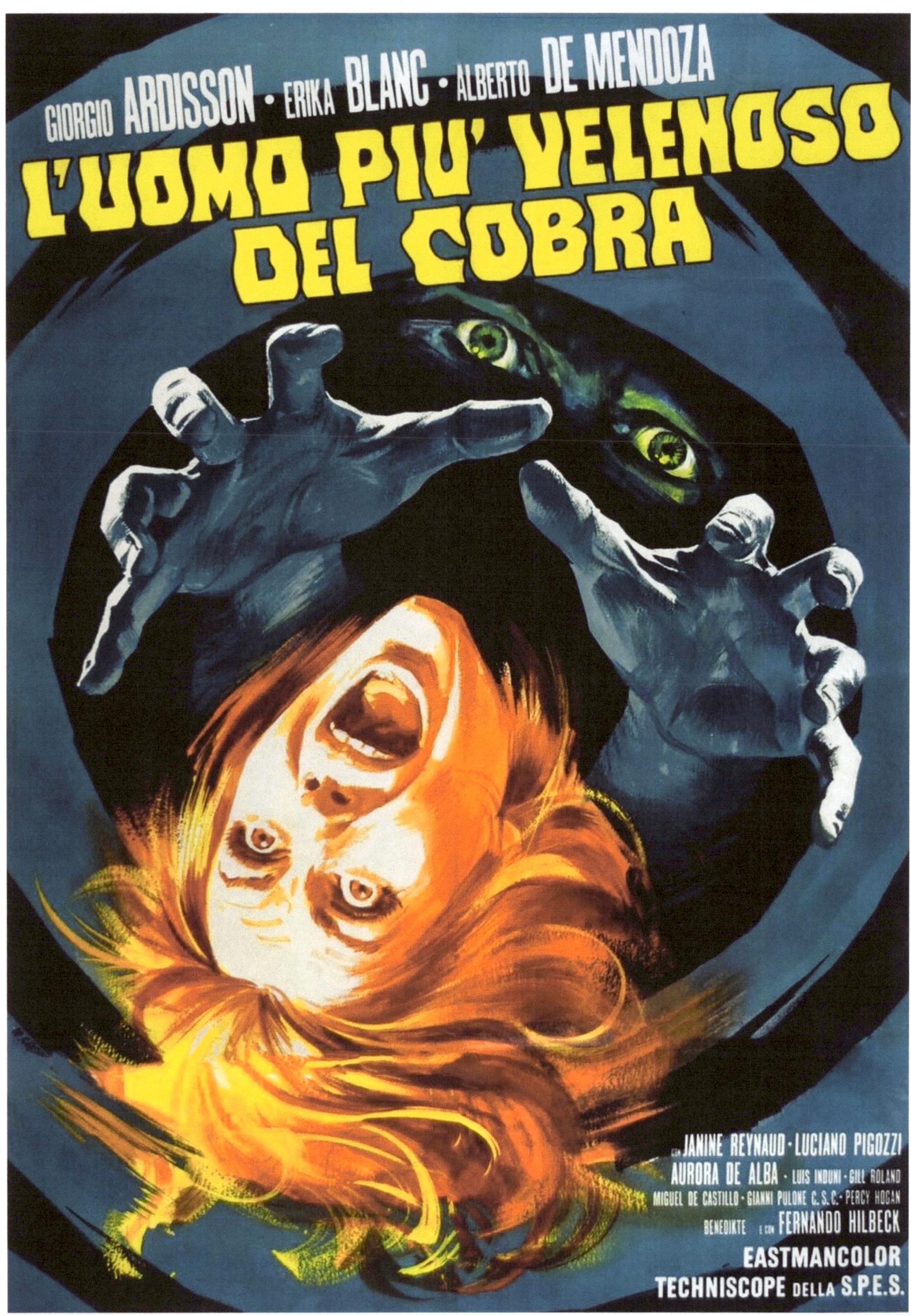

L'UOMO PIÙ VELENOSO DEL COBRA

("The Man More Poisonous Than A Cobra"; Italy/Spain, 1971). Artist: unsigned.

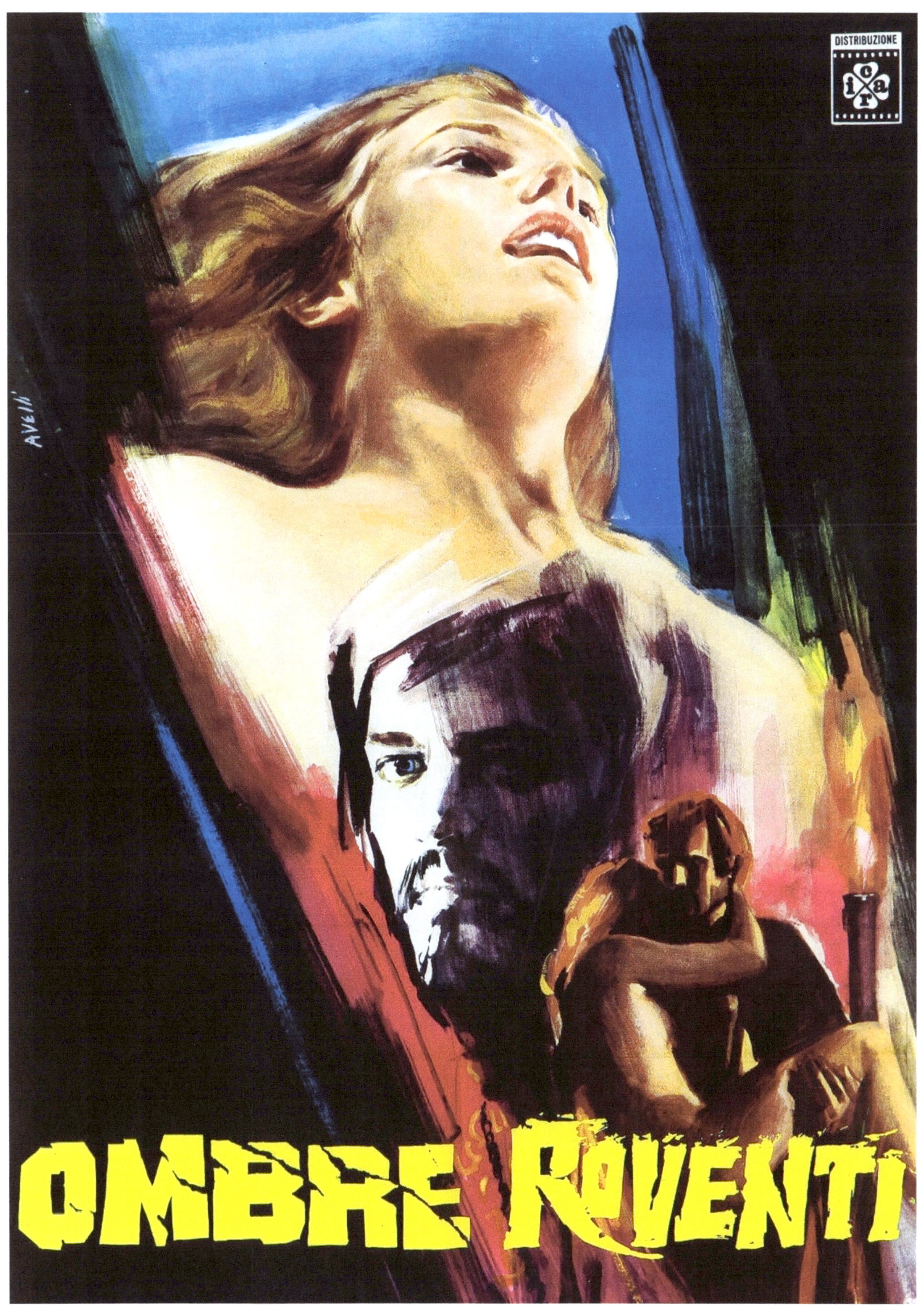

("Scorching Shadow"; Italy, 1970). Artist: Tino Avelli.

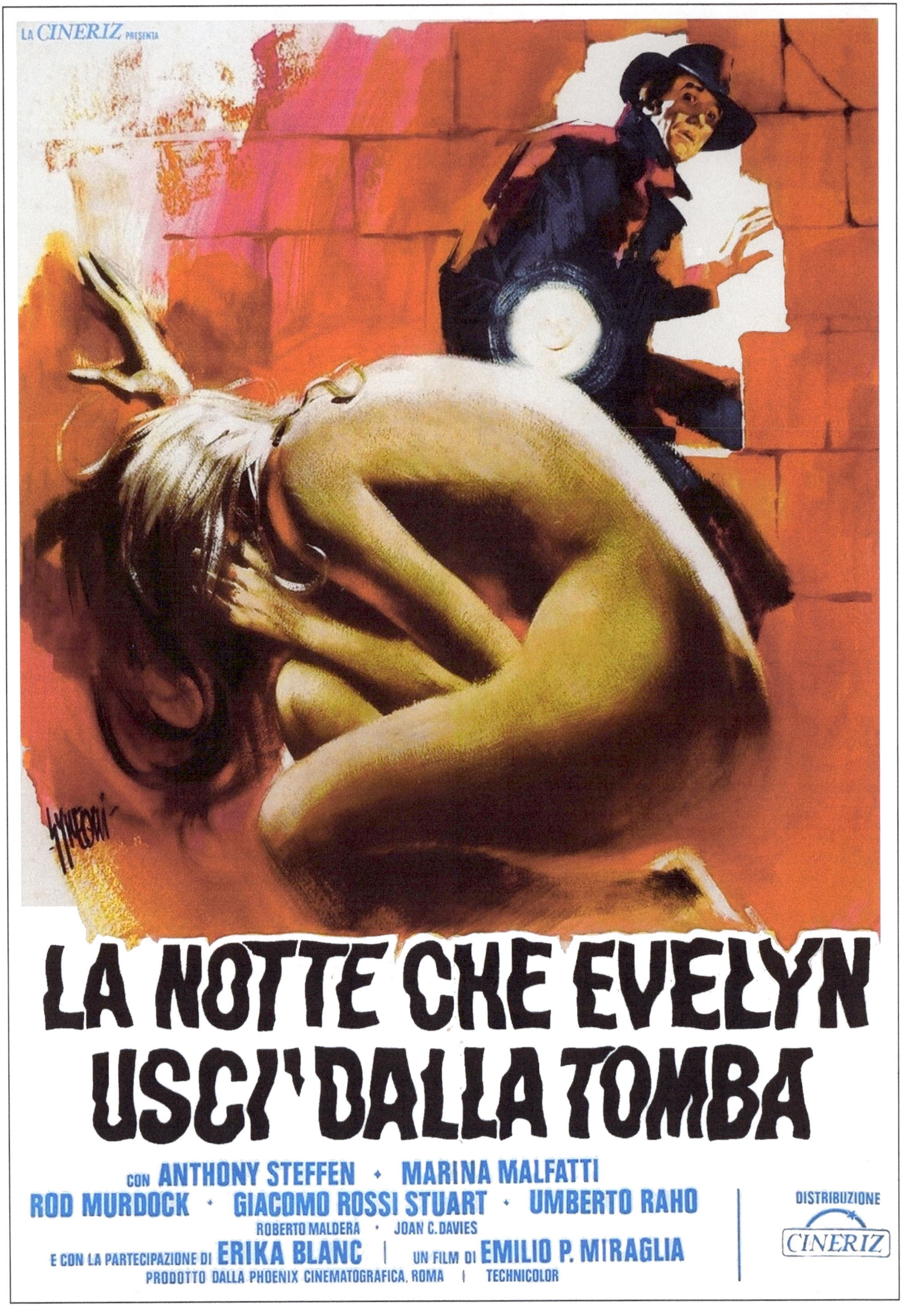

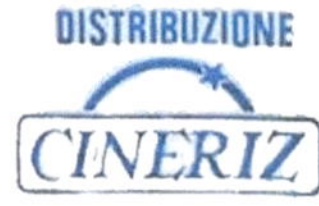

LA NOTTE CHE EVELYN USCI DALLA TOMBA

("The Night Evelyn Rose From The Tomb"; Italy, 1971). Artist: Sandro Symeoni.

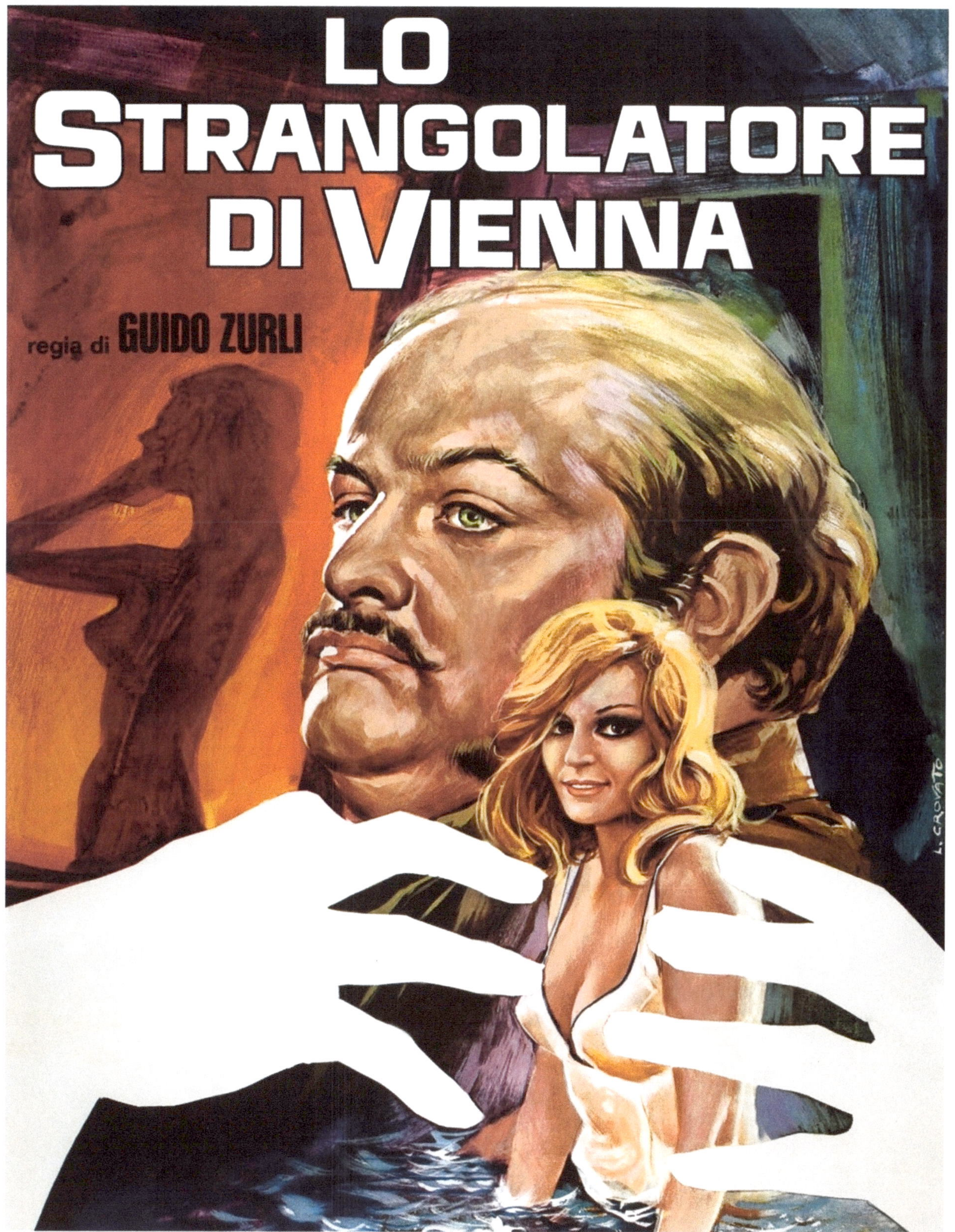

LO STRANGOLATORE DI VIENNA

("The Vienna Strangler"; Italy/Germany, 1971). Artist: Luca Crovato.

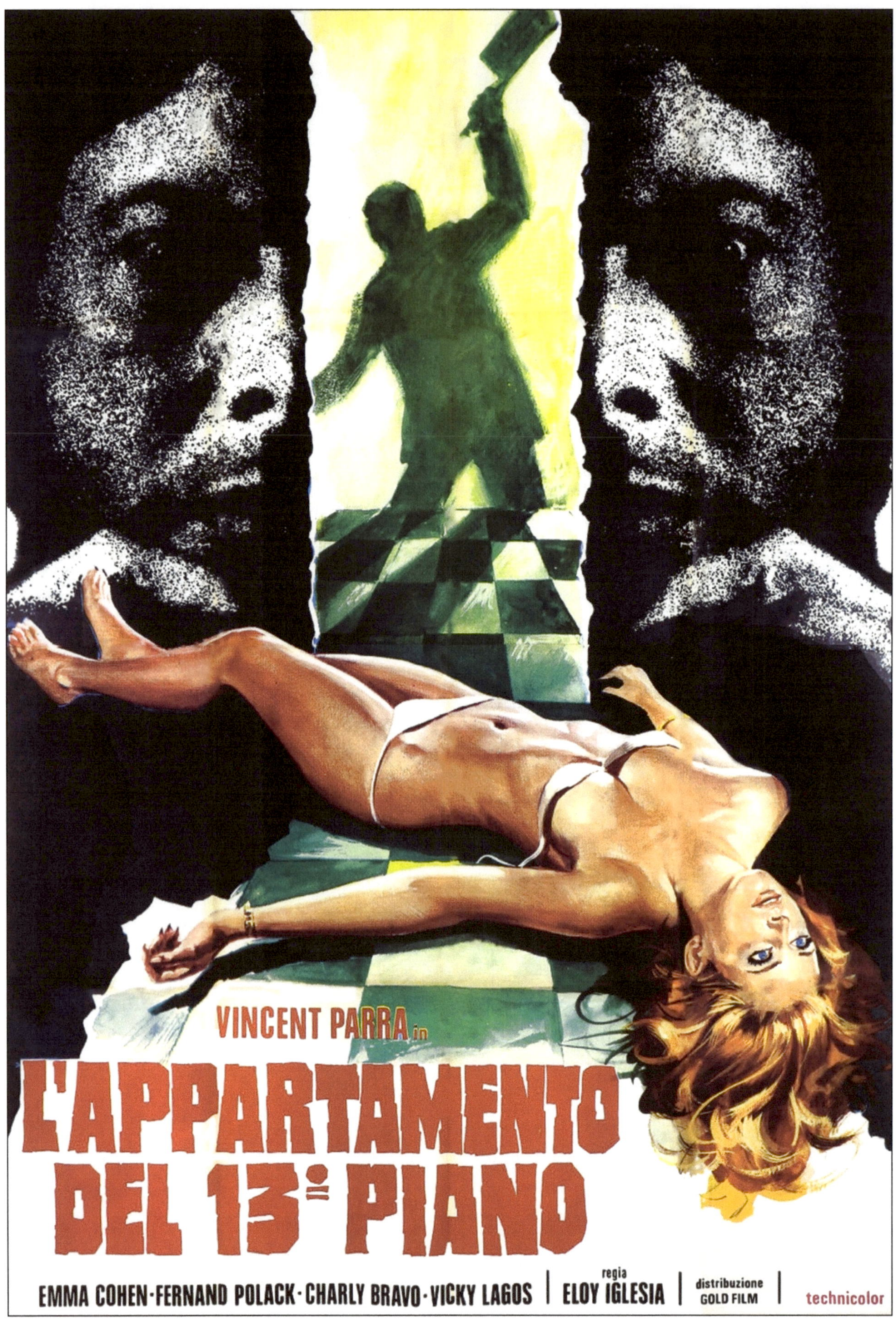

L'APPARTAMENTO DEL 13° PIANO

("The 13th Floor Apartment"; Spain, 1971). Artist: unsigned. Original Title: "La Semana Del Asesino".

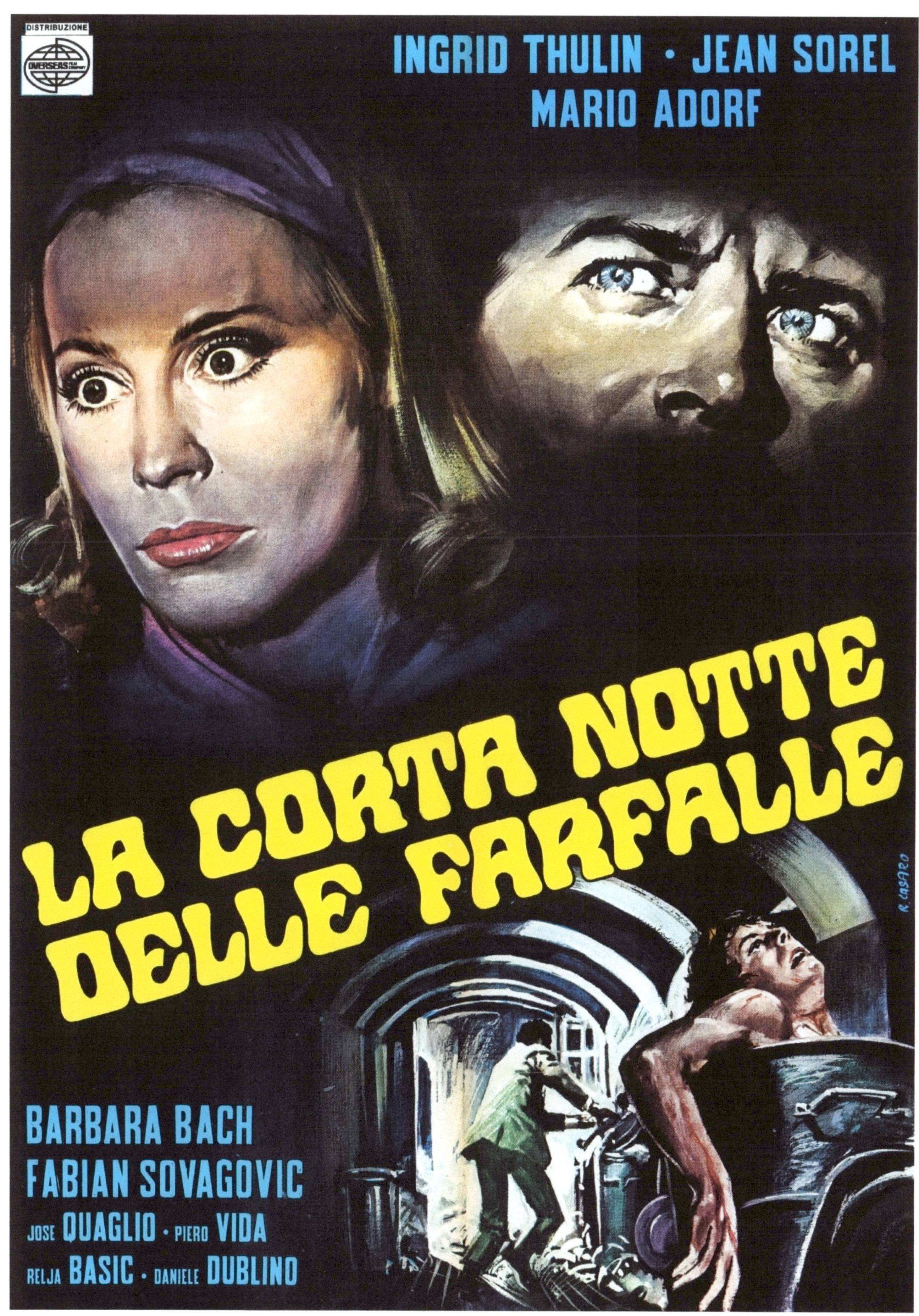

("The Short Night Of The Butterflies"; Italy/Germany, 1971). Artist: Renato Casaro. Release Title: "La Corta Notte Delle Bambole Di Vetro".

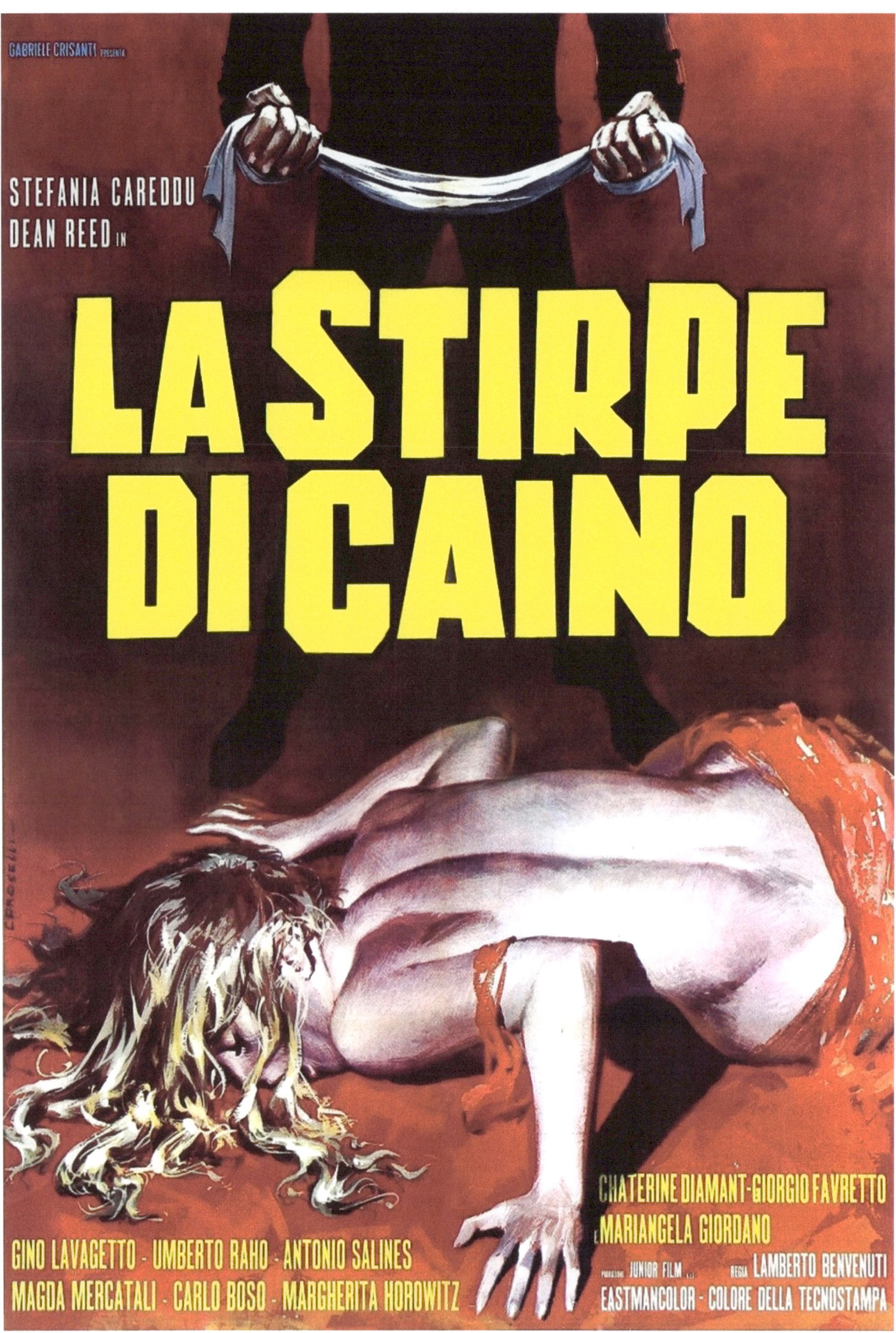

LA STIRPE DI CAINO

("The Bloodline Of Cain"; Italy, 1969-71). Artist: Caroselli.

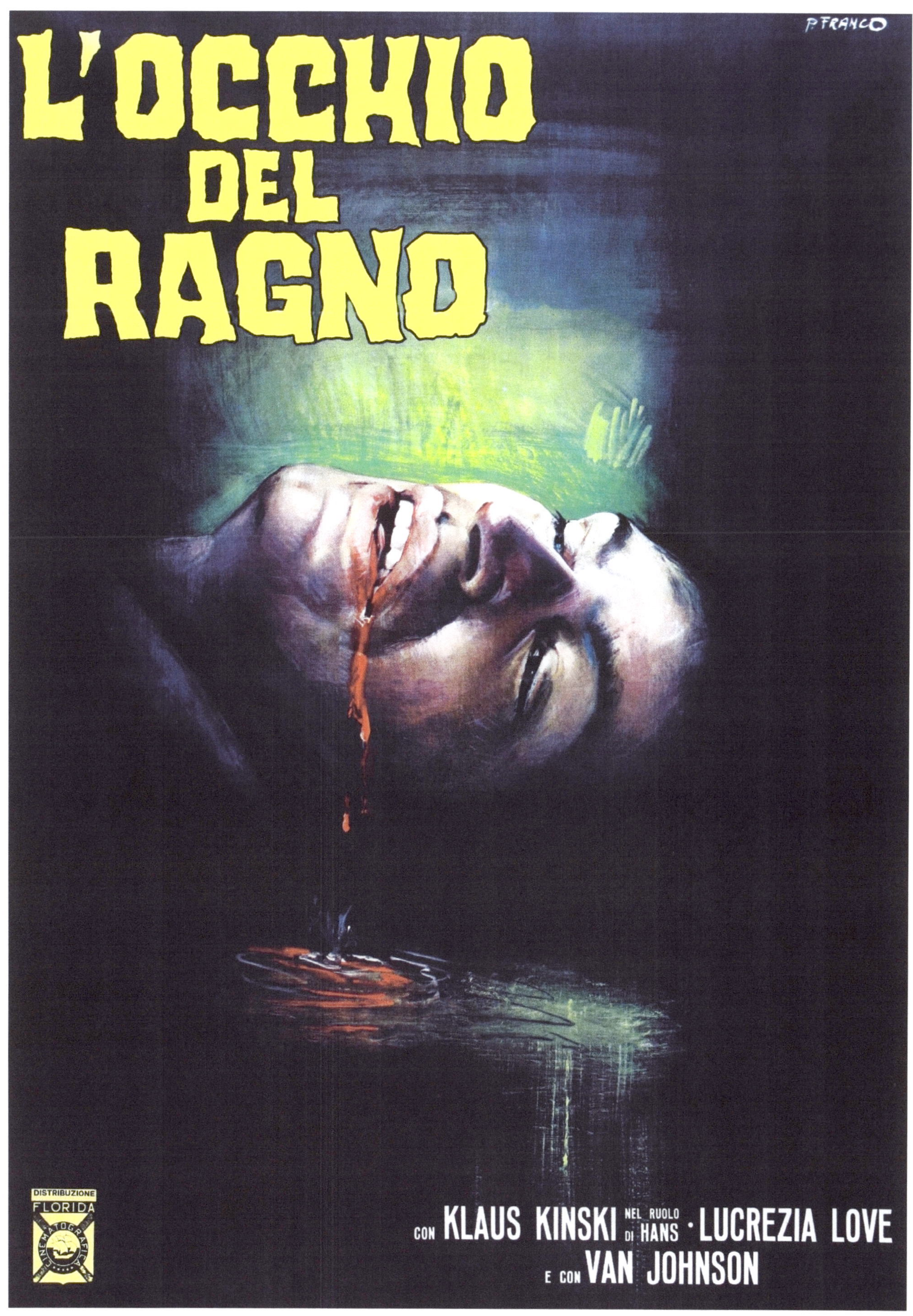

L'OCCHIO DEL RAGNO
(''Eye Of The Spider''; Italy, 1971). Artist: P. Franco.

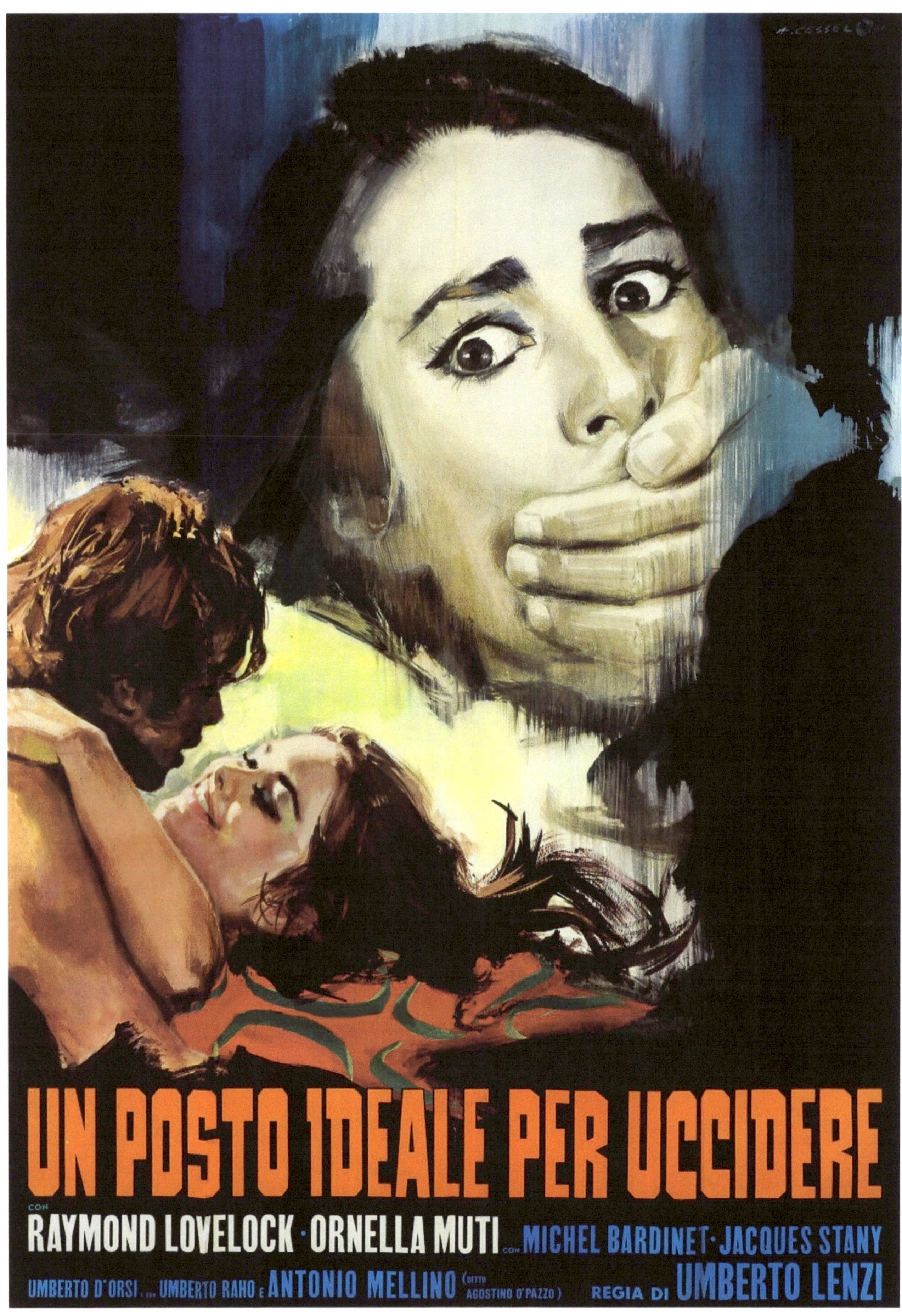

UN POSTO IDEALE PER UCCIDERE

("A Perfect Place For Murder"; Italy, 1971). Artist: Angelo Cessalon.

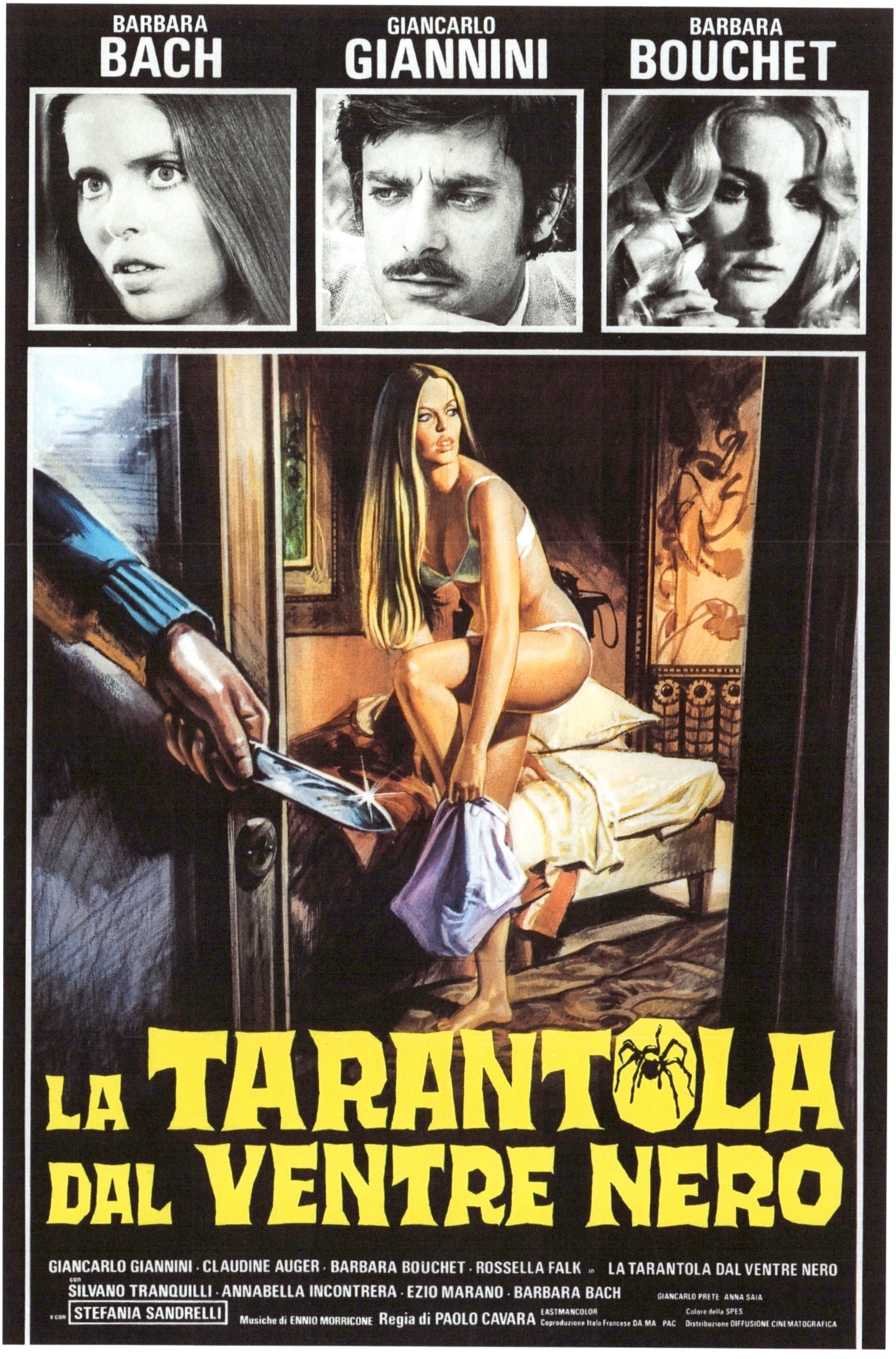

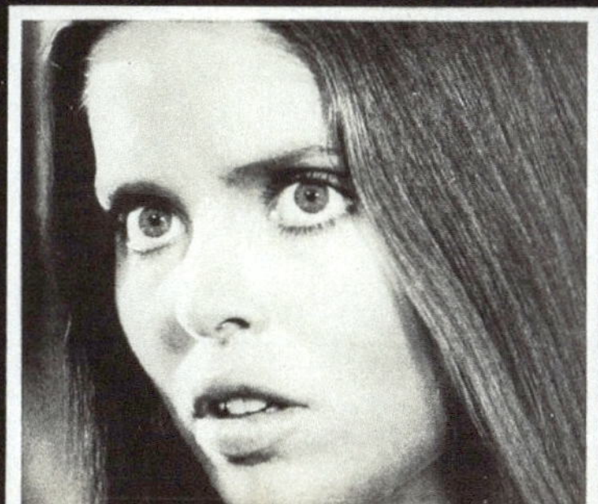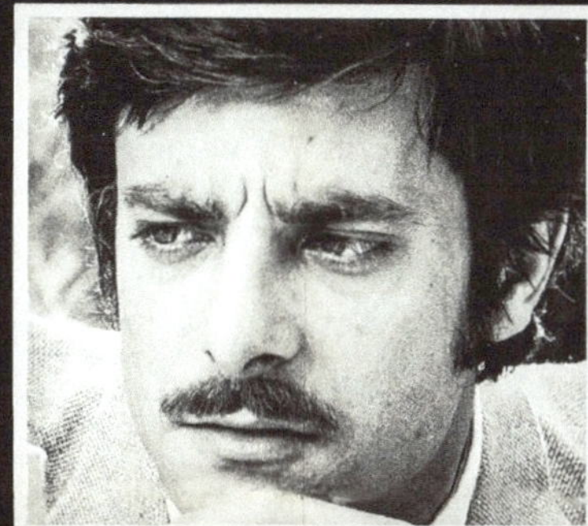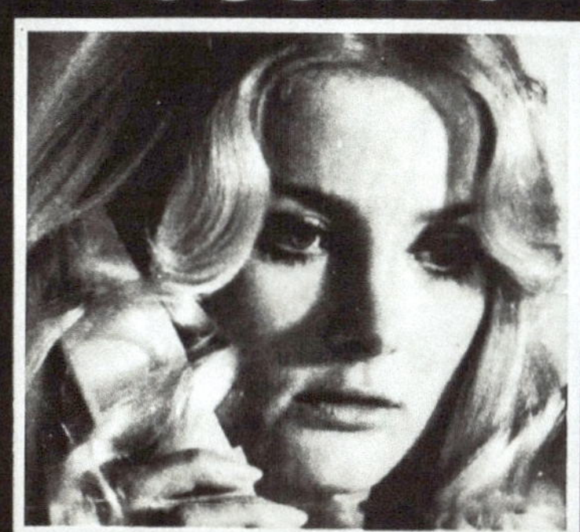

LA TARANTOLA DAL VENTRE NERO

("The Black-Bellied Tarantula"; Italy/France, 1971). Artist: unsigned.

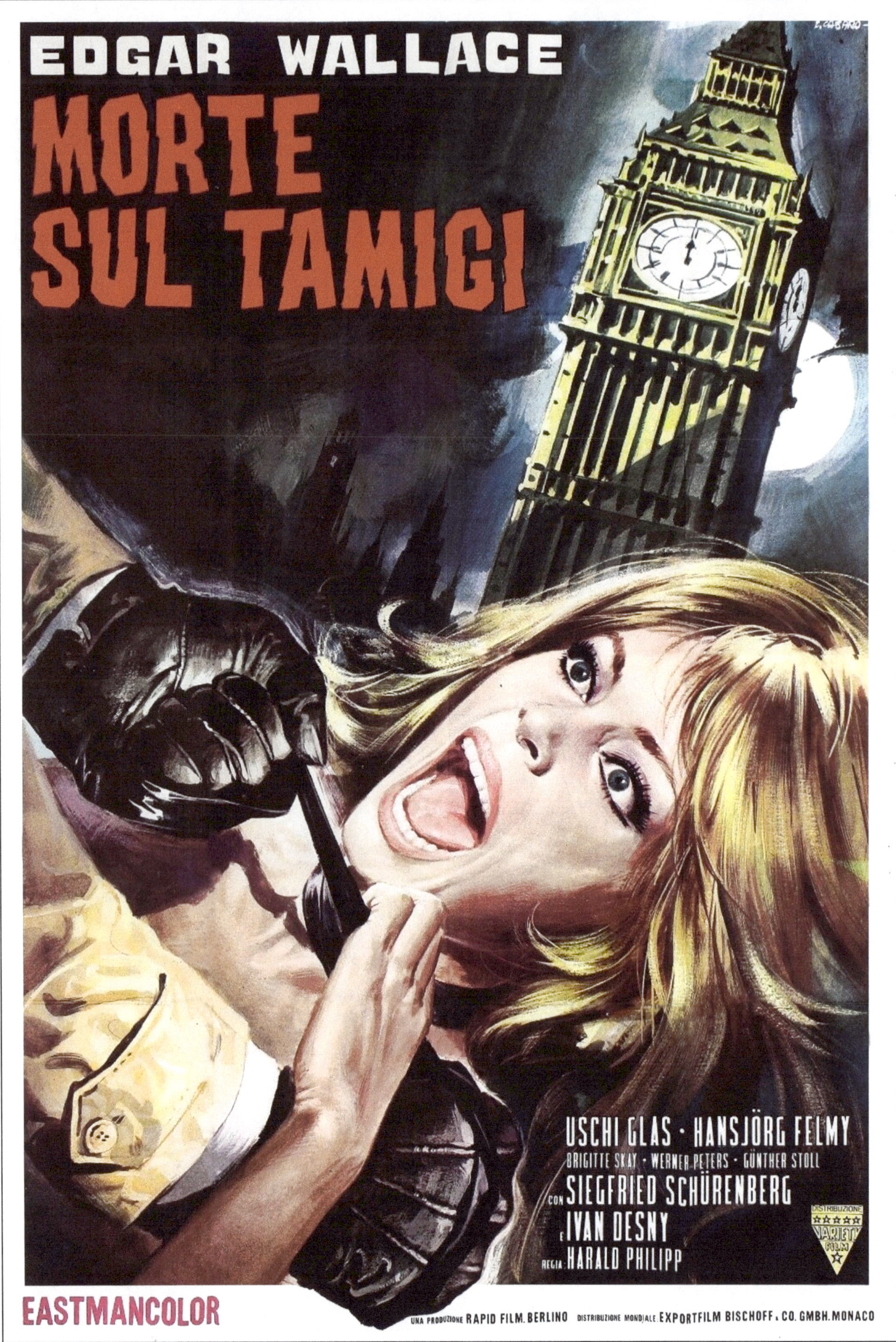

("Death On The Thames"; Germany/UK, 1971). Artist: Renato Casaro. Original Title: **Die Tote Aus Der Themse**.

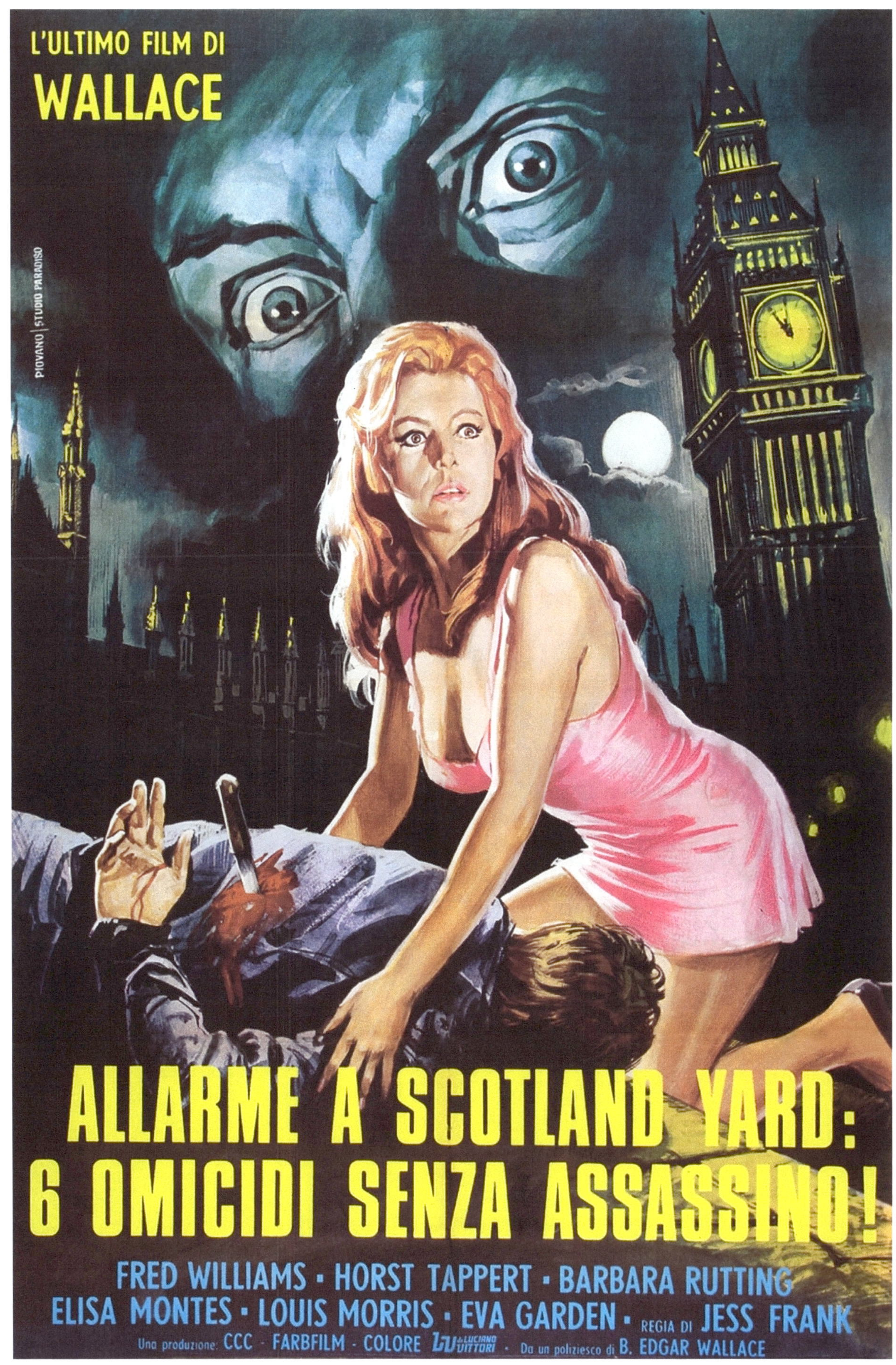

("Alarm At Scotland Yard: 6 Murders, No Killer!"; Germany/Spain/UK, 1972). Artist: Mario Piovano. Original Title: **Der Todesrächer Von Soho**.

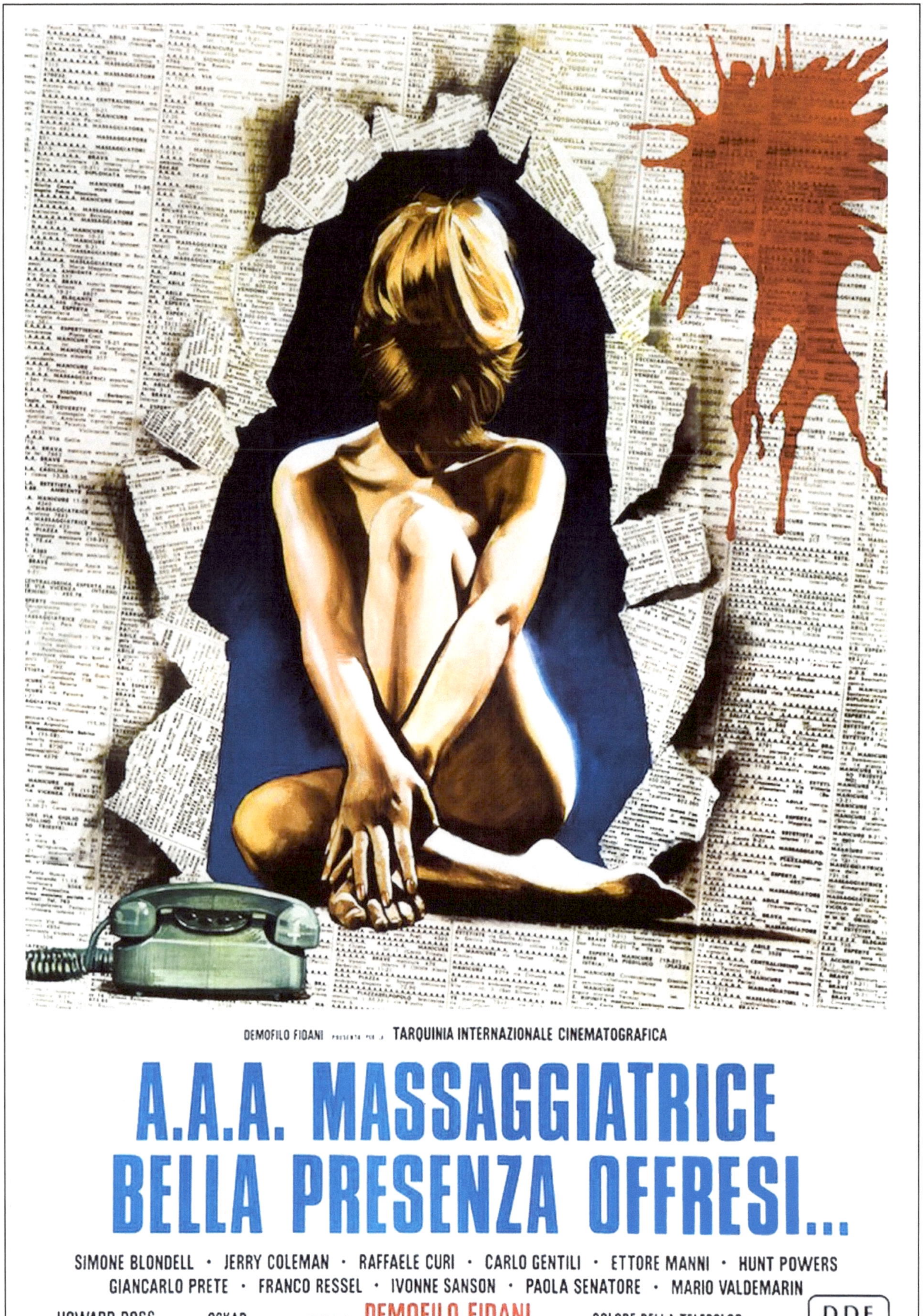

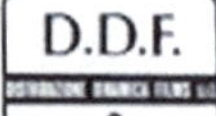

A.A.A. MASSAGGIATRICE BELLA PRESENZA OFFRESI

("A.A.A. Beautiful Masseuse For Hire"; Italy, 1972). Artist: unsigned.

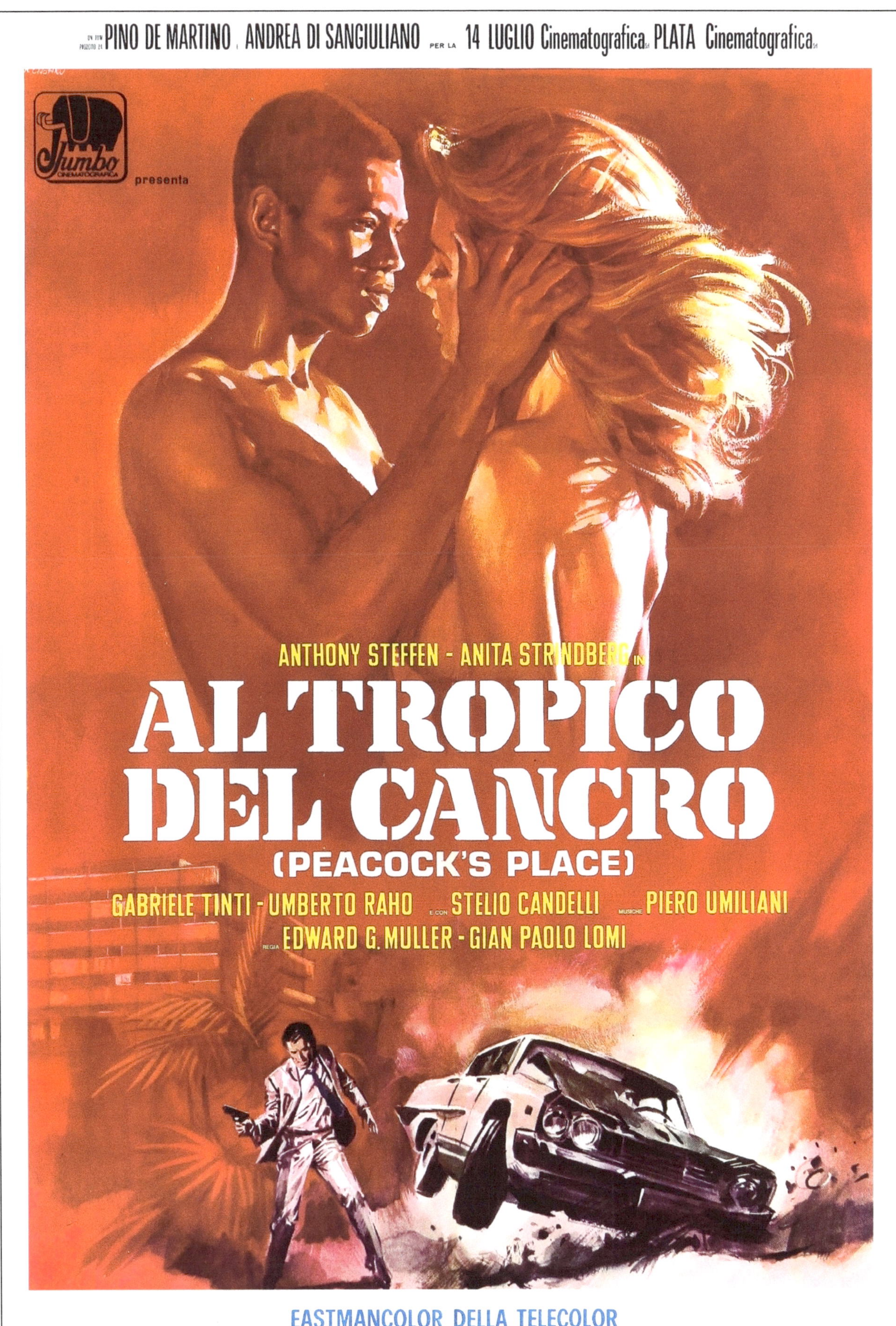

AL TROPICO DEL CANCRO

("At The Tropic Of Cancer"; Italy, 1972). Artist: Renato Casaro.

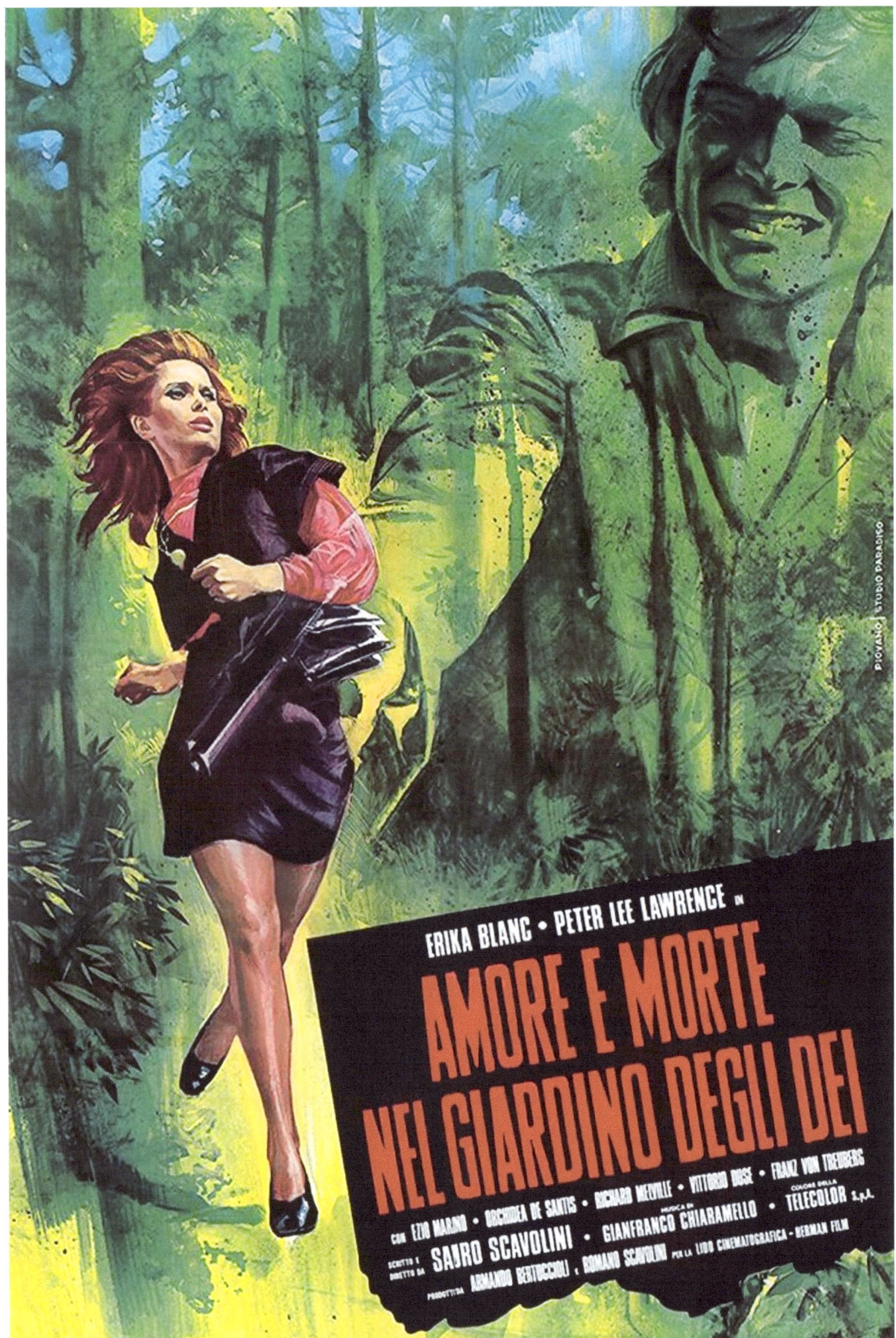

AMORE E MORTE NEL GIARDINO DEGLI DEI

(''Love And Death In The Garden Of The Gods''; Italy, 1972). Artist: Mario Piovano.

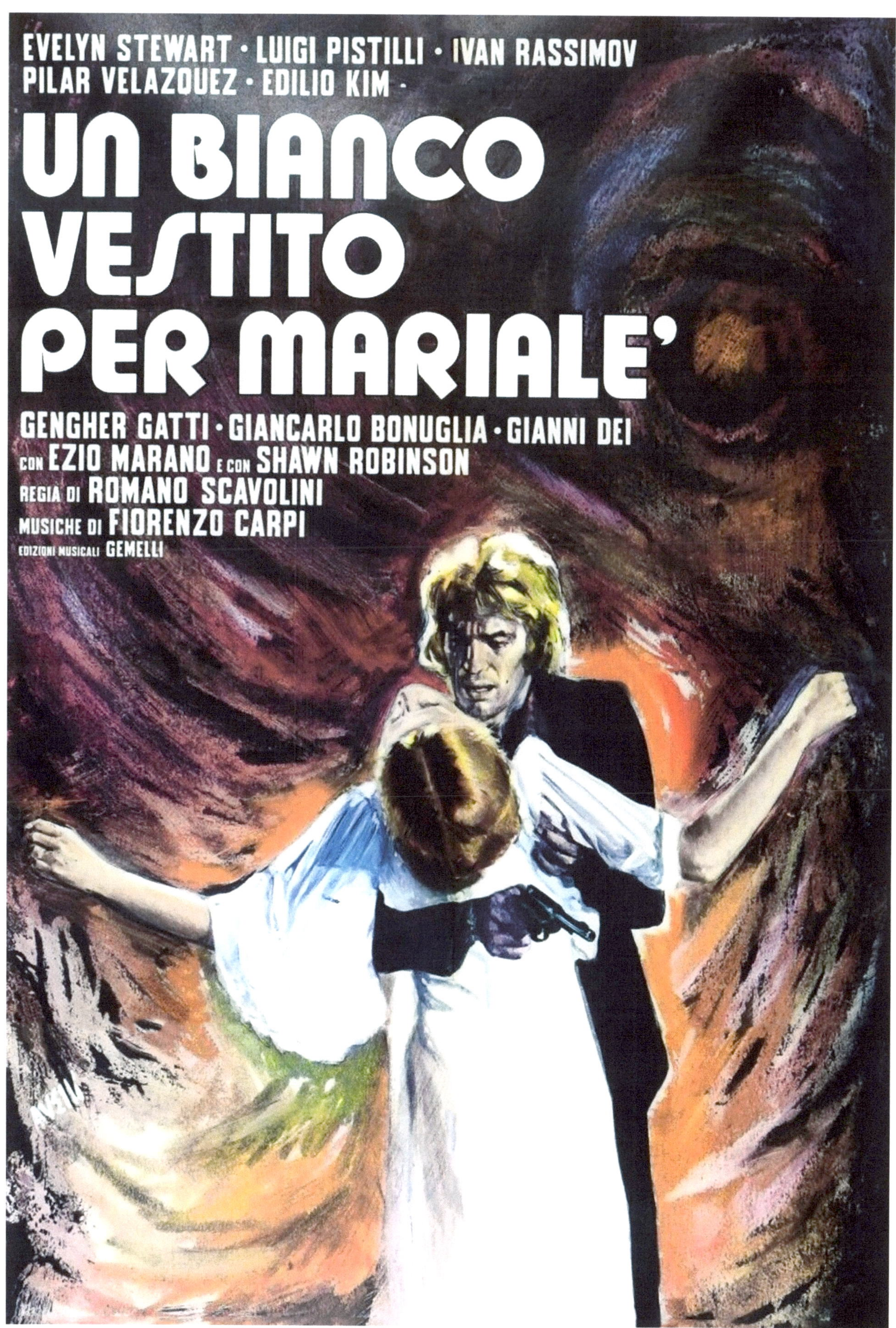

(''A White Gown For Marialé''; Italy, 1972). Artist: Tino Avelli.

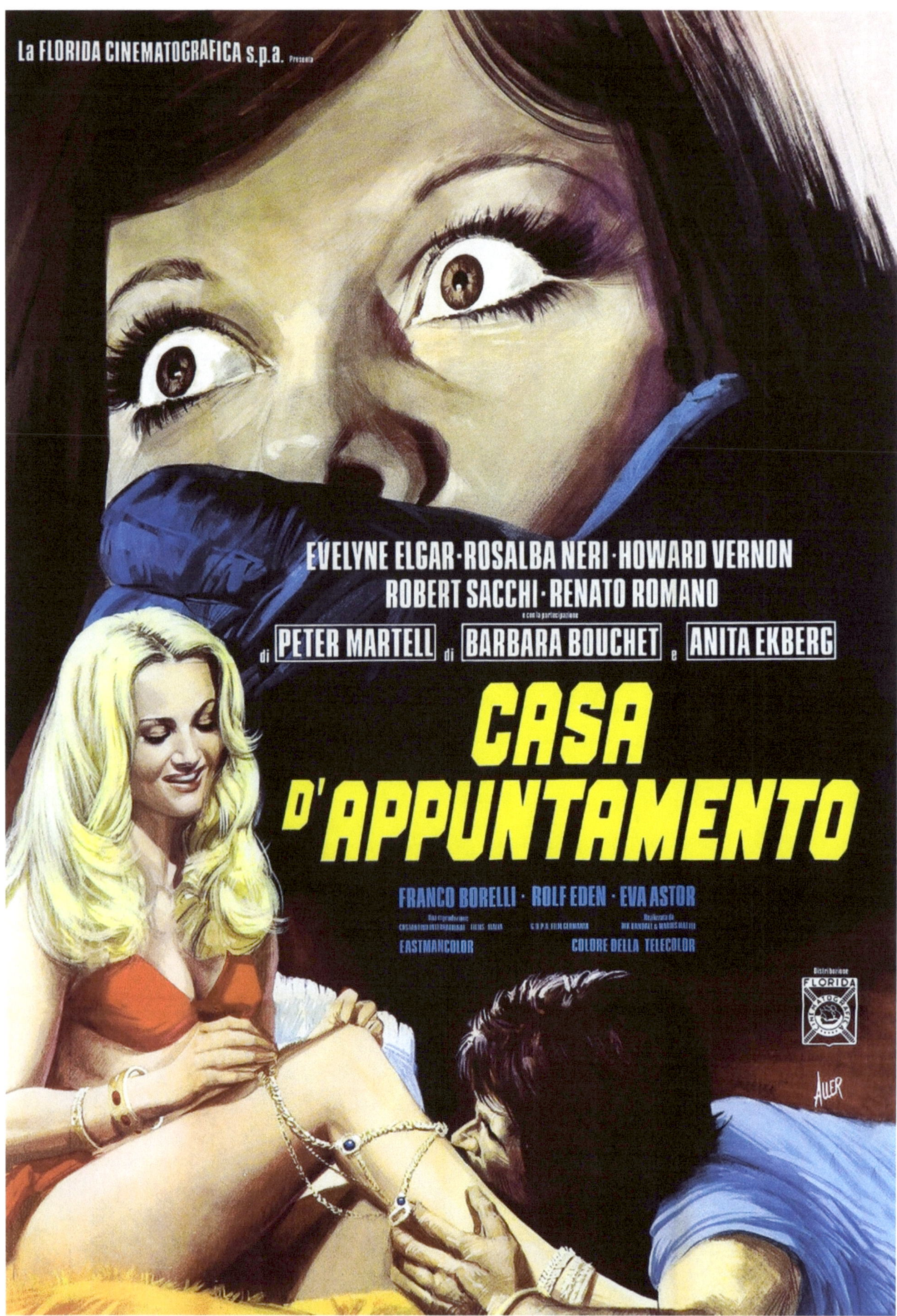

CASA D'APPUNTAMENTO

("Whorehouse"; Italy/Germany, 1972). Artist: Aller.

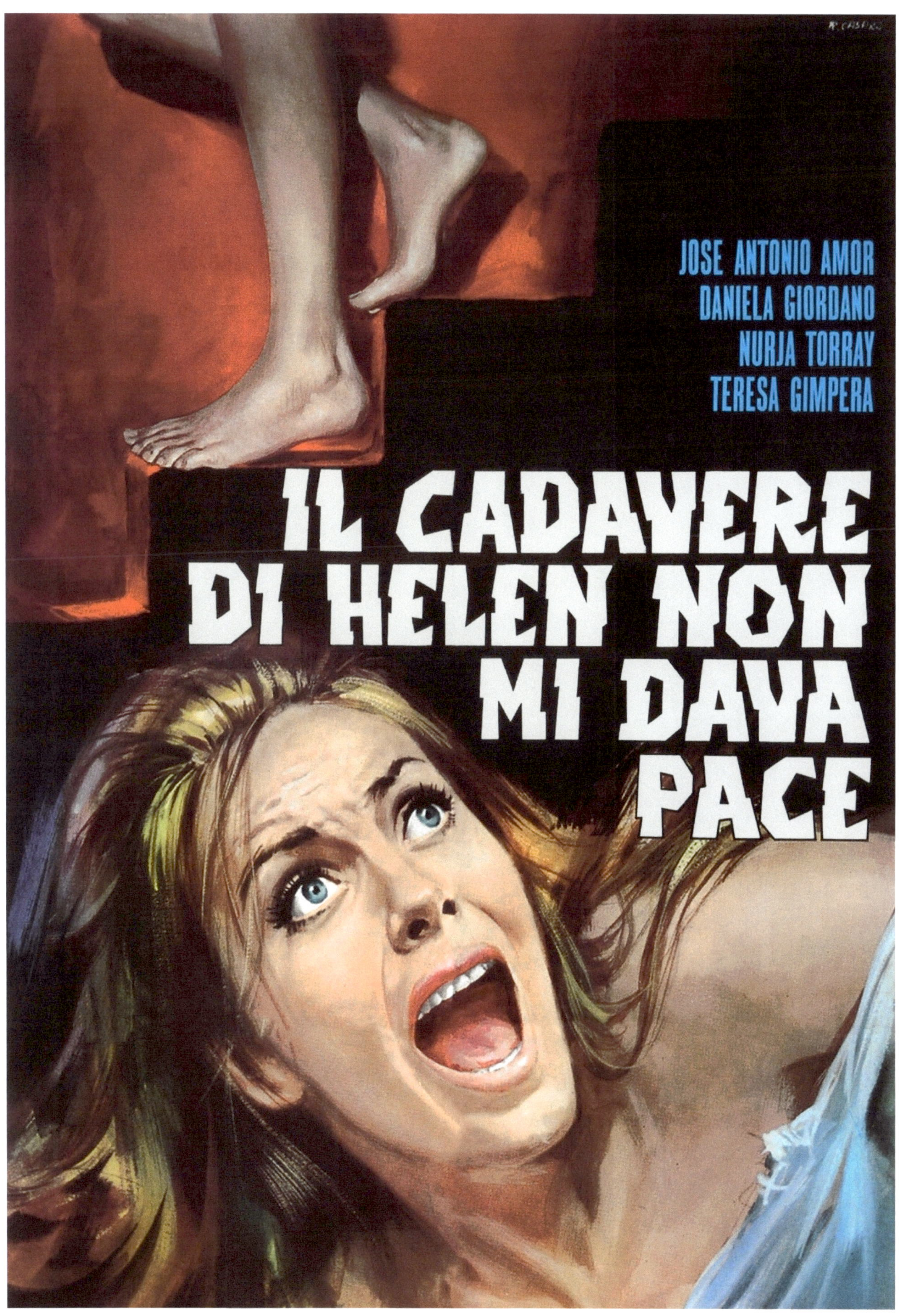

IL CADAVERE DI HELEN NON MI DAVA PACE

("Helen's Corpse Won't Let Me Rest"; Italy/Spain, 1972). Artist: Renato Casaro.

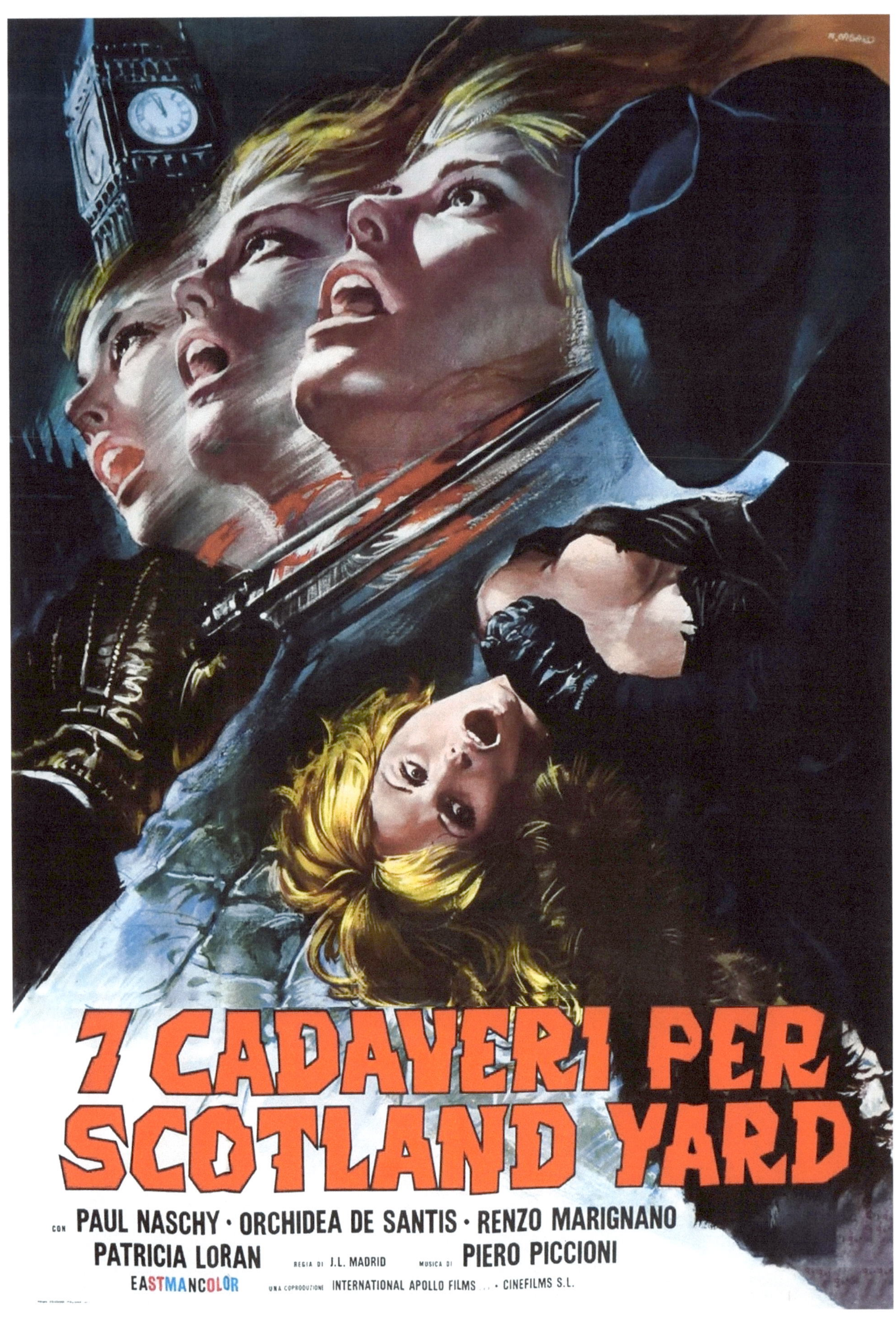

7 CADAVERI PER SCOTLAND YARD

(''7 Corpses For Scotland Yard''; Italy/Spain, 1972). Artist: Renato Casaro.

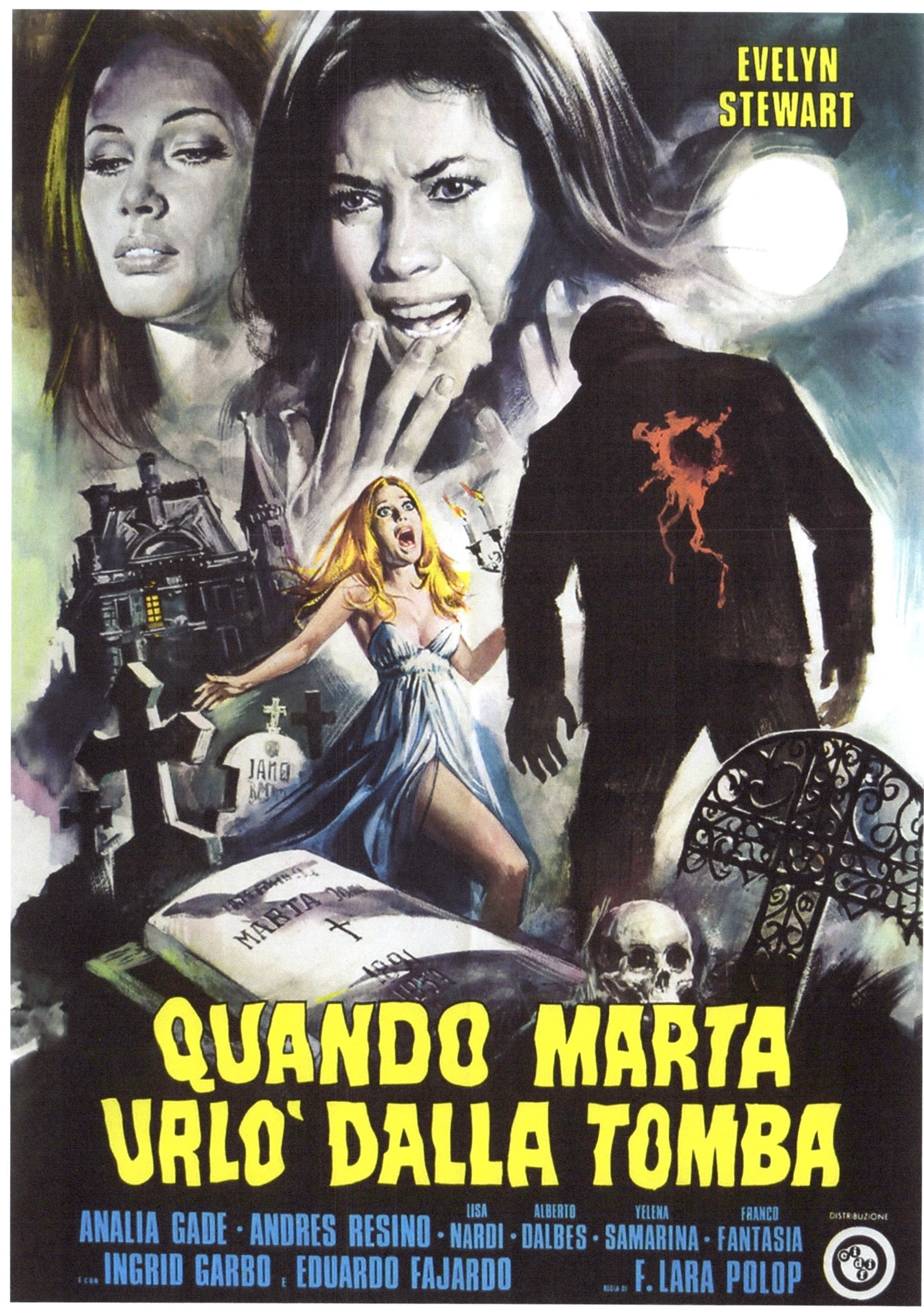

("When Marta Screamed From The Tomb"; Italy/Spain, 1972). Artist: unsigned.

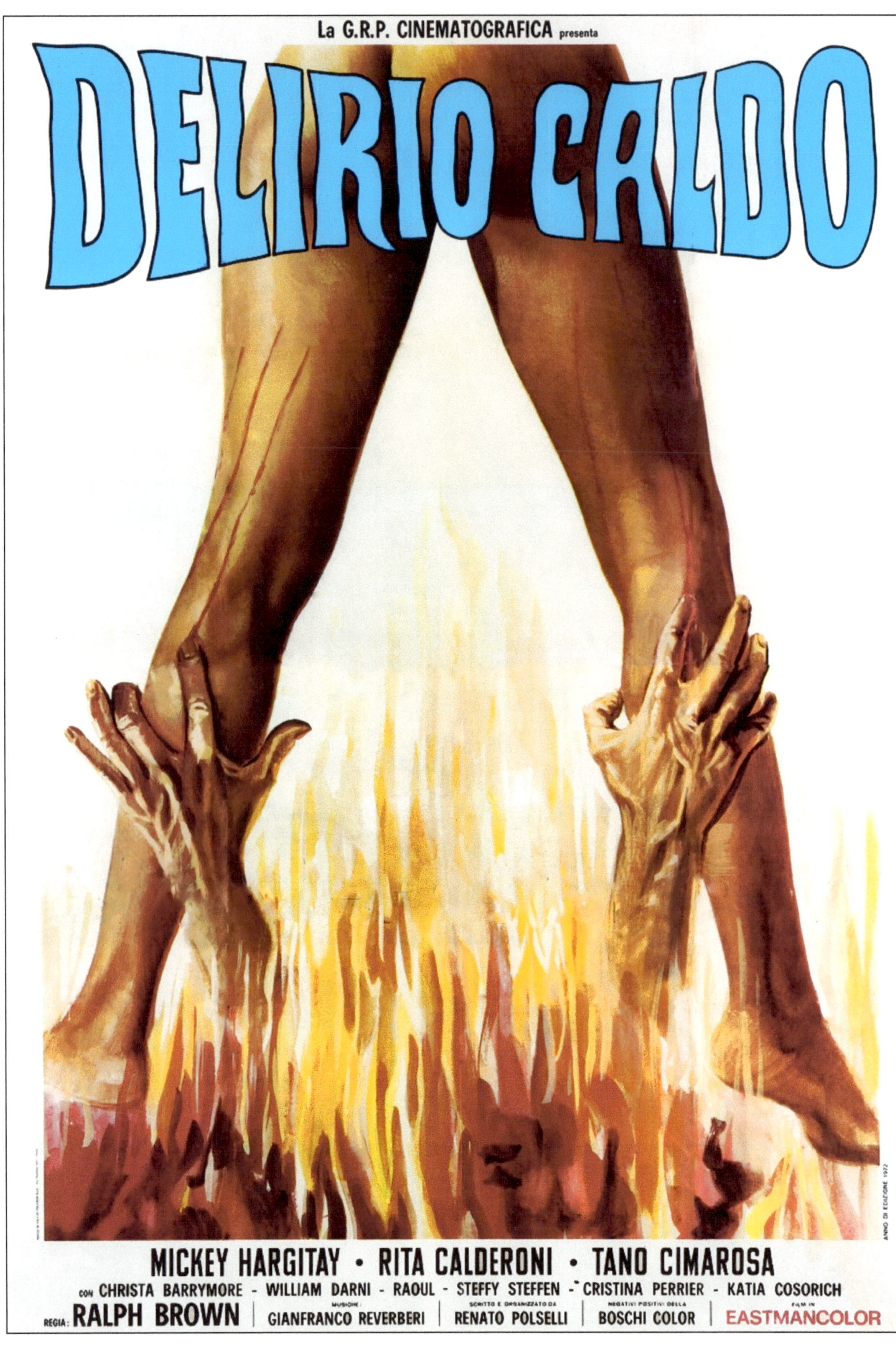

DELIRIO CALDO

("Hot Delirium"; Italy, 1972). Artist: unsigned.

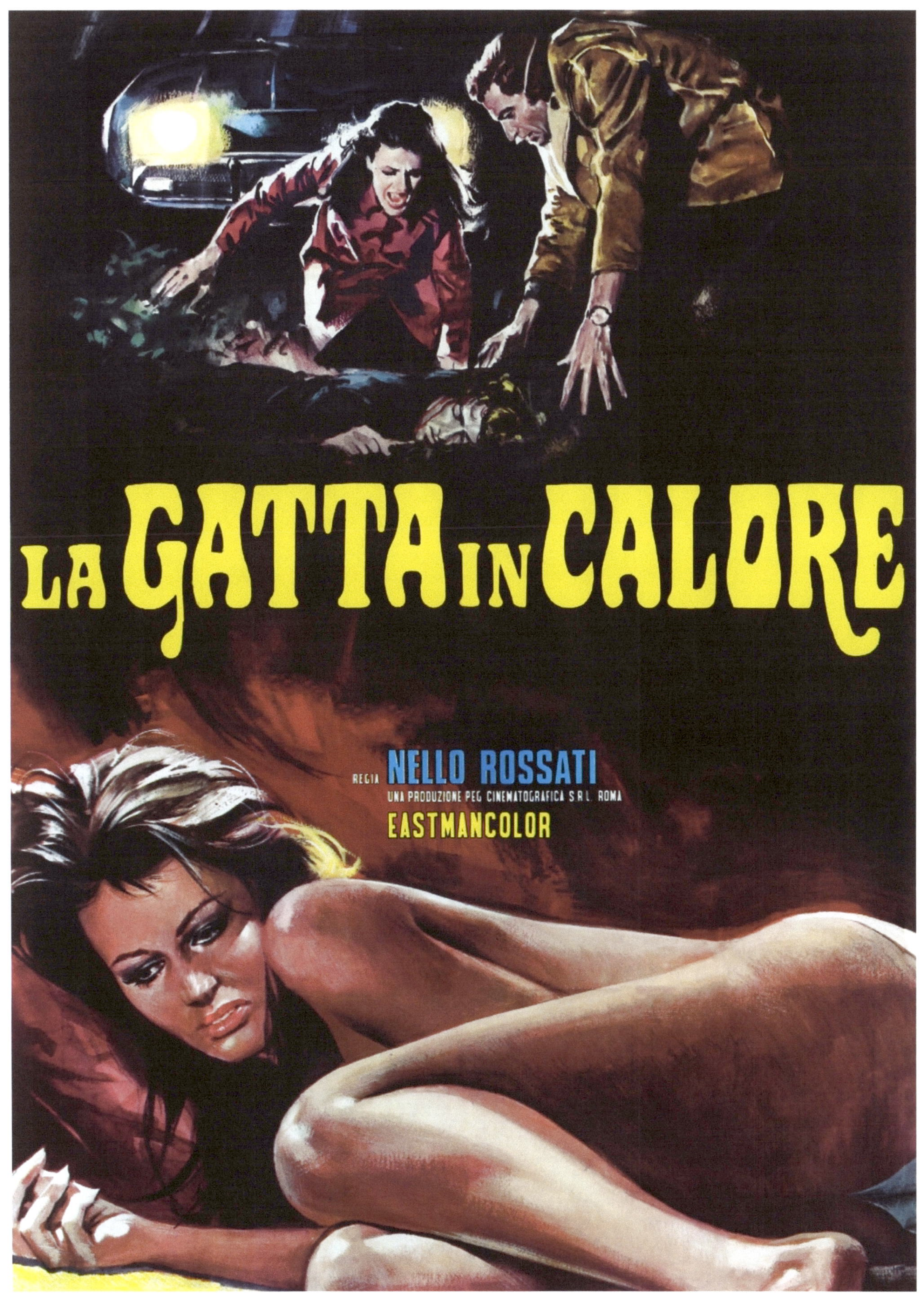

("She-Cat In Heat"; Italy, 1972). Artist: unsigned.

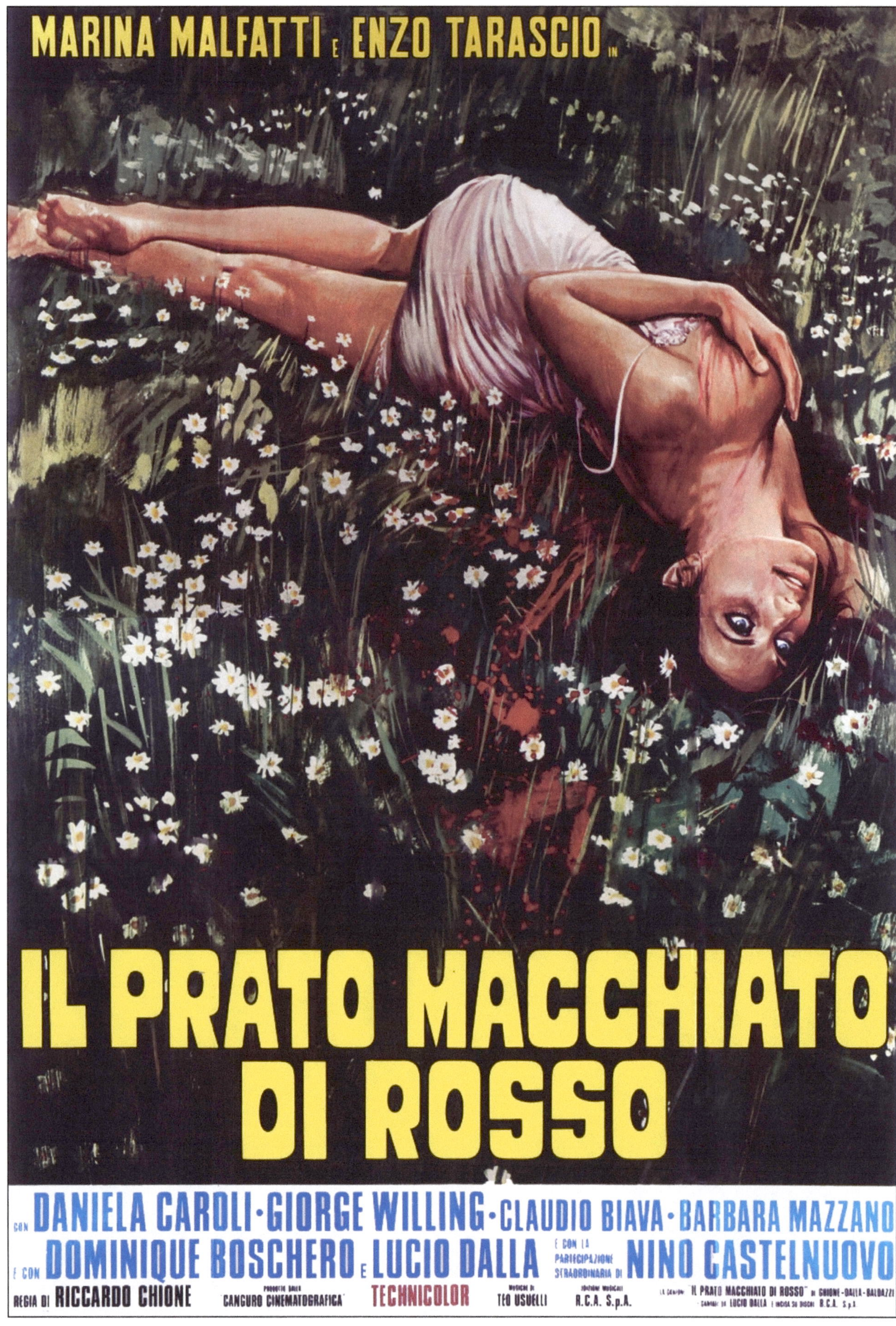

IL PRATO MACCHIATO DI ROSSO

(''The Red-Stained Meadow''; Italy, 1972). Artist: unsigned.

74

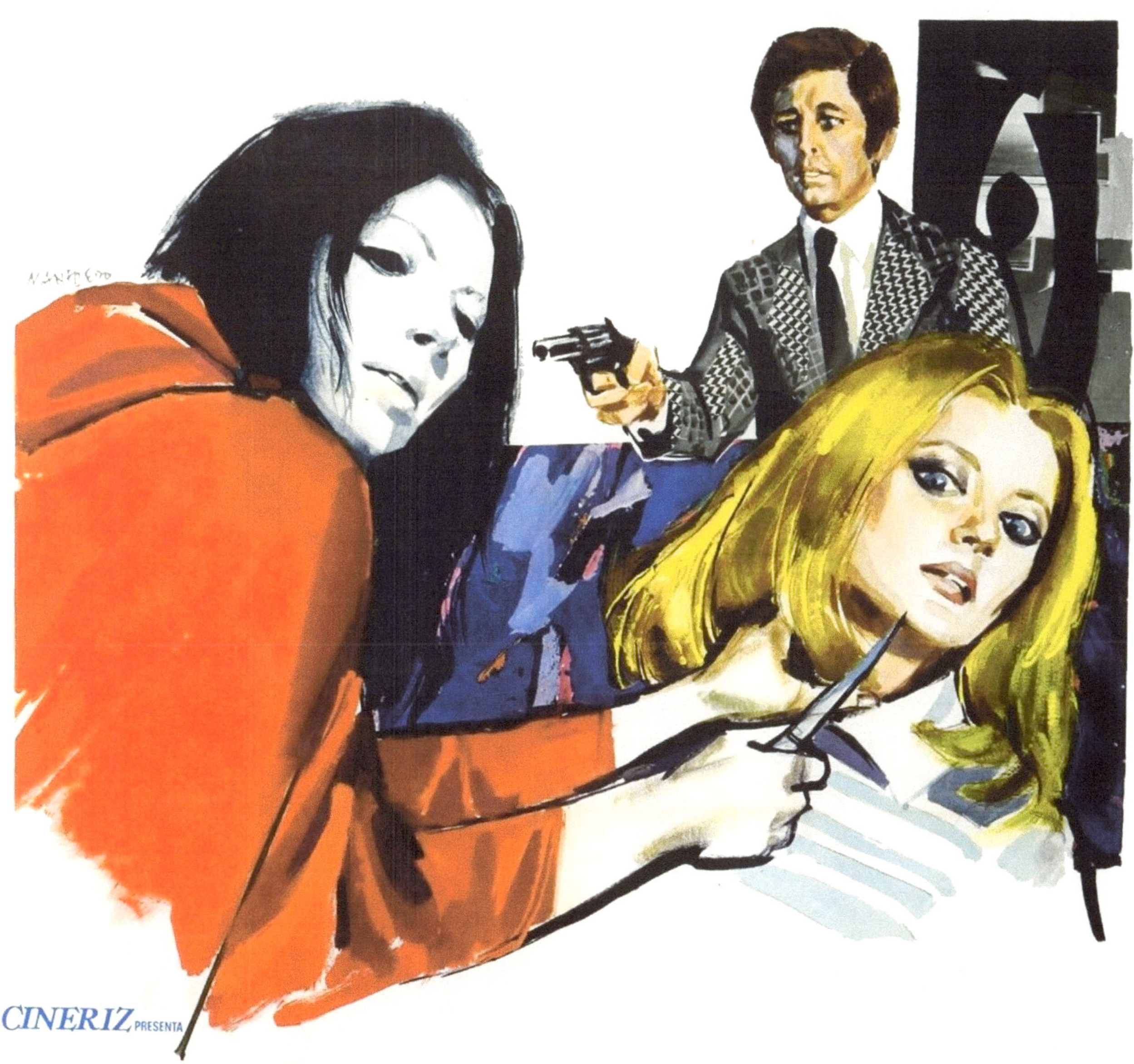

LA DAMA ROSSA UCCIDE SETTE VOLTE

("The Red Lady Kills Seven Times"; Italy/Germany, 1972). Artist: Manfredo.

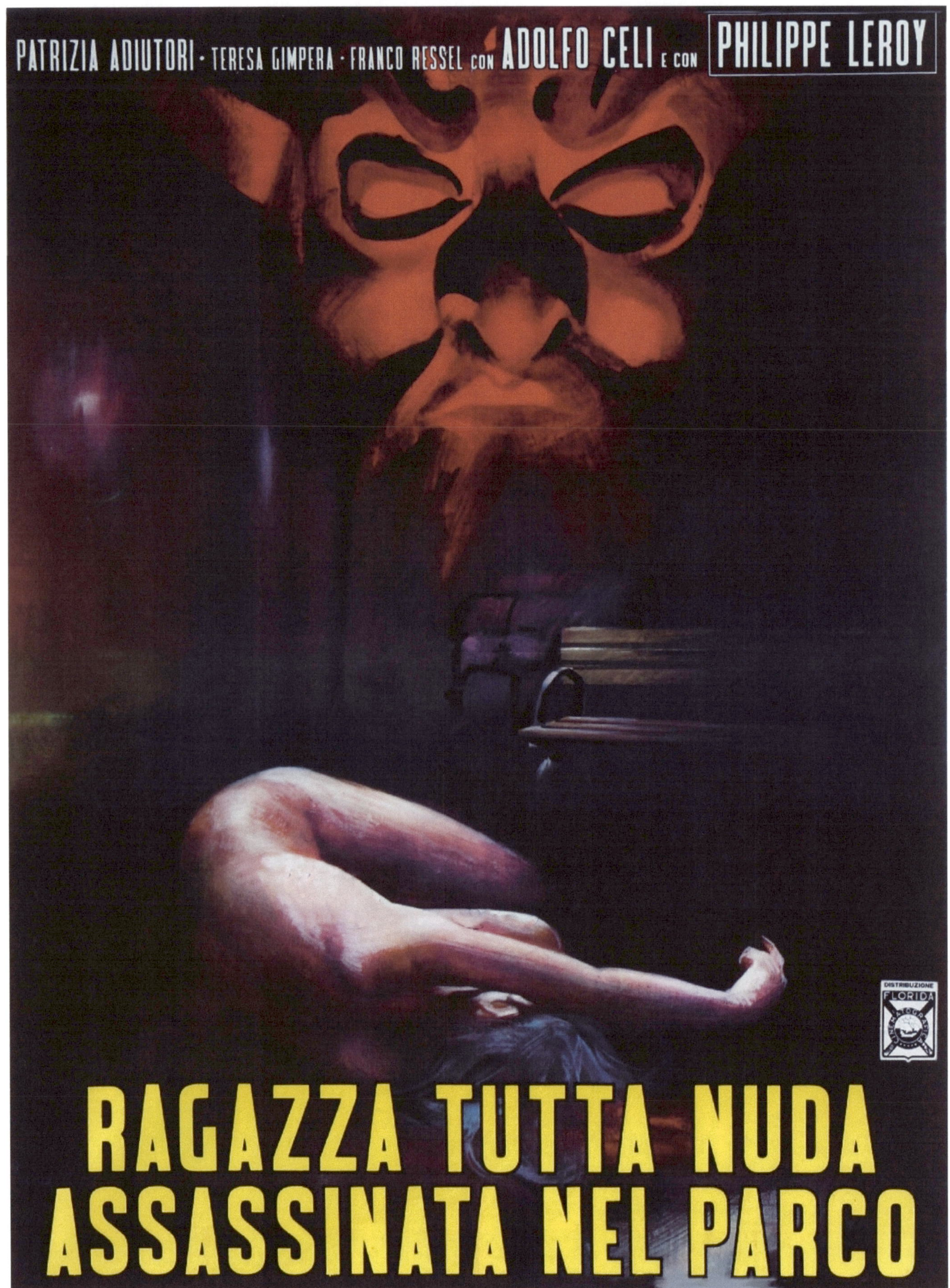

RAGAZZA TUTTA NUDA ASSASSINATA NEL PARCO

("Stark Naked Girl Murdered In The Park"; Italy/Spain, 1972). Artist: unsigned.

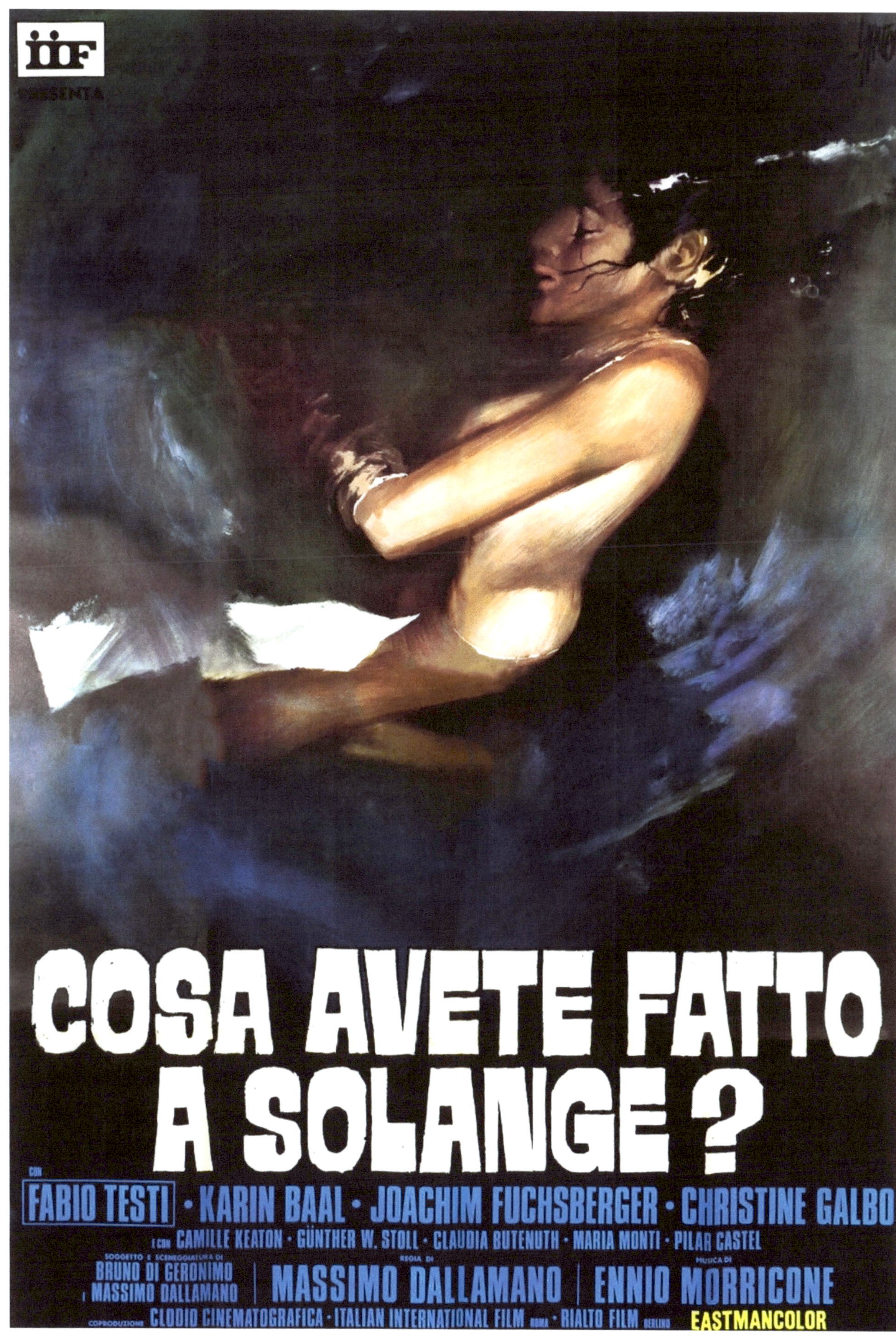

COSA AVETE FATTO A SOLANGE?

("What Have You Done To Solange?"; Italy/Germany, 1972). Artist: Sandro Symeoni.

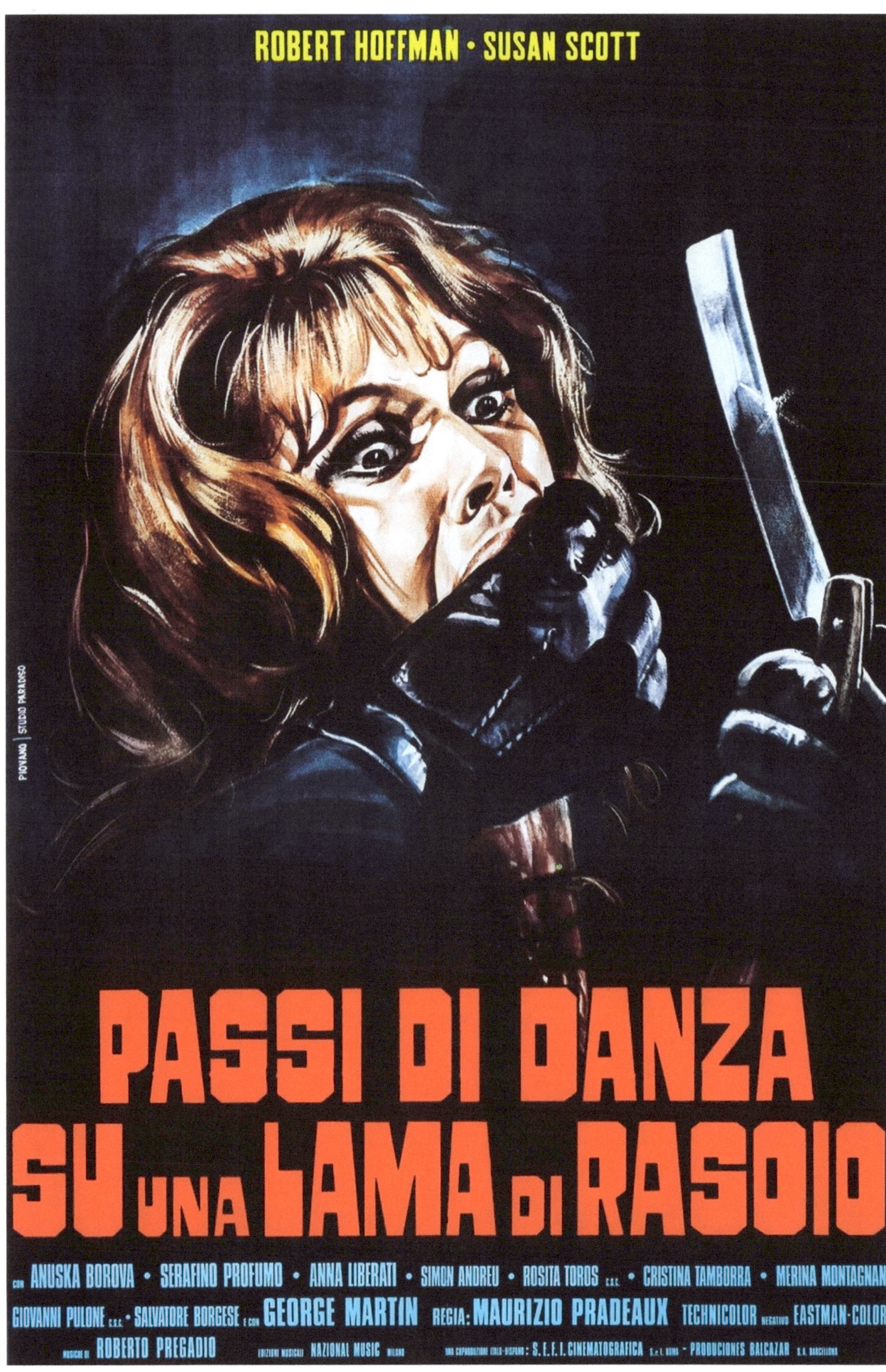

PASSI DI DANZA SU UNA LAMA DI RASOIO

("Dance-Steps On A Razor's Edge"; Italy/Spain, 1972). Artist: Mario Piovano.

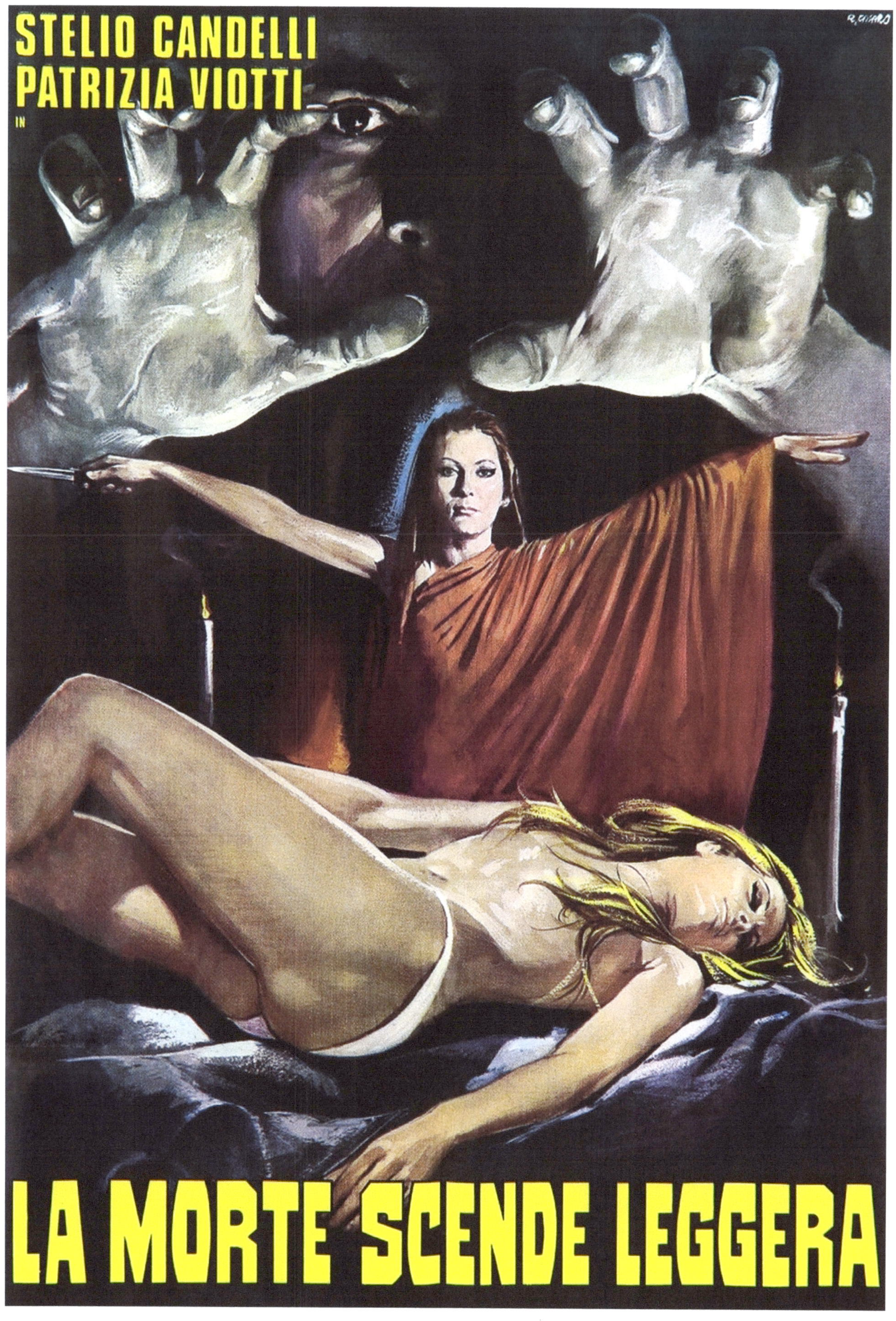

("Death Descends Lightly"; Italy, 1972). Artist: Renato Casaro.

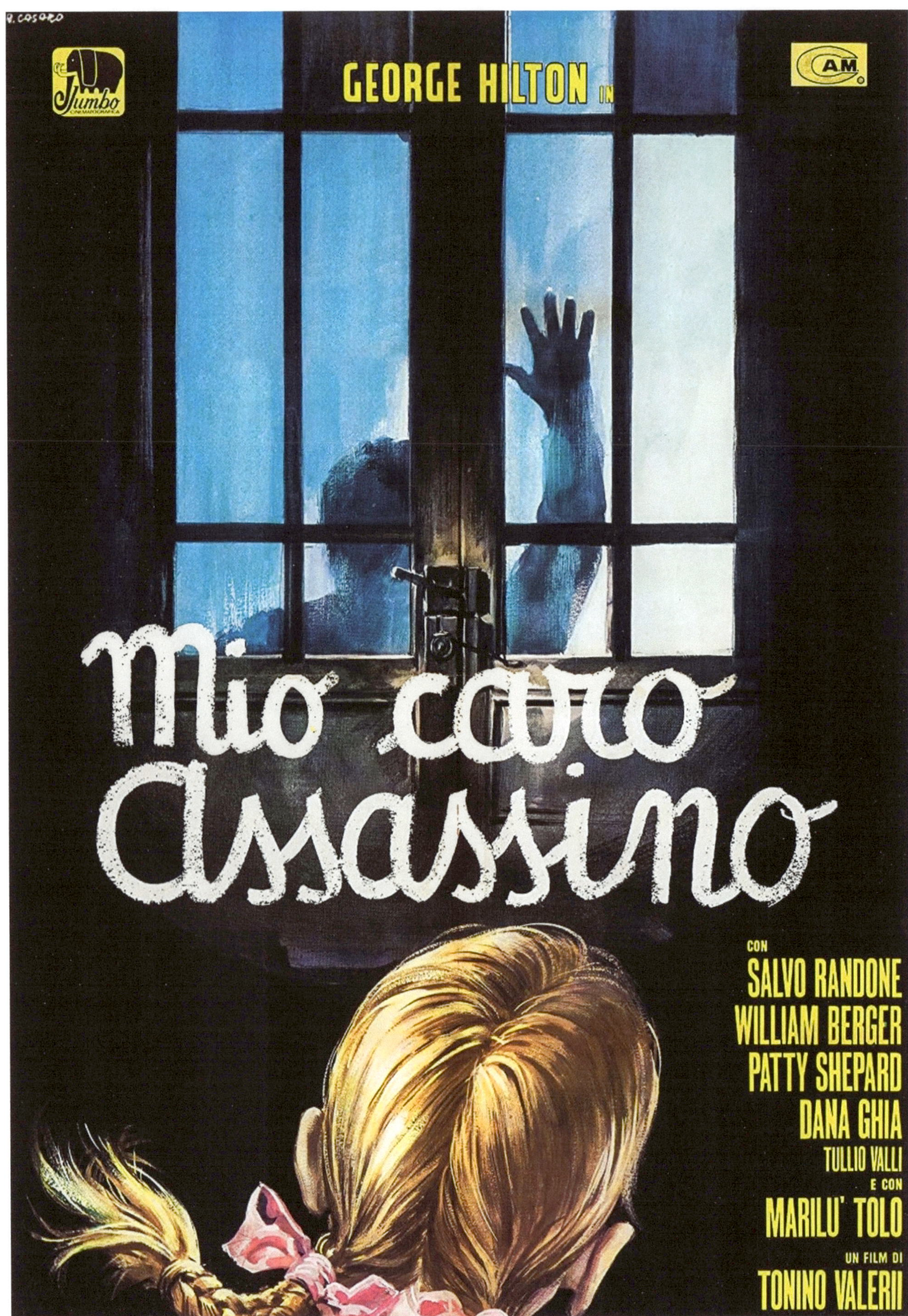

MIO CARO ASSASSINO

("My Dear Killer"; Italy/Spain, 1972). Artist: Renato Casaro.

80

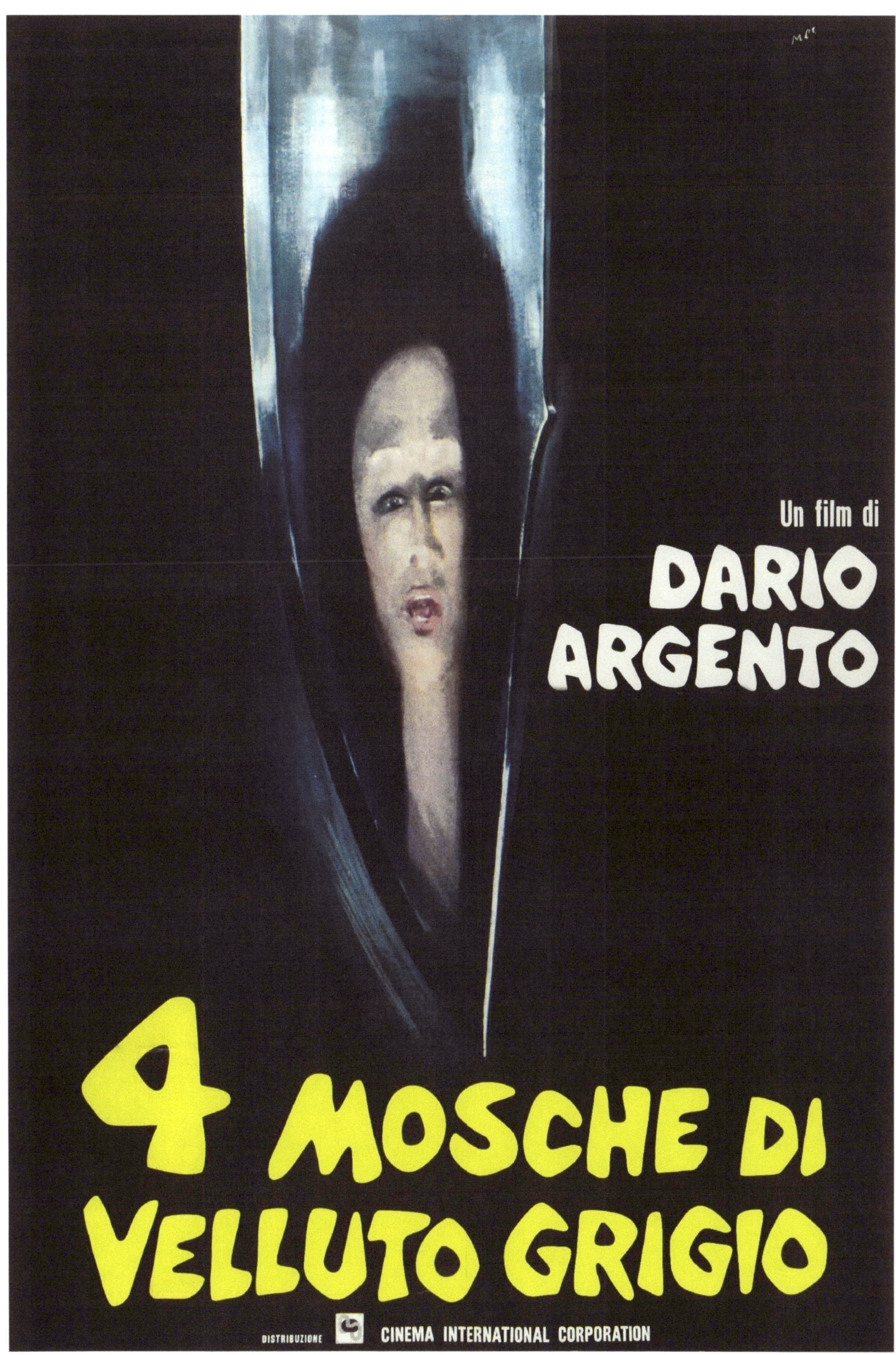

("4 Grey Velvet Flies"; Italy, 1972). Artist: Moz.

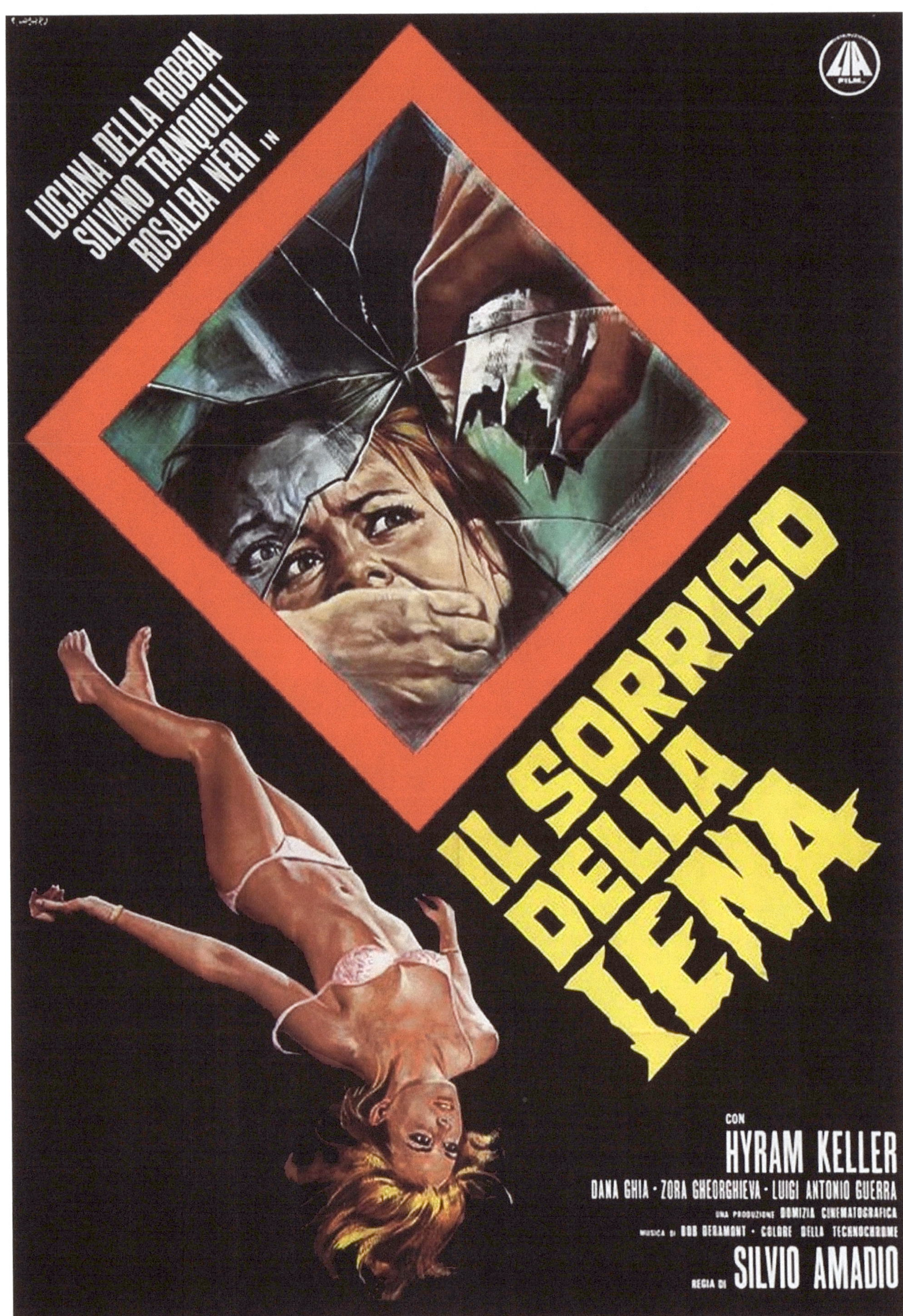

IL SORRISO DELLA IENA

(''The Rictus Of The Beast''; Italy, 1972). Artist: Renato Casaro.

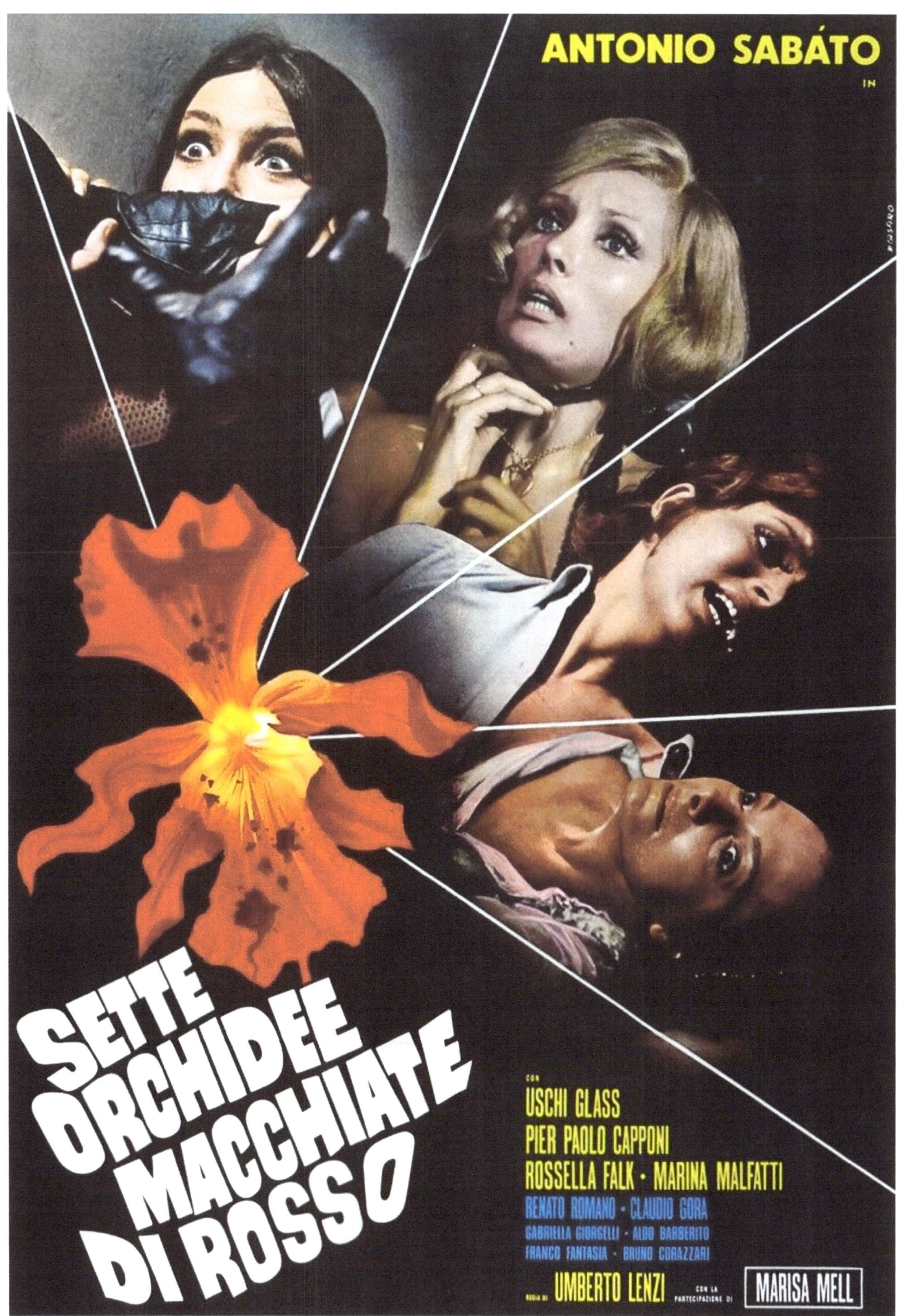

SETTE ORCHIDEE MACCHIATE DI ROSSO

("Seven Red-Stained Orchids"; Italy, 1972). Artist: Renato Casaro.

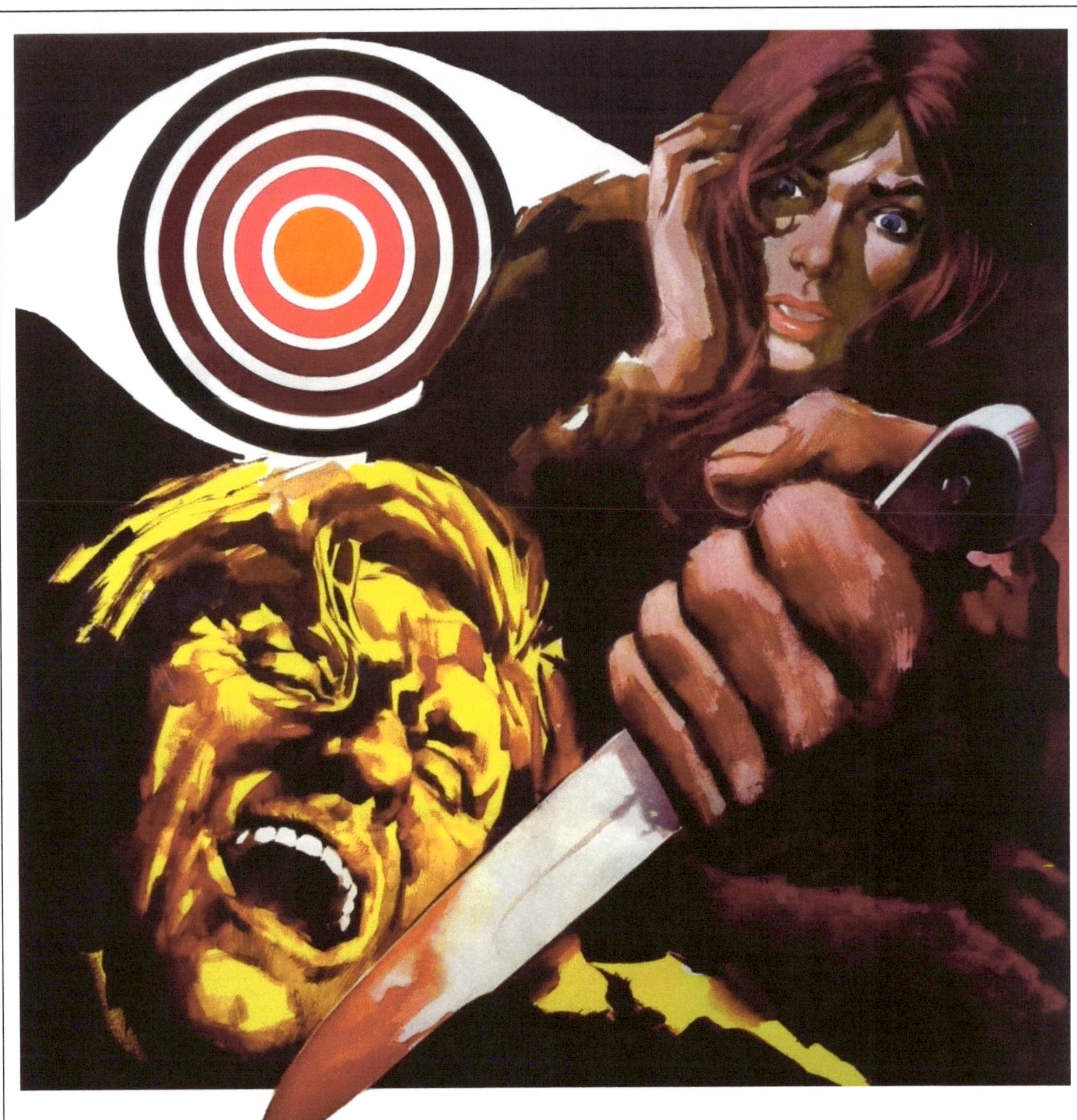

L'OCCHIO NEL LABIRINTO

(''The Eye In The Labyrinth''; Italy/Germany, 1972). Artist: Sandro Symeoni.

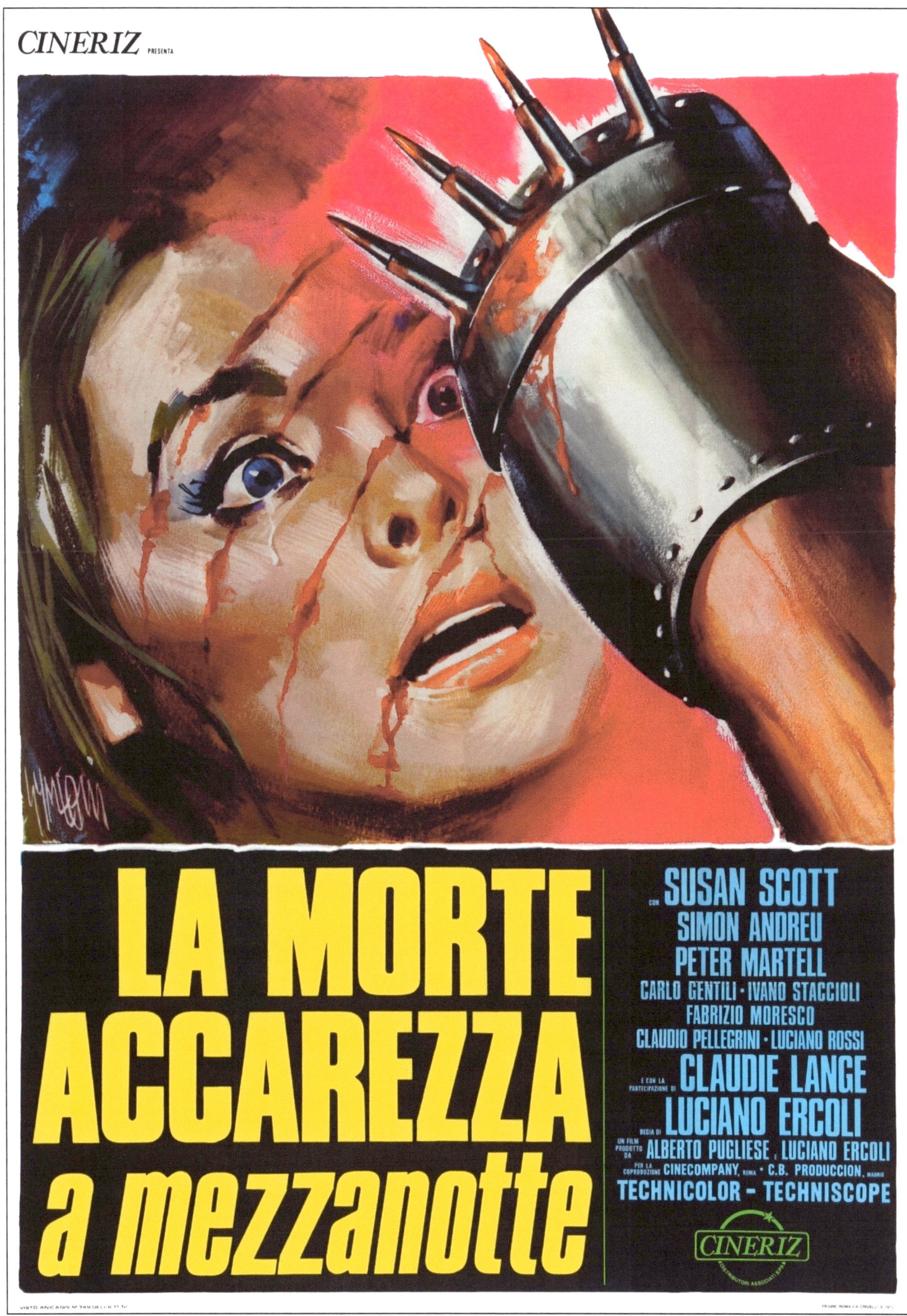

LA MORTE ACCAREZZA A MEZZANOTTE

("Death Caresses At Midnight"; Italy/Spain, 1972). Artist: Sandro Symeoni.

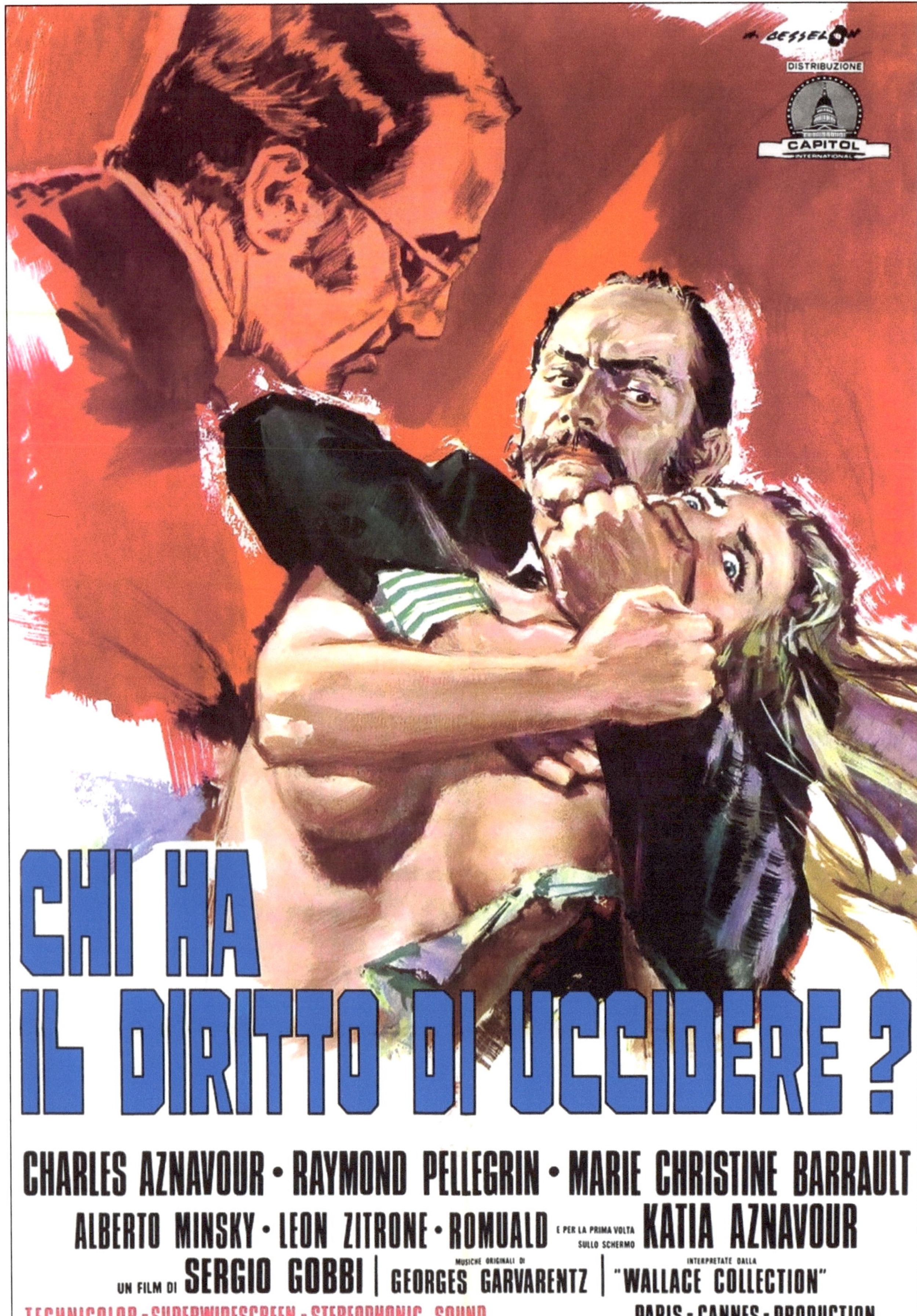

CHI HA IL DIRITTO DI UCCIDERE?

(''Who Has The Right To Kill?''; France, 1972). Artist: Angelo Cessalon. Original Title: Les **Intrus**.

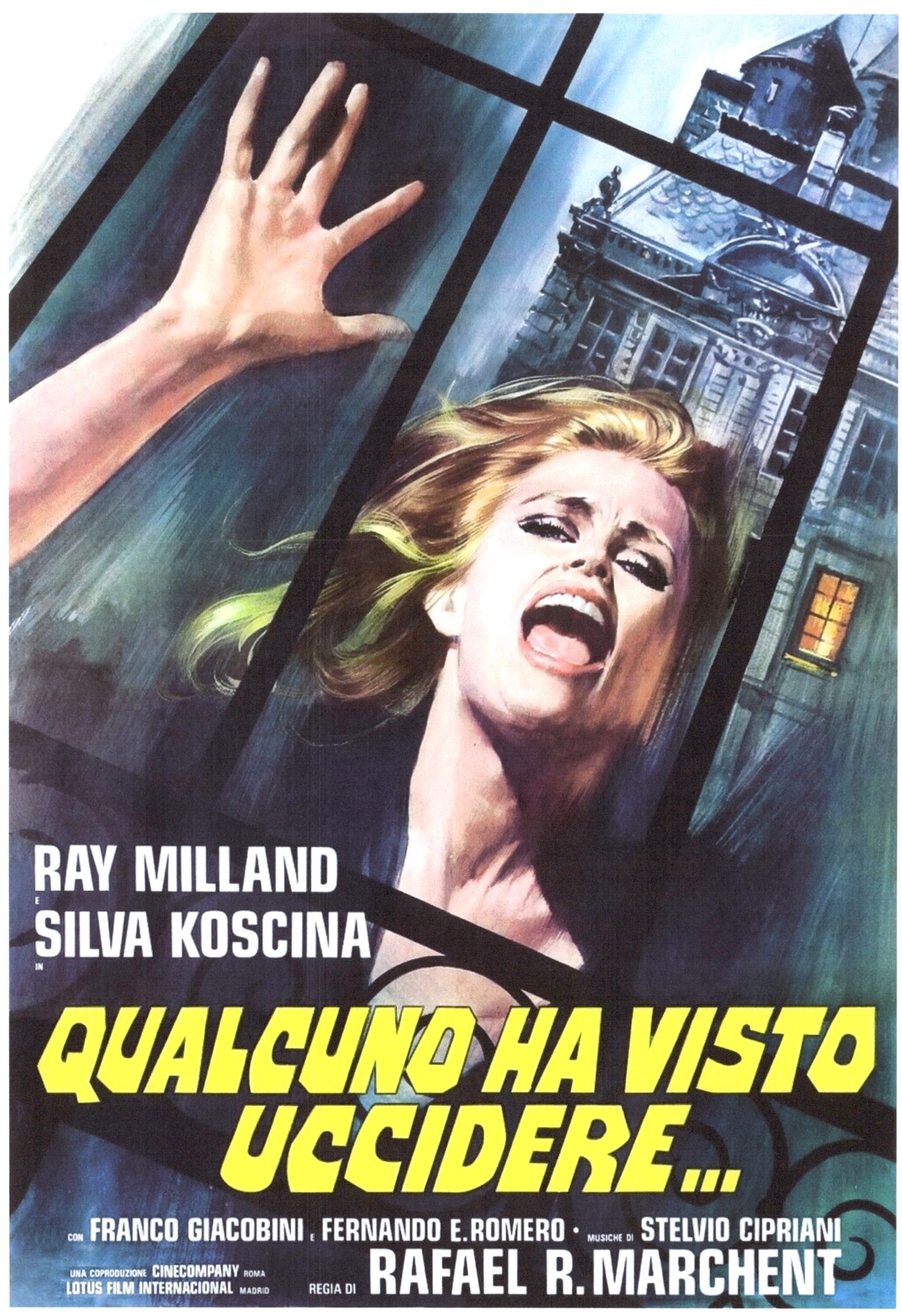

("Someone Saw Murder"; Italy/Spain, 1973). Artist: unsigned.

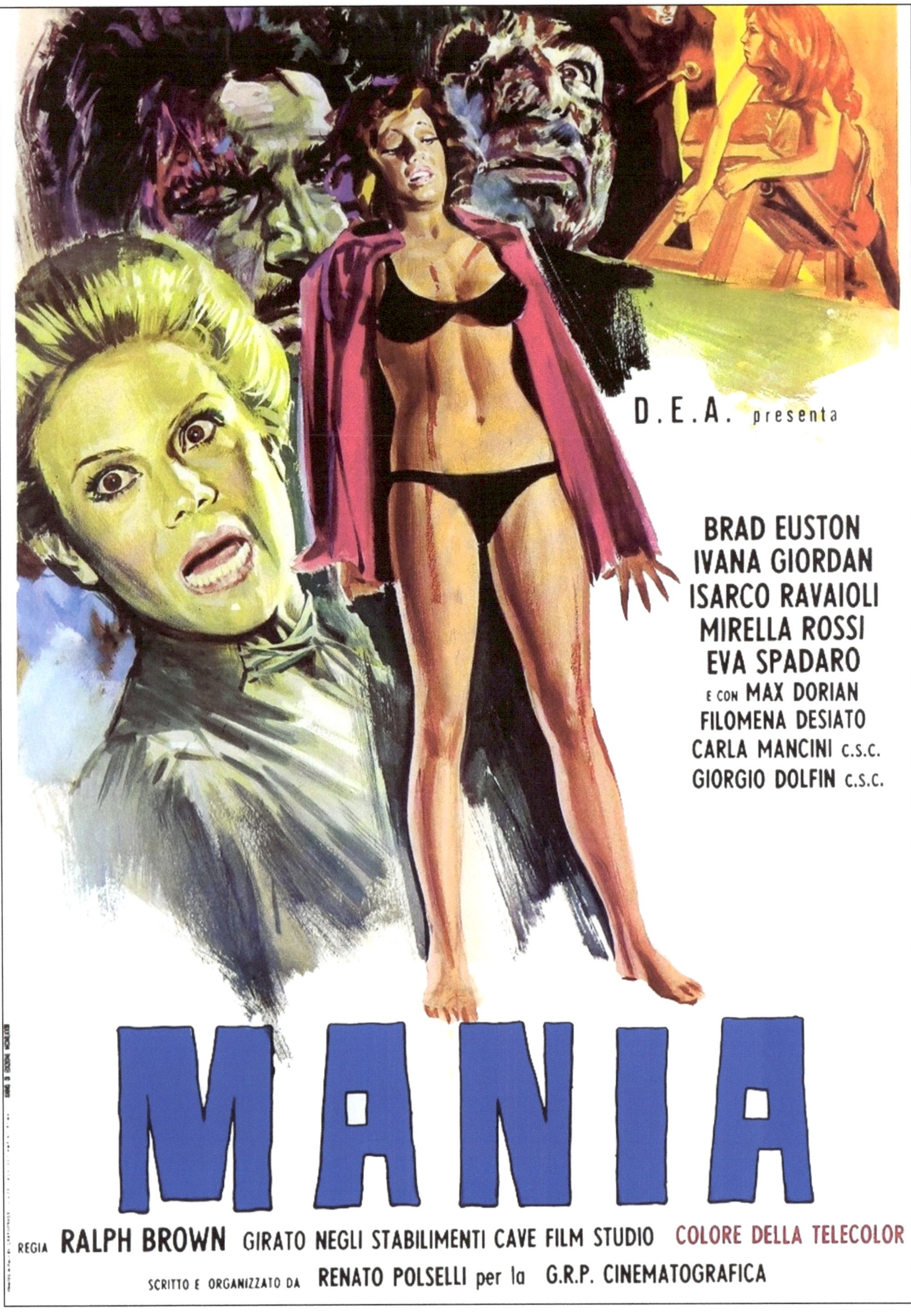

MANIA

("Mania"; Italy, 1973). Artist: unsigned.

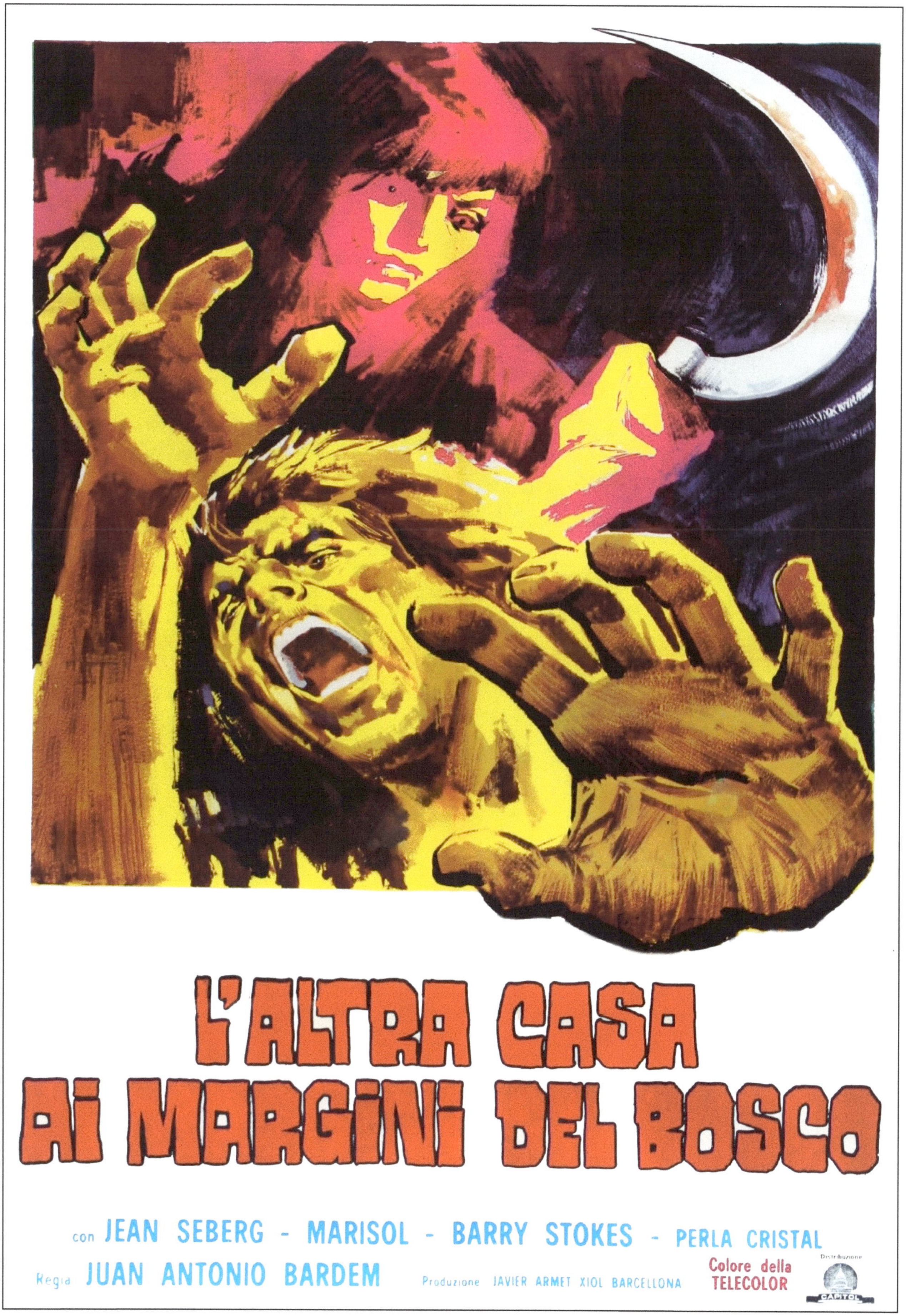

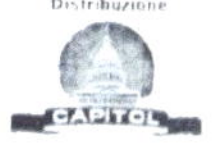

L'ALTRA CASA AI MARGINI DEL BOSCO

("The Other House At The Edge Of The Woods"; Spain, 1973). Artist: unsigned. Original Title: **La Corrupción De Chris Miller.**

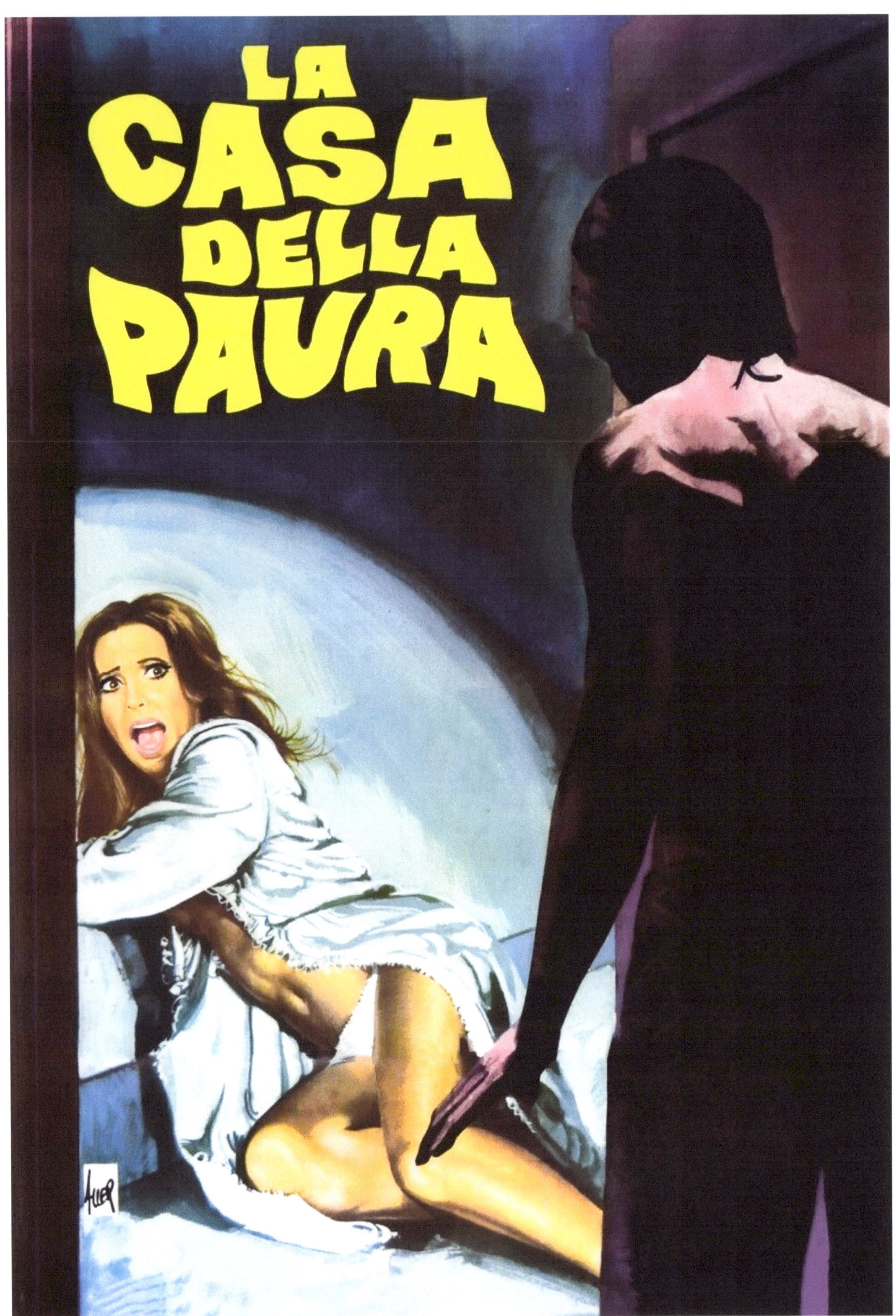

LA CASA DELLA PAURA

("The House Of Fear"; Italy, 1974). Artist: Aller.

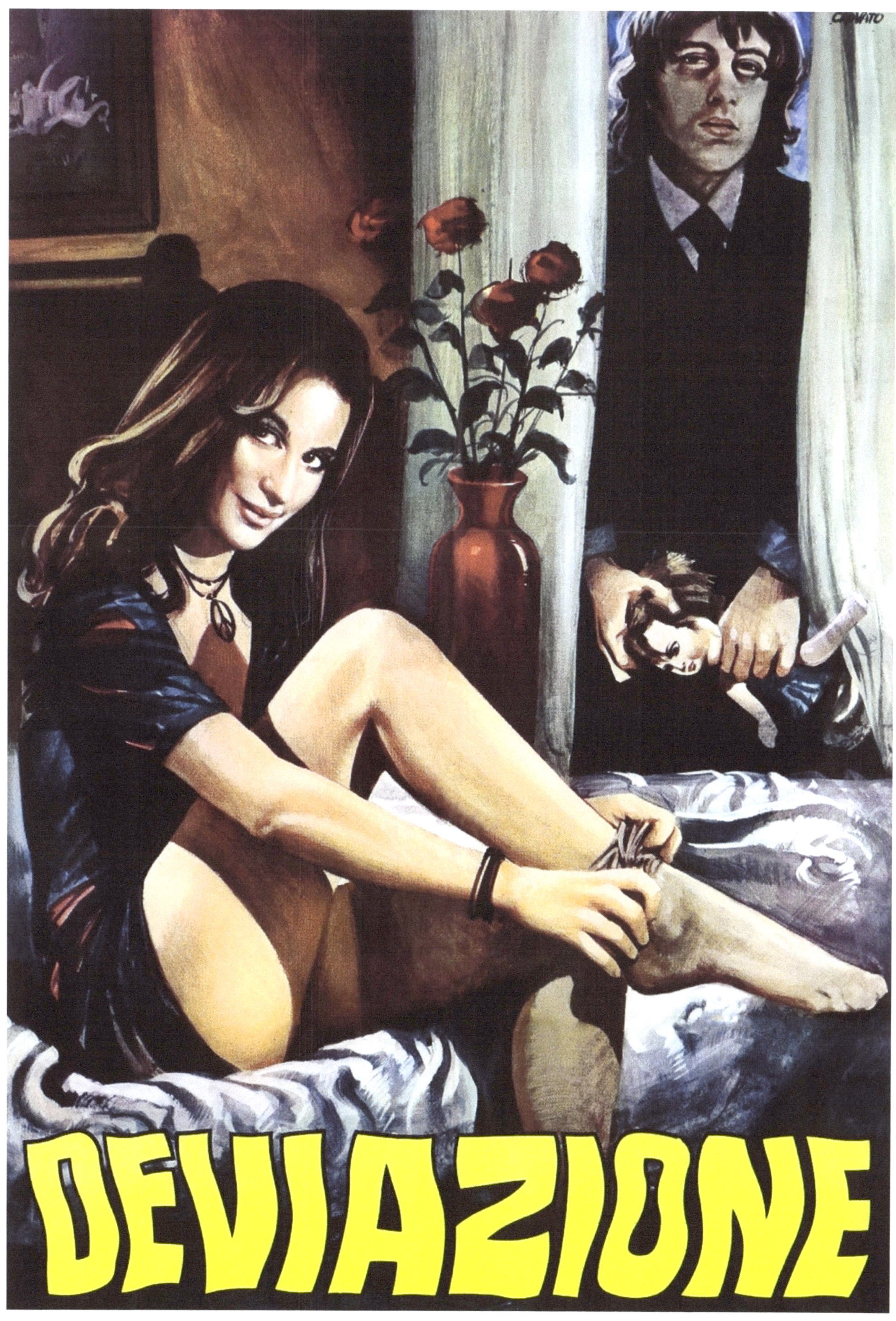

("El Espectro Del Terror"; Spain, 1974). Artist: Luca Crovato.

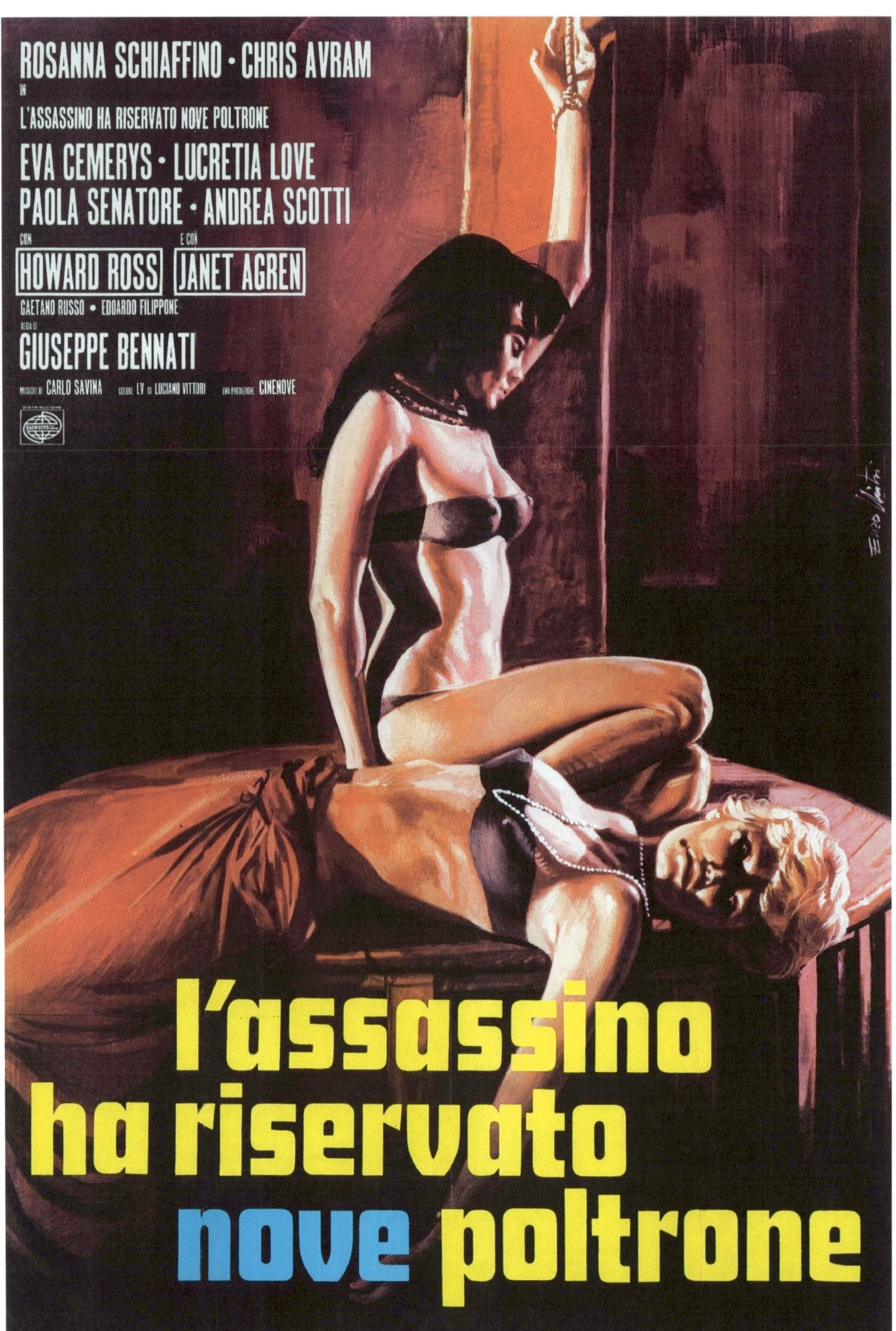

L'ASSASSINO HA RISERVATO NOVE POLTRONE

("The Killer Reserved Nine Seats"; Italy, 1974). Artist: Enzo Nistri.

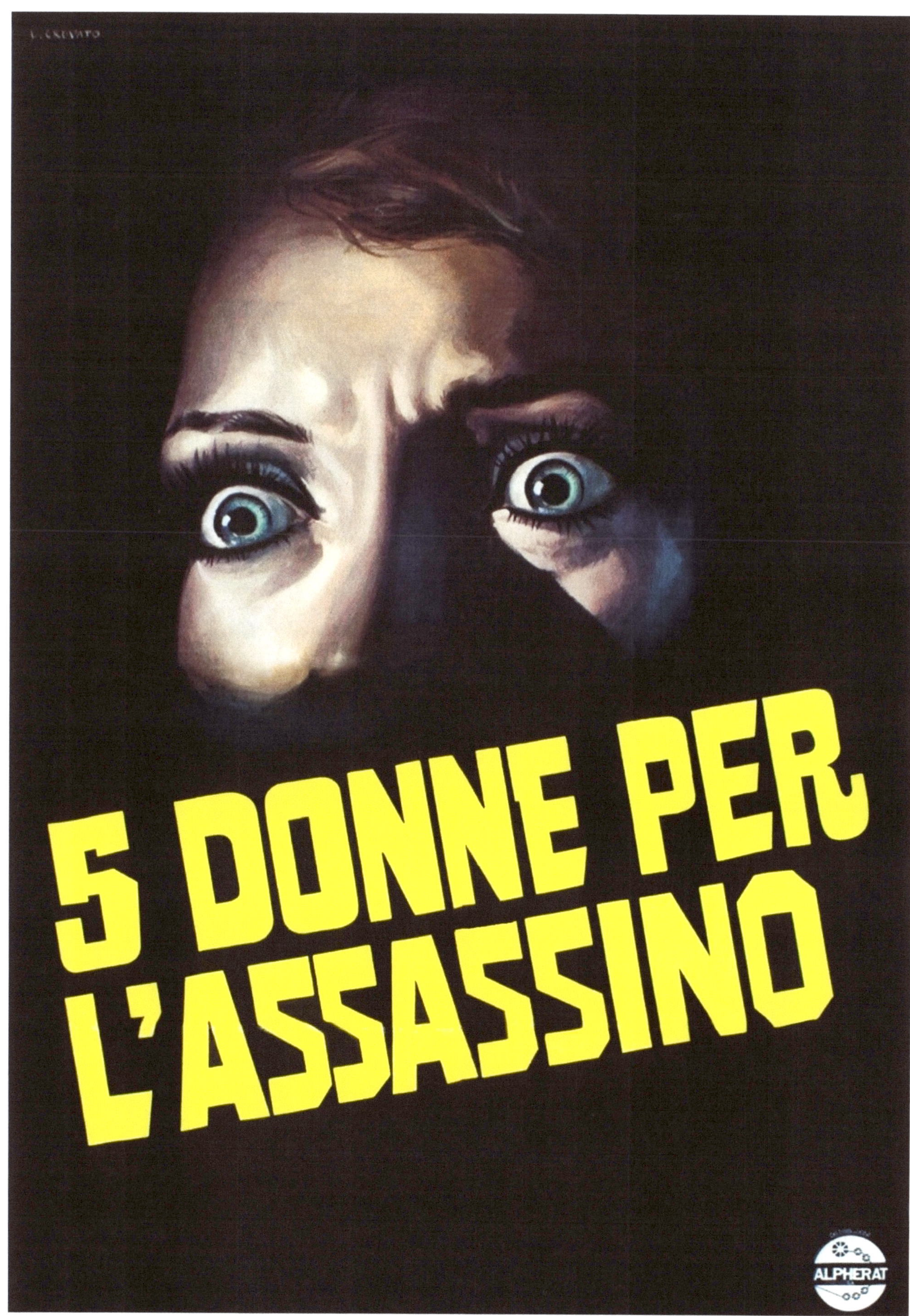

5 DONNE PER L'ASSASSINO
("5 Women For The Killer"; Italy/France, 1974). Artist: Luca Crovato.

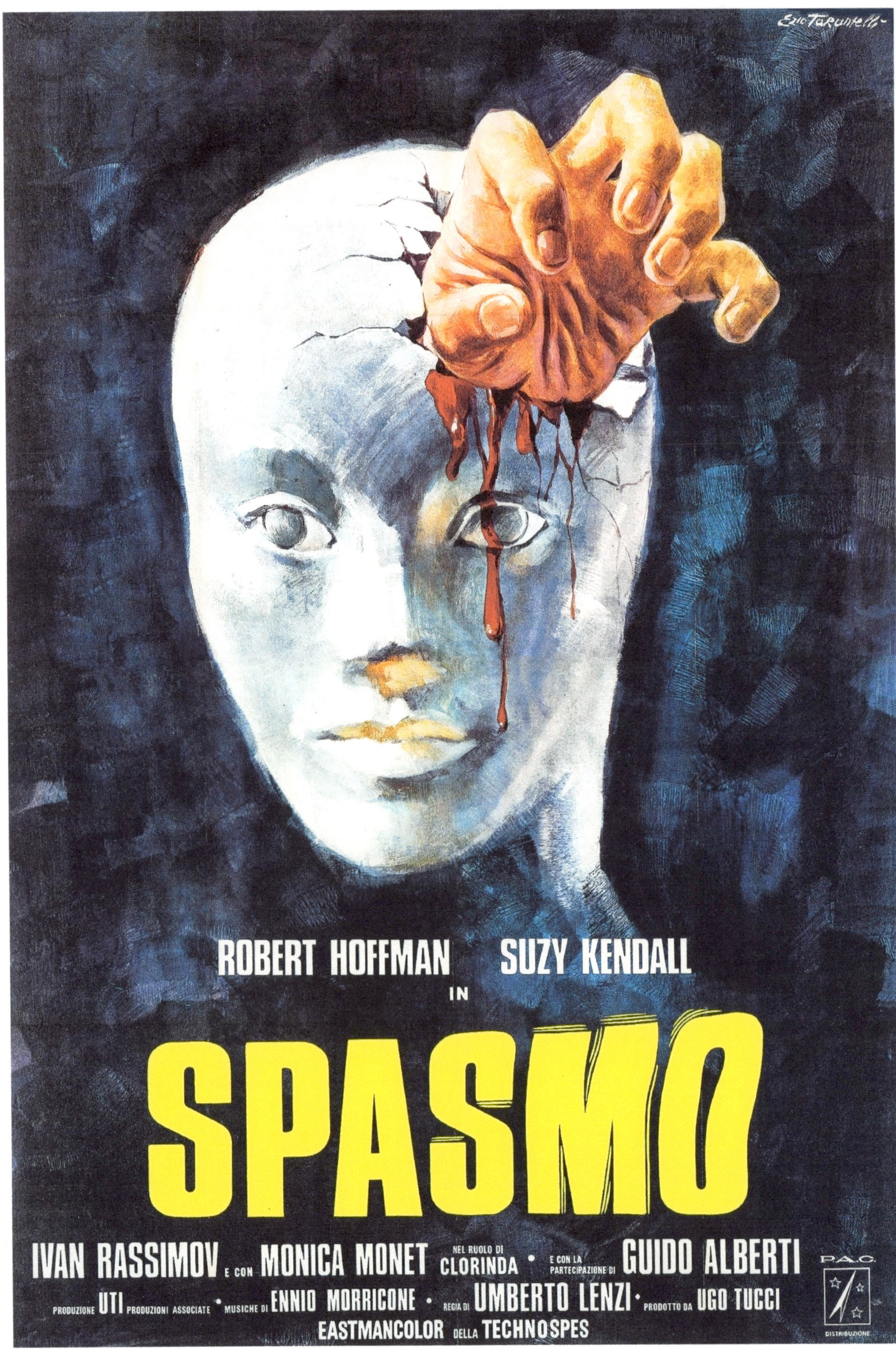

SPASMO

("Spasmo"; Italy, 1974). Artist: Ezio Tarantelli.

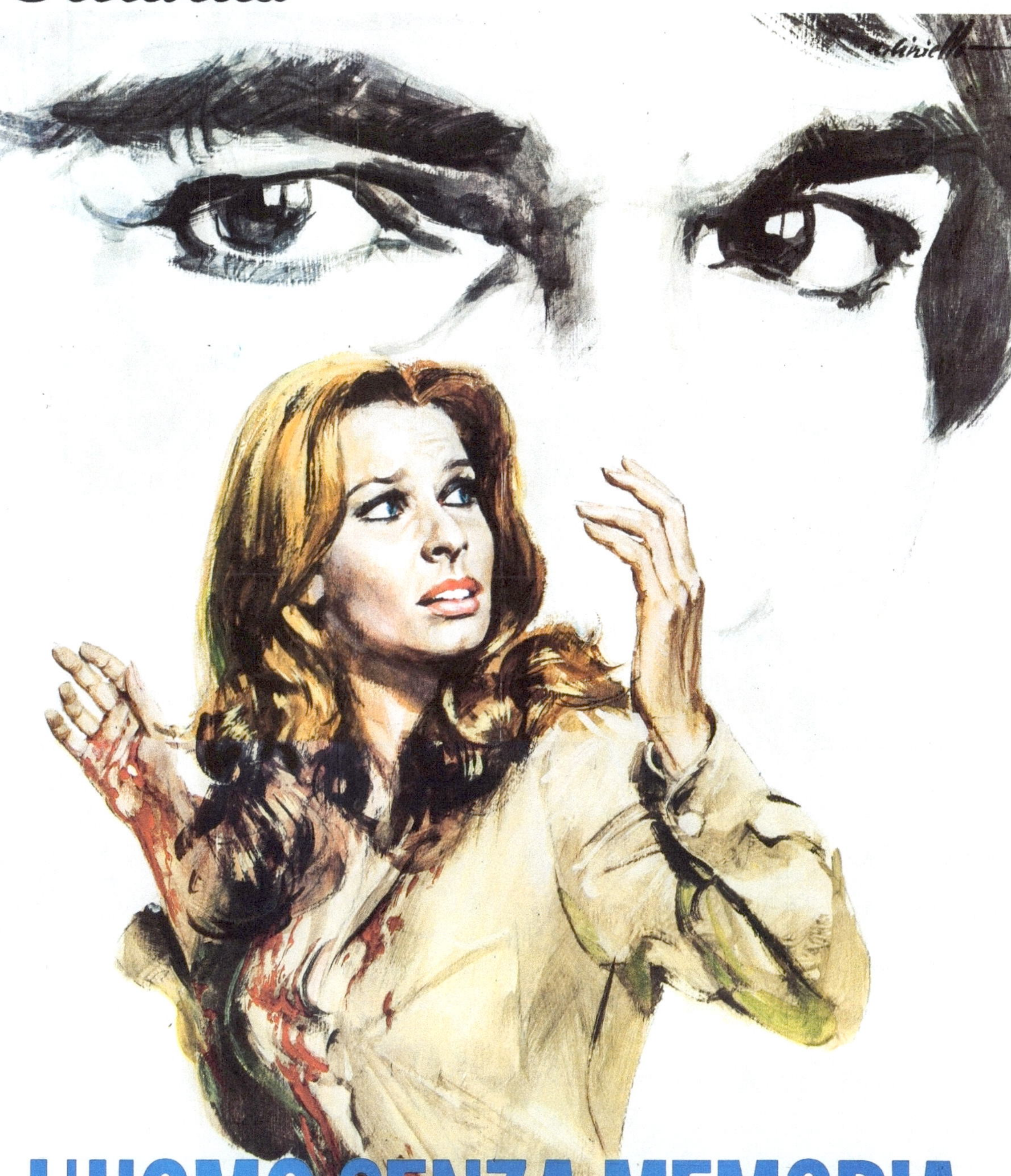

L'UOMO SENZA MEMORIA

("The Man With No Memory"; Italy, 1974). Artist: Averado Ciriello.

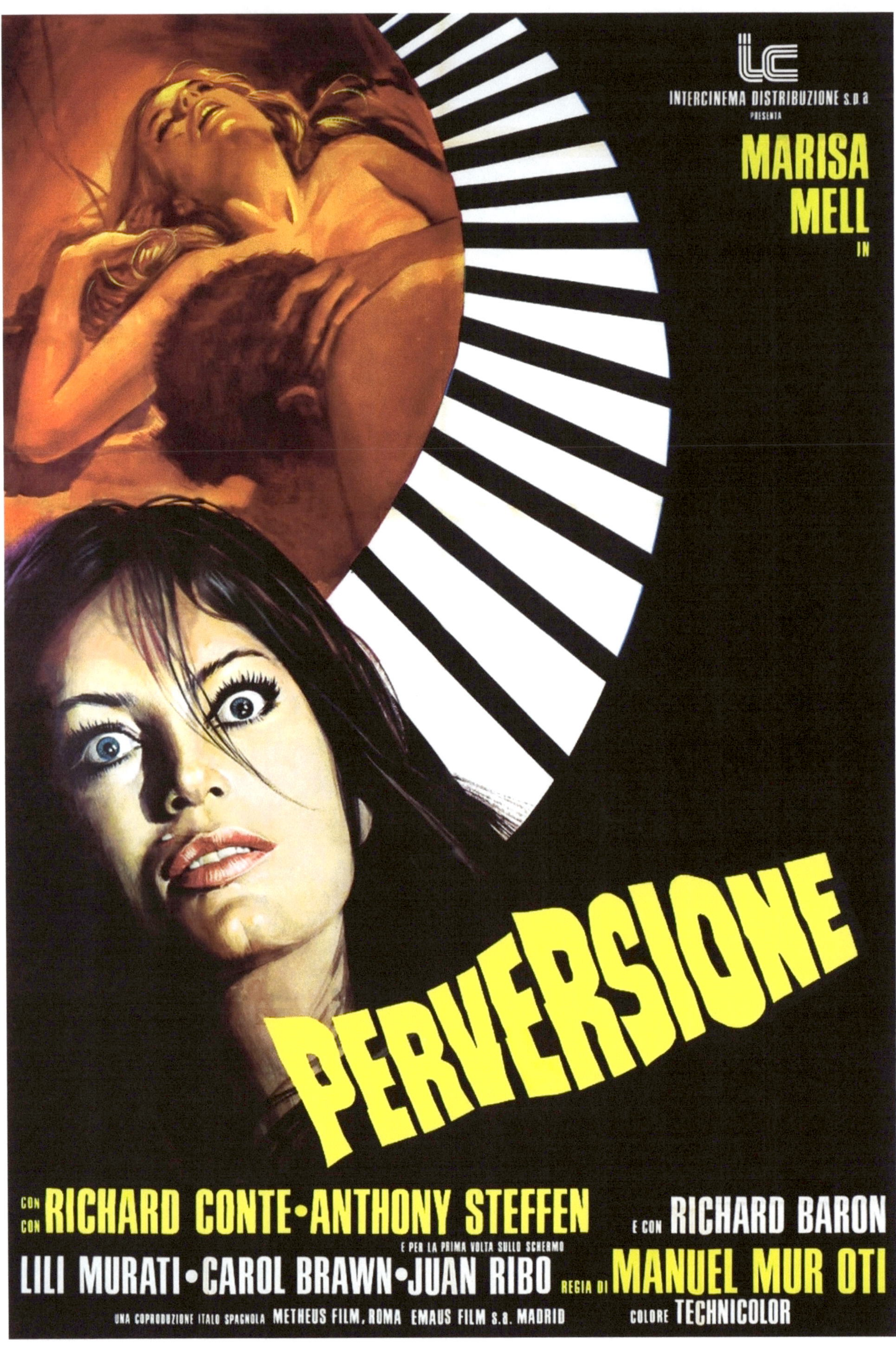

PERVERSIONE

("Perversion"; Italy/Spain, 1974). Artist: unsigned.

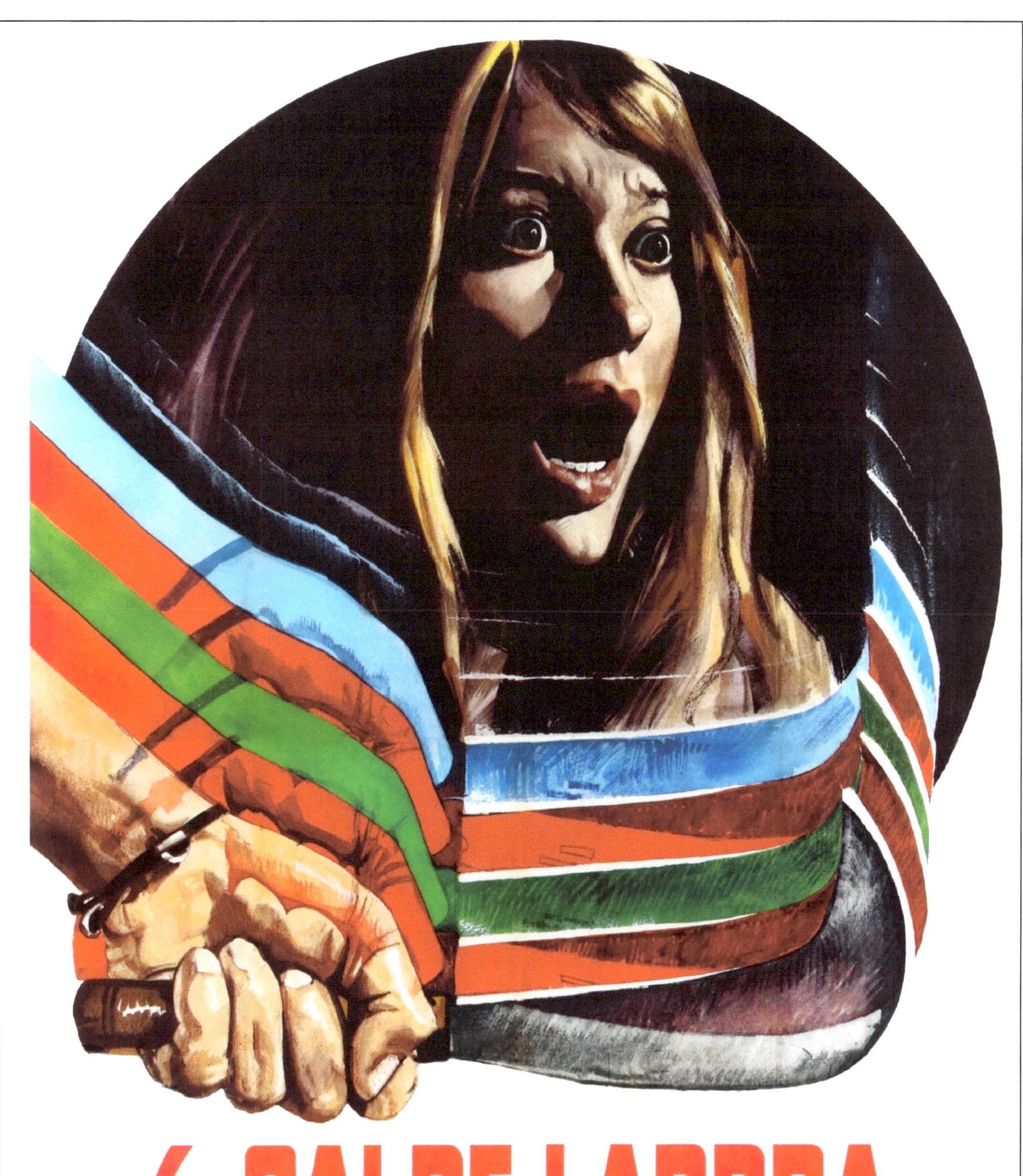

LE CALDE LABBRA DEL CARNEFICE
("Hot Lips Of The Executioner"; Italy/Spain, 1974). Artist: unsigned.

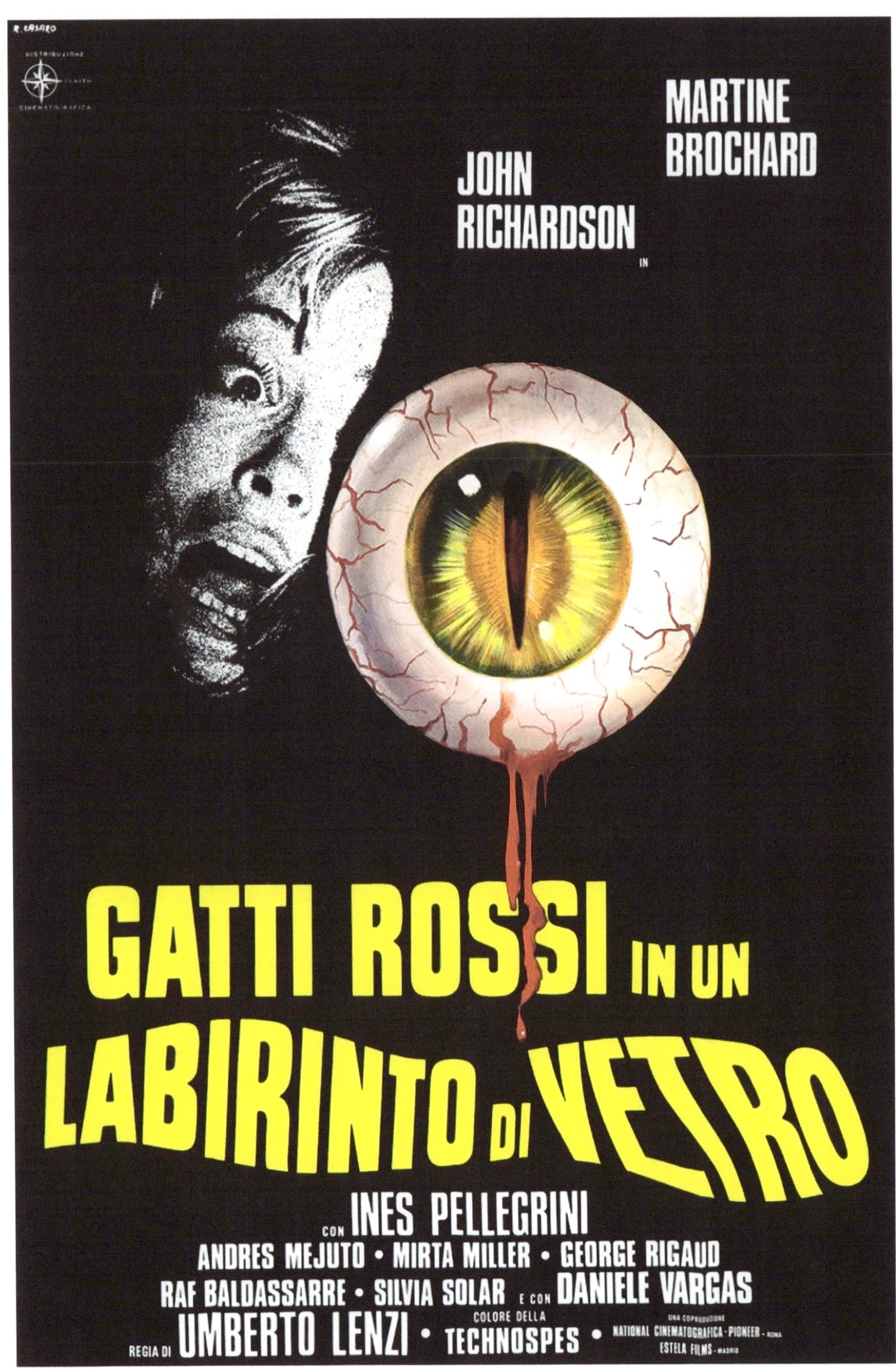

GATTI ROSSI IN UN LABIRINTO DI VETRO

("Red Cats In A Glass Labyrinth"; Italy/Spain, 1975). Artist: Renato Casaro.

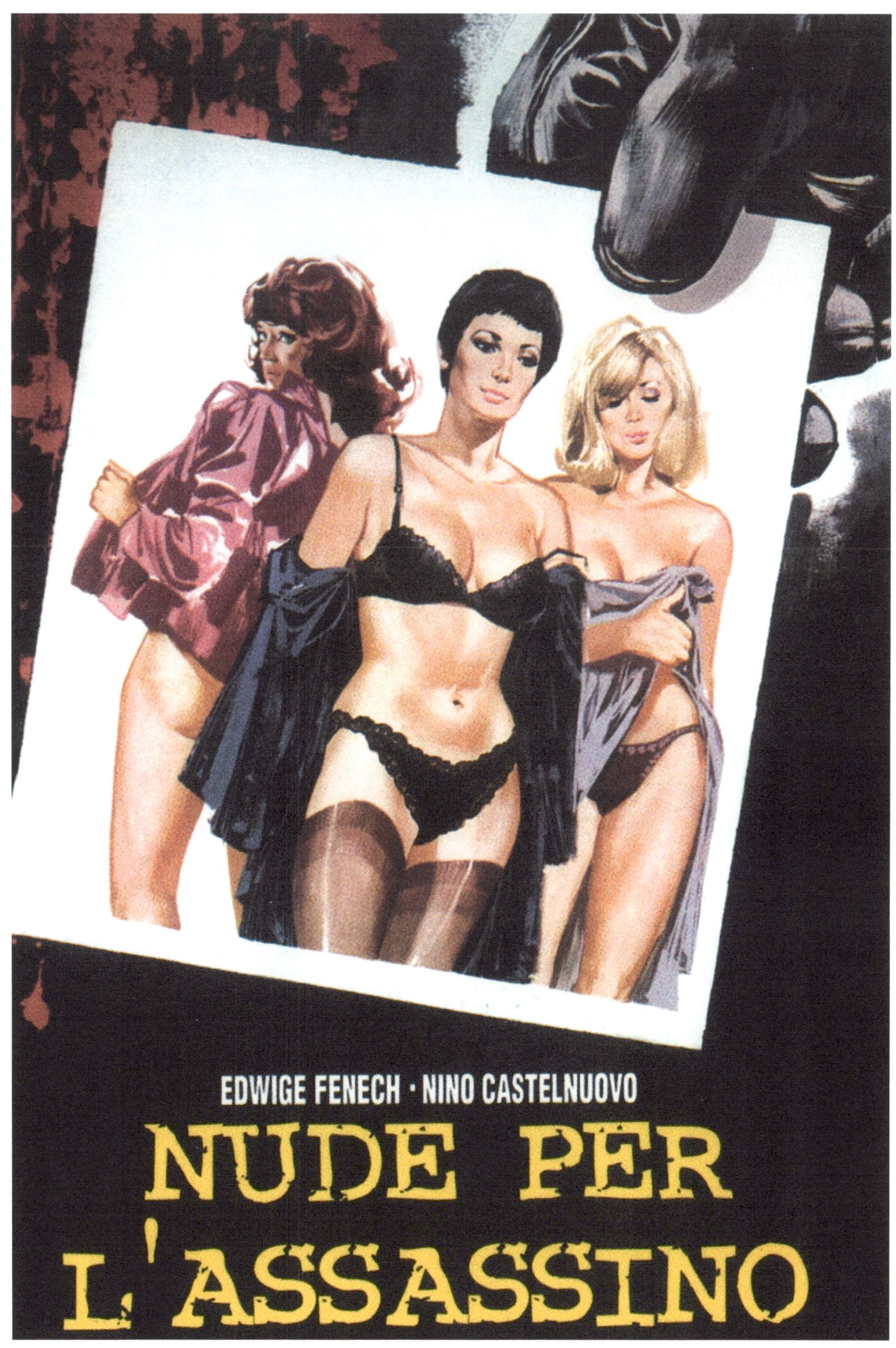

NUDE PER L'ASSASSINO
("Naked For The Killer"; Italy, 1975). Artist: unsigned.

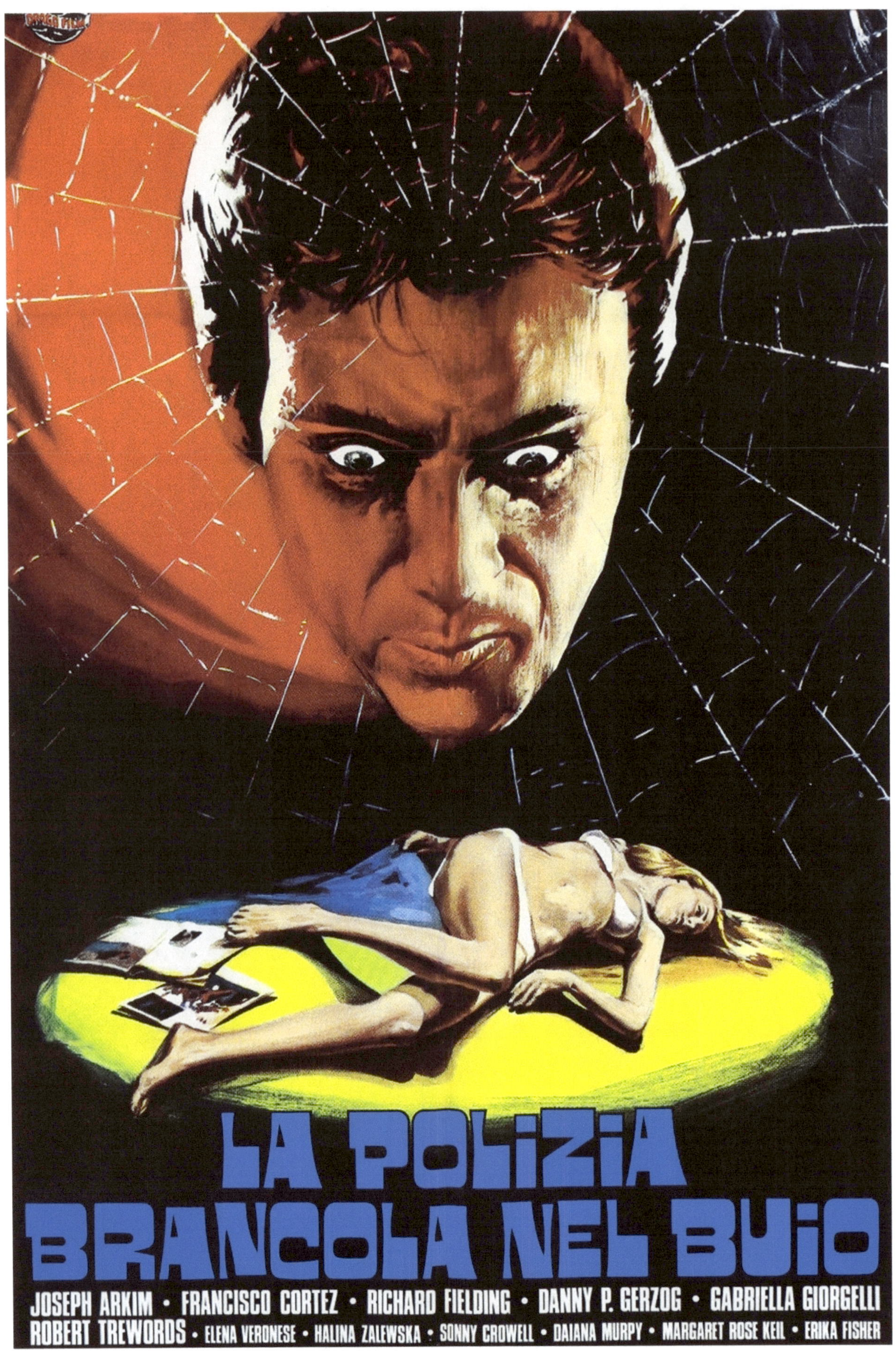

LA POLIZIA BRANCOLA NEL BUIO

("The Police Are Groping In The Dark"; Italy, 1975). Artist: unsigned.

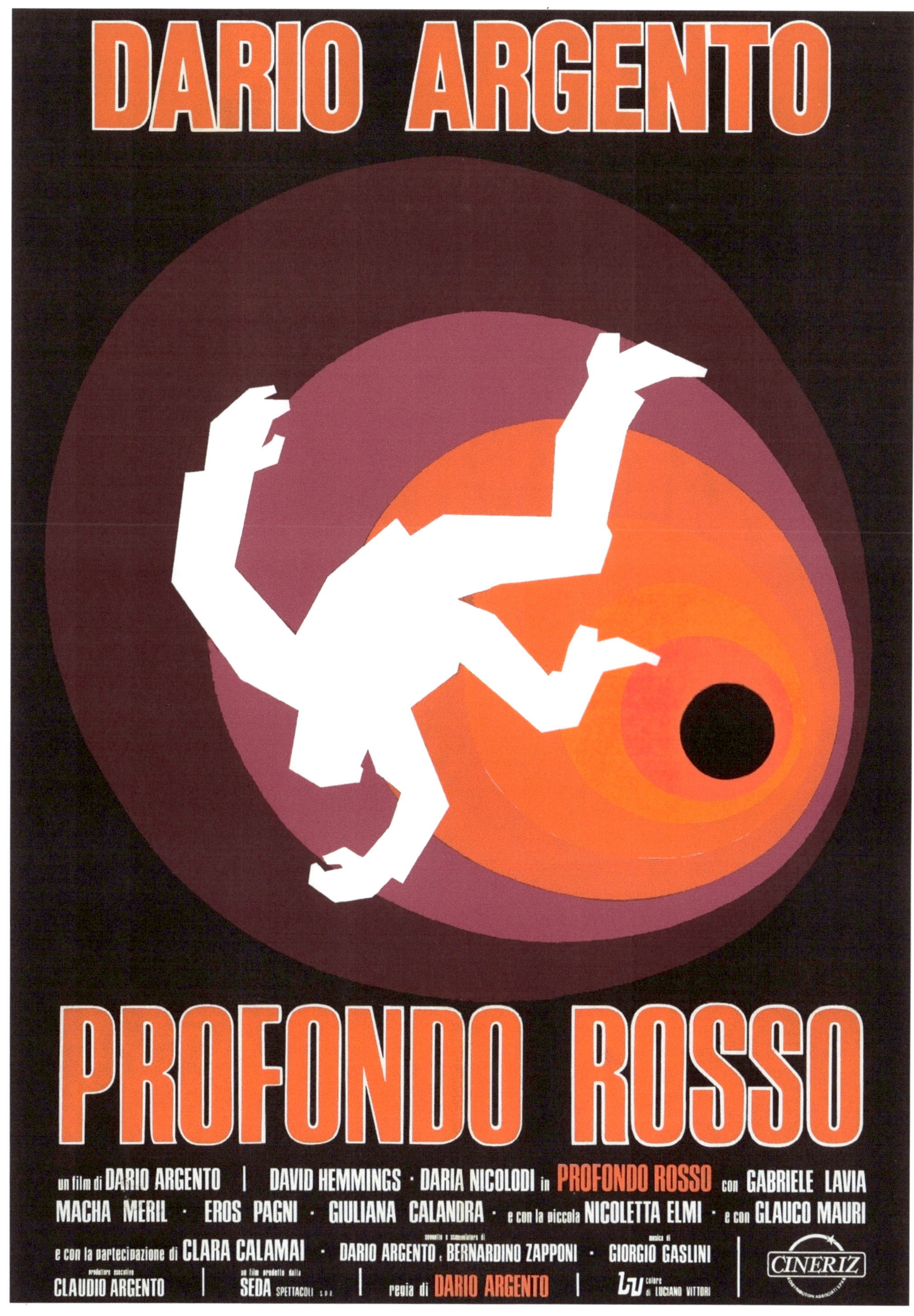

PROFONDO ROSSO

("Deep Red"; Italy, 1975). Artist: unsigned.

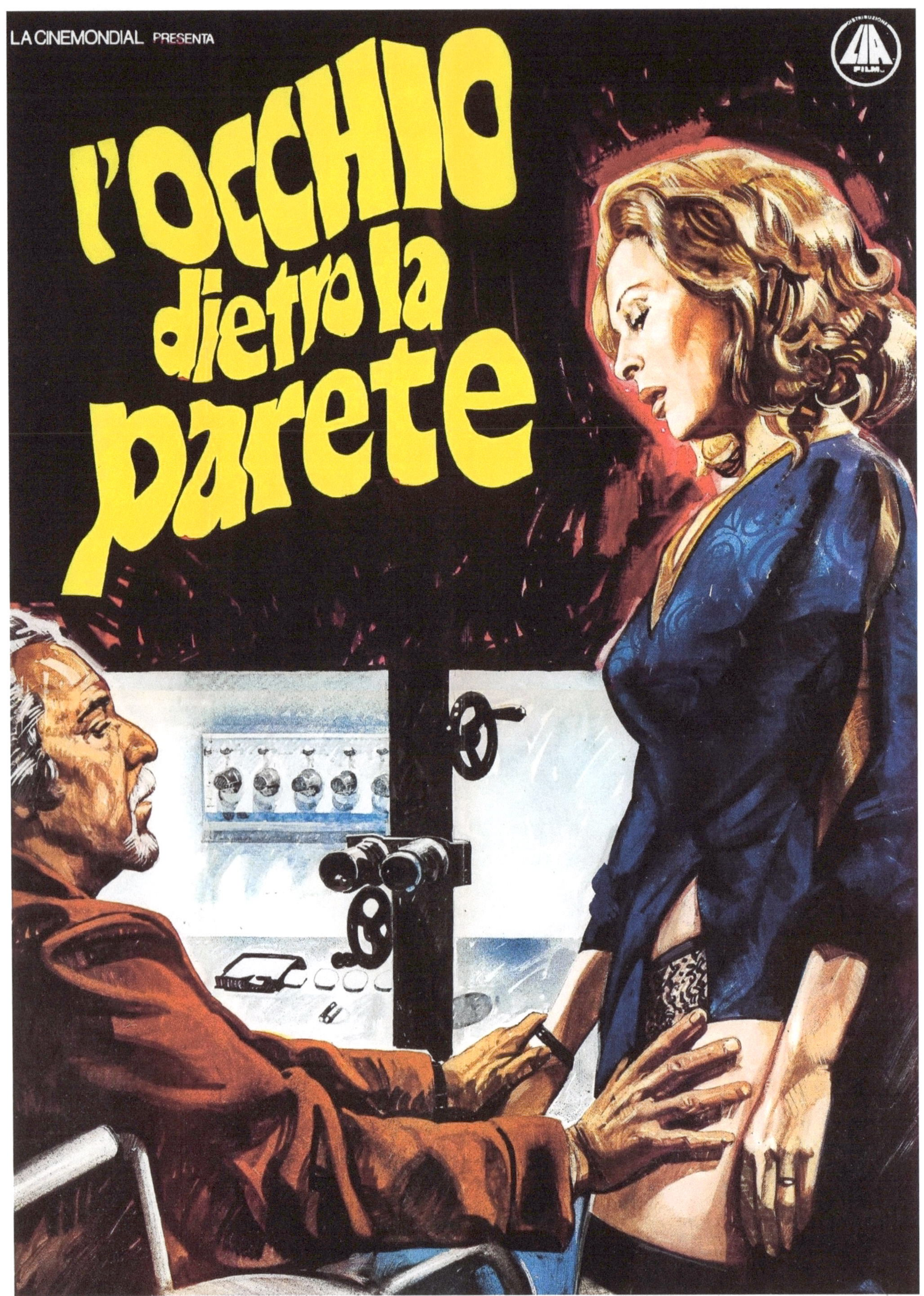

L'OCCHIO DIETRO LA PARETE

("The Eye Behind The Wall"; Italy, 1977). Artist: unsigned.

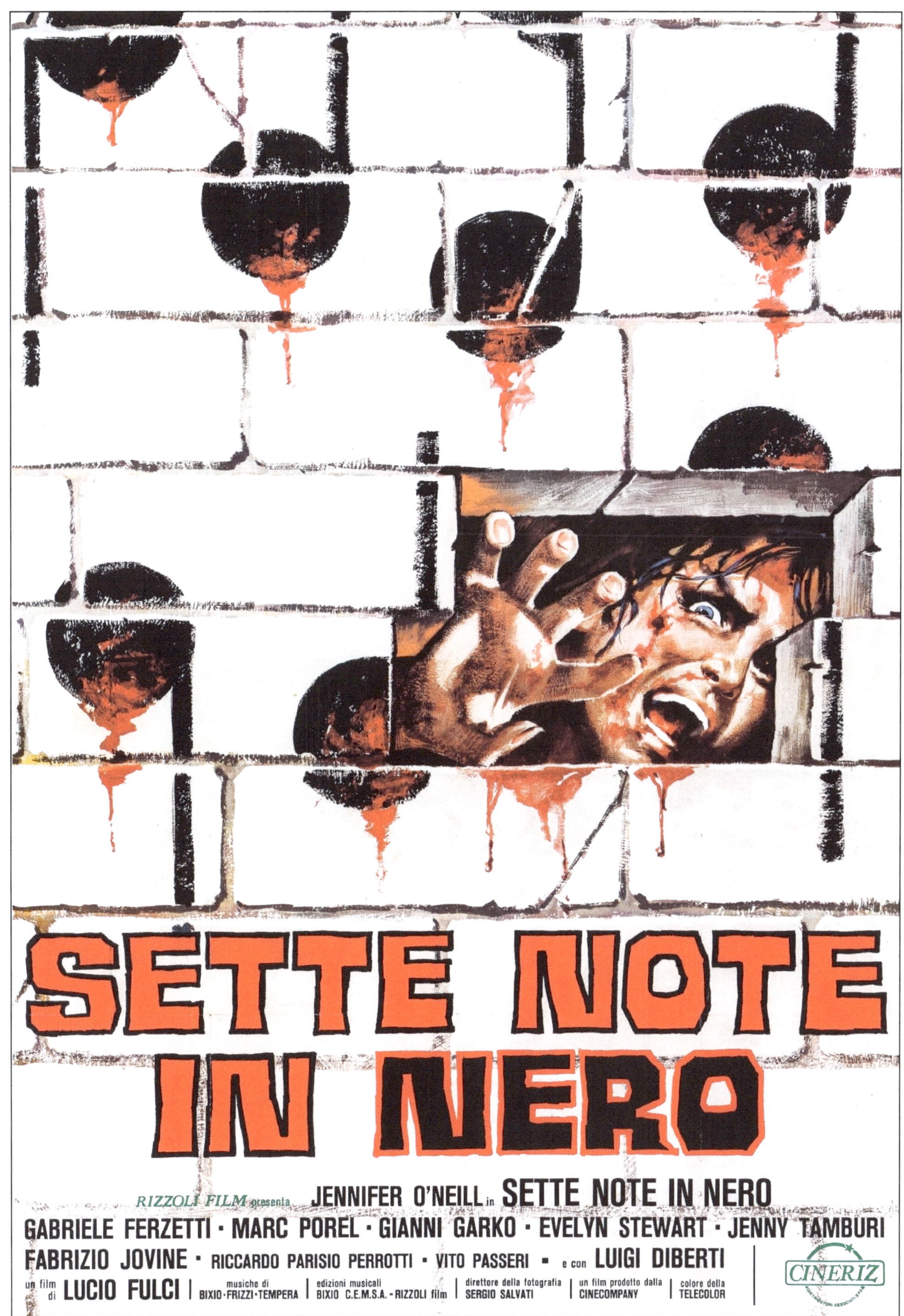

SETTE NOTE IN NERO

("Seven Notes In Black"; Italy, 1977). Artist: unsigned.

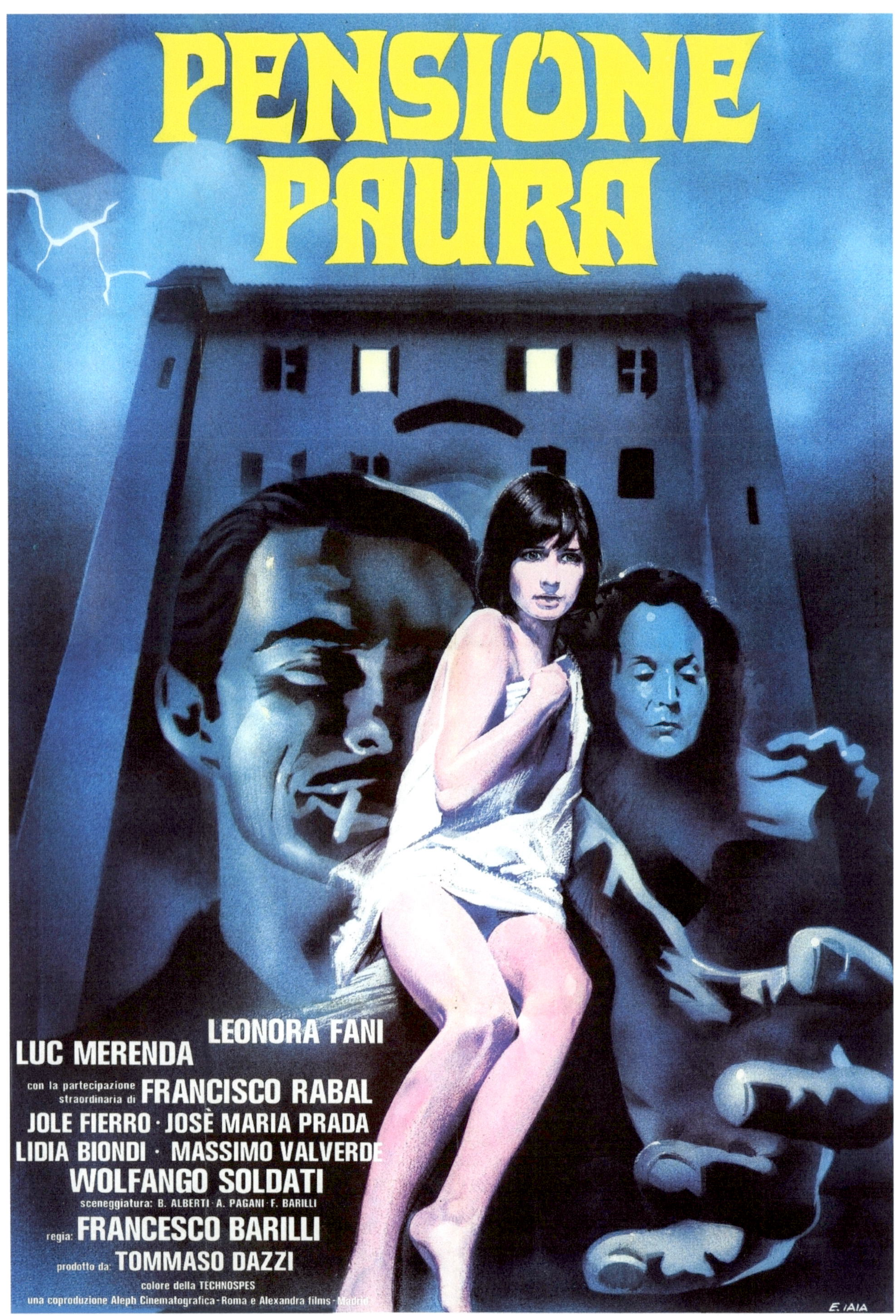

PENSIONE PAURA

("Hotel Fear"; Italy/Spain, 1978). Artist: Ermanno Iaia.

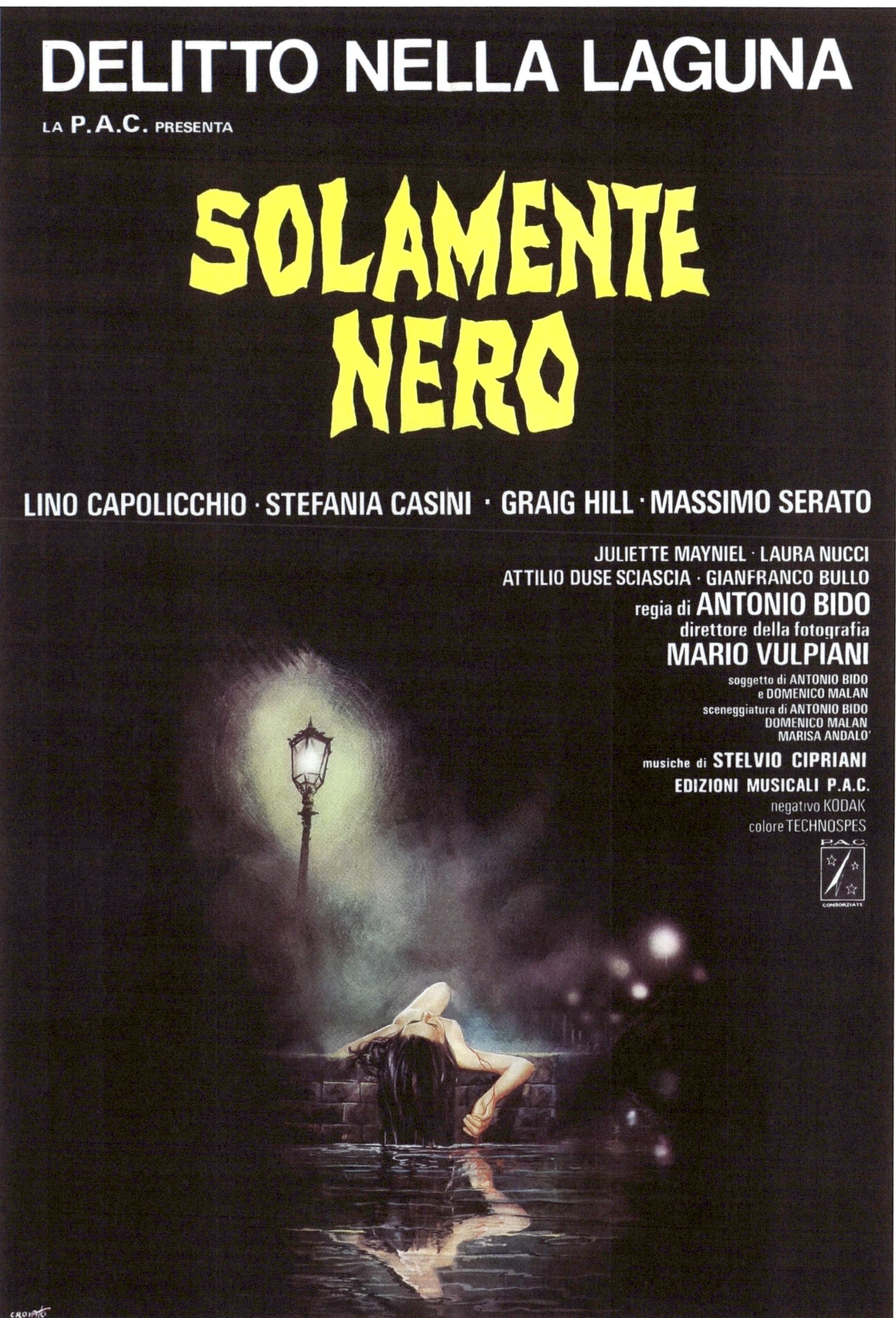

SOLAMENTE NERO
("Absolute Black"; Italy, 1978). Artist: Luca Crovato.

ALSO BY G.H. JANUS

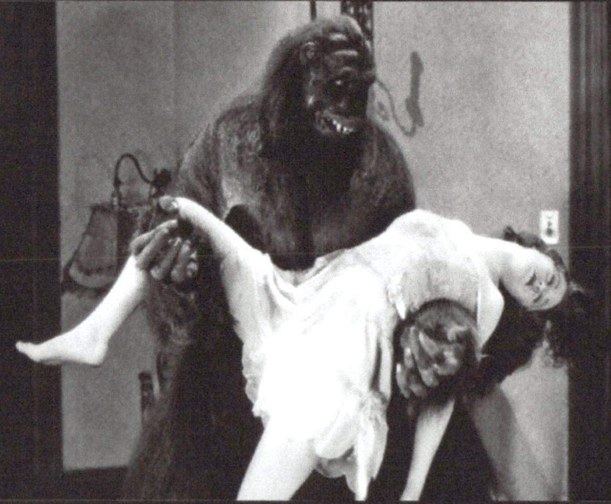

BEASTS AND BEAUTIES
CINEMA'S GOLDEN AGE OF GORILLA MEN, KILLER APES & MISSING LINKS

A major source of inspiration for early film-makers was provided by the often grotesque mystery-horror tales of Edgar Allan Poe, notably "The Murders In The Rue Morgue" (1841), not only a prototype of the modern detective story but also the debut of another vivid cultural trope, the killer ape – in Poe's tale, a trained orang-utan that slashes the throats of its female human victims to the bloody bone. Usually portrayed by actors in costume or heavy prosthetics, early cinema's killer apes were soon joined by rampaging gorillas – either jungle-wild, circus-tamed or trained to serve wicked masters – and even a rising crop of ape-human hybrids, either evolutionary "missing links" or creatures spawned by medical experimentation and radical surgeries. While the first examples of these engineered anomalies tended to be the subject of absurdist comedies, later films would posit them as murderous haunters of the shadows.

Another key inspiration for this body of cinema was the populist trope of gorillas as abductors and ravishers of human females, a fear which arose from early European expeditions into Africa. This idea found its apex expression in RKO's King Kong (1932) – with Fay Wray as the blonde snatched away by a giant ape – while its unspoken logical conclusion, a grotesque miscegenation of species, was shown in the infamous Ingagi (1931).

Charles Gemora, Ray "Crash" Corrigan, Emil Van Horn and Hollywood's other delinquent gorilla men – seen in feature films, shorts and serials alike – persisted into the 1940s and only began to slow with the mass advent of colour cinema, marking the period up until 1949 as the golden age of beasts and beauties. This book documents that period with an annotated filmography of informative texts and a stunning array of over

CRYPT OF CARNAL TERRORS
100 ARTWORKS FOR ITALIAN HORROR & GIALLO FILM POSTERS

Classic Italian film poster art is renowned as being among the most accomplished, creative and dynamic of its kind. From the post-war period through to the 1980s, Italian artists consistently produced posters with sumptuously stunning designs and imagery – not least in the horror and giallo genres, for which compositions almost invariably included curvaceous female figures in jeopardy, juxtaposed with the iconography of blood and terror.

Crypt Of Carnal Terrors is a book volume that showcases 100 classic artworks crafted for film posters by a wide range of acclaimed Italian artists, created for both indigenous and foreign-language film productions. Classic horror and giallo scenes figure in full-color, full-page images highlighting some of the world's most innovative and seductive movie poster art.

Edited by G.H. Janus.

ISBN 978-1-838-3595-2-2

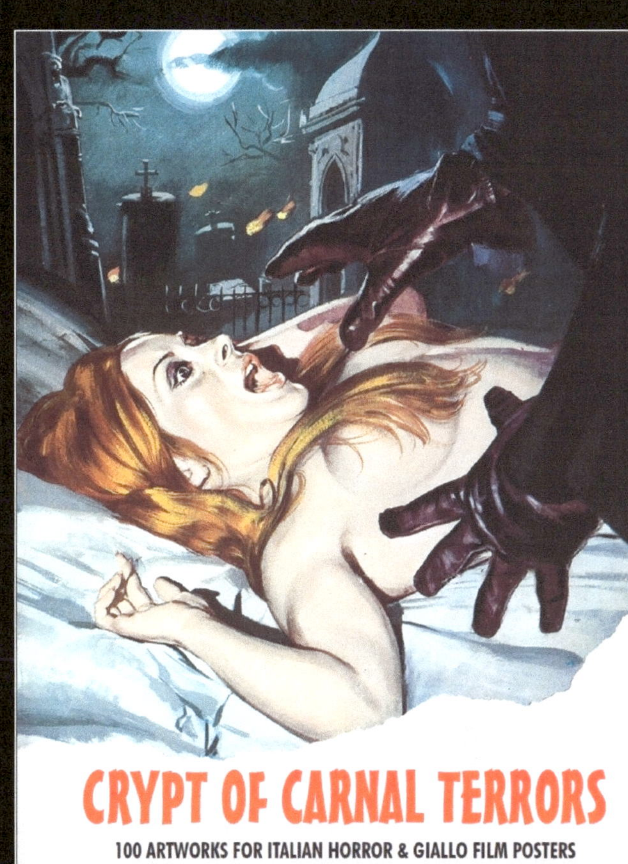

TERRORS FROM WORLDS UNKNOWN
150 CLASSIC SCIENCE FICTION FILM POSTERS FROM ITALY

Classic Italian film poster art is renowned as being among the most innovative, creative and dynamic of its kind. From the post-war period through to early 1990s, Italian artists consistently produced posters with sumptuously stunning designs and seductive imagery – not least in the science fiction genre, for which compositions often included curvaceous female figures in jeopardy, juxtaposed with the iconography of unreal terrors.

Terrors From Worlds Unknown collects 150 science fiction film posters by a wide range of acclaimed Italian artists, created for both indigenous and world-wide film productions. The collection features full-color, full-page reproductions illustrating classic SF tropes from space exploration and alien invasions to aberrant experimentation and bizarre human mutations, as well as science fantasy sub-genres such as lost worlds, giant monsters and fumetto-inspired superhero narratives. **Terrors From Worlds Unknown** presents a vivid pictorial history of science fiction cinema expressed in its most immediate and eye-catching form.

Edited by G.H. Janus.

ISBN 978-1-8383595-3-9

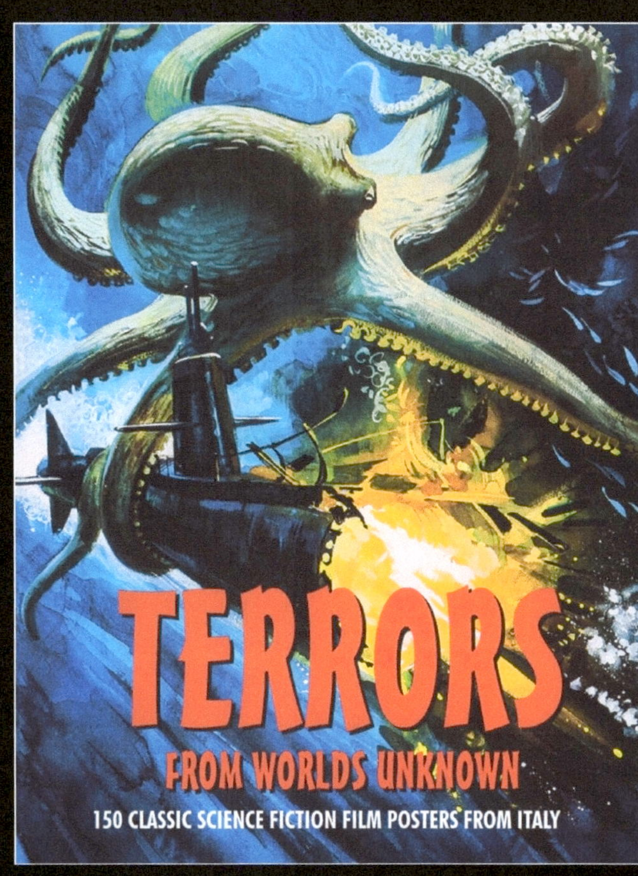

ALSO FROM BONEFYRE BOOKS

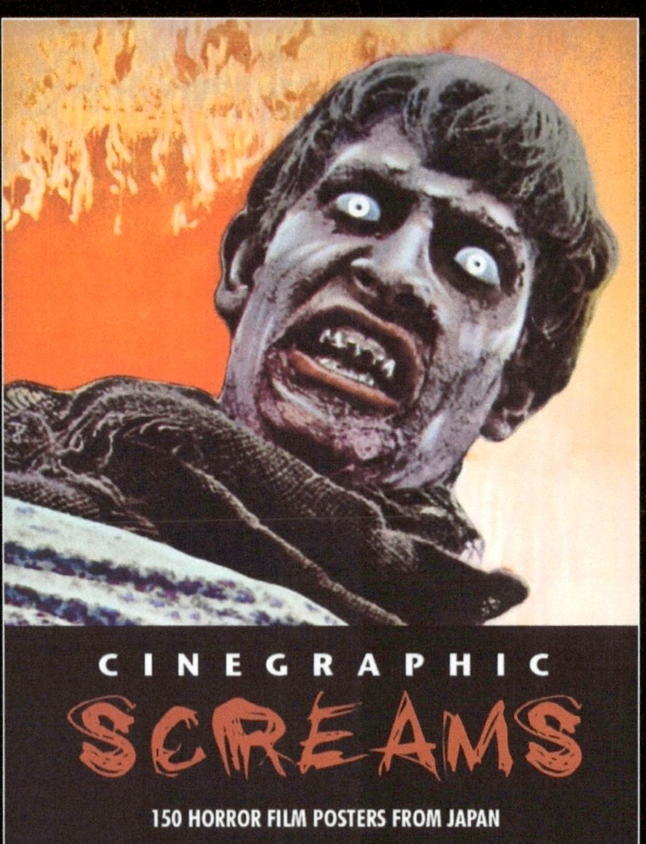

CINEGRAPHIC SCREAMS
150 HORROR FILM POSTERS FROM JAPAN

Film poster art and design from Japan is renowned as being among the most striking and dynamic in the world, with kanji logograms adding an extra dimension of graphic integration for the Western eye.

CINEGRAPHIC SCREAMS presents 150 of the very best horror film posters created in Japan in the latter decades of the 20th century, the peak years of creativity for this art-form. This volume focuses on posters designed to promote international productions.

The artworks are reproduced in full-colour, full-page format, with films ranging from classic American horror to gothic Hammer phantasies and gore-splattered Italian cine-nightmares of cannibalism and zombie mayhem.

Edited by Kagami Jigoku Kobayashi.

ISBN 978-1-8383595-5-3

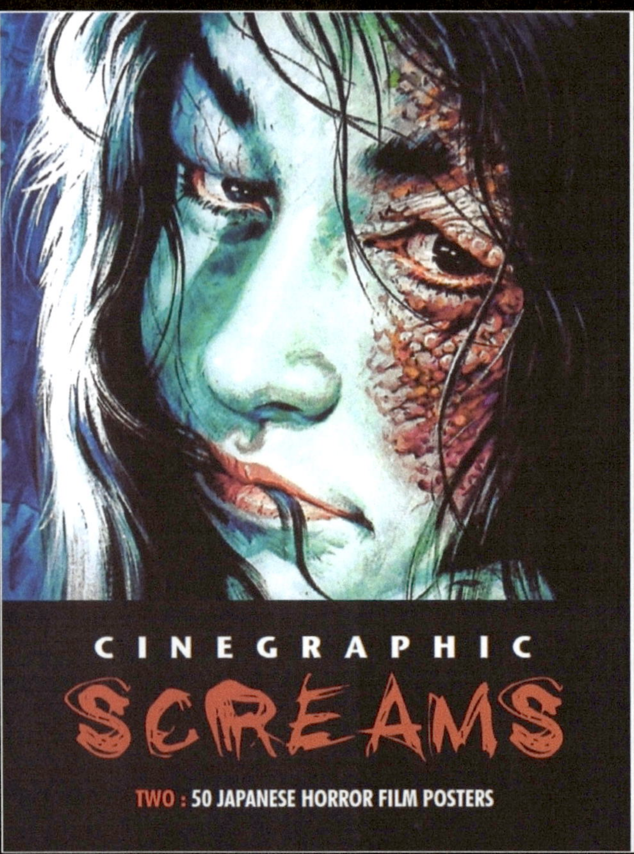

CINEGRAPHIC SCREAMS 2
50 JAPANESE HORROR FILM POSTERS

Film poster art and design from Japan is renowned as being among the most striking and dynamic in the world, with kanji logograms adding an extra dimension of graphic integration for the Western eye.

CINEGRAPHIC SCREAMS 2 presents 50 of the very best horror film posters created in Japan in the latter decades of the 20th century, the peak years of creativity for this art-form. This volume focuses on posters designed to promote indigenous Japanese productions.

The artworks are reproduced in full-colour, full-page format, with films ranging from classic interpretations of Japanese ghost stories to more modern variations steeped in visceral terror.

Edited by Kagami Jigoku Kobayashi.

ISBN 978-1-8383595-6-0

ALSO FROM BONEFYRE BOOKS

TEENAGE TIMBERWOLVES: LUST FOR LIGHTNING

In 1795, the survivors of a murderous torture orgy at a remote French castle were attacked by rabid wolves. Badly bitten, Guillaume Garou surfaced a century later as a necrophagous cannibal in New Orleans, where he was recruited by white knights to carry out acts of atrocity and carnage. Now, after another hundred years have elapsed, he emerges as Billy Timberwolf, a shaman of electric corpse magick and leader of a lightning-addicted gang of graveyard shape-shifters, roaming the southern states in search of flesh and bones and vying for survival in a nightmarish grindhouse underworld of vampiric sex covens, serial killers, hellfire lunatics, sadistic bounty-hunters, acid-damaged circus freaks, and the resurrected spectres of his former masters.

A color graphic novel by Daniele Serra and James Havoc. 100 pages.

New edition including bonus strip **Dead Black Bones Of Idiot Bill**.

Foreword by G.H. Janus.

ISBN 978-1-838-3595-4-6

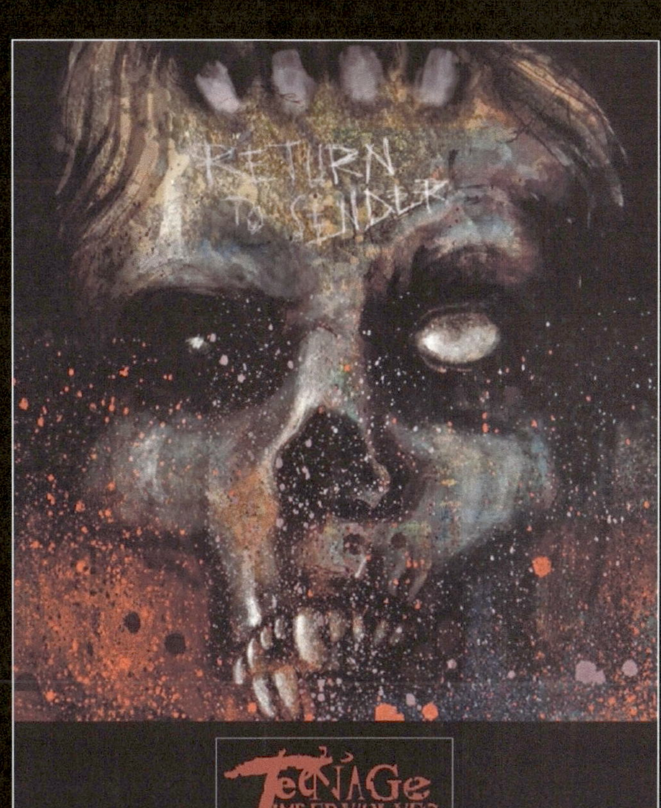

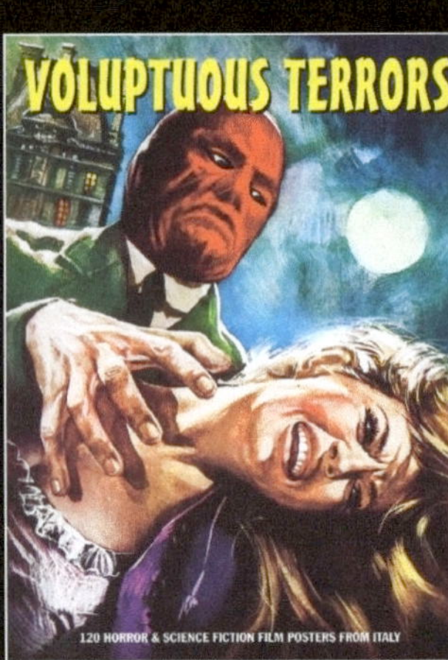
VOLUPTUOUS TERRORS
120 HORROR & SCIENCE FICTION FILM POSTERS FROM ITALY

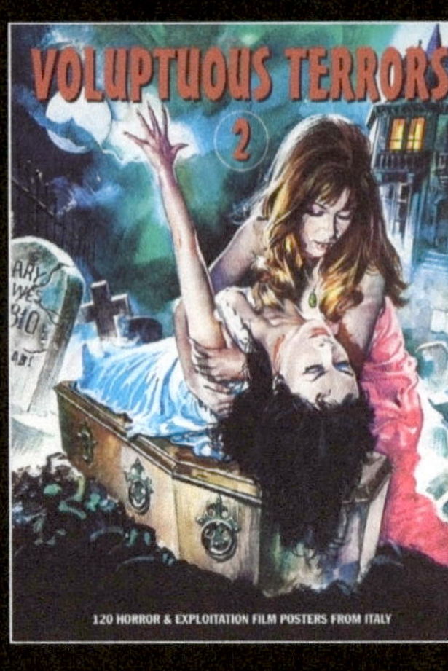
VOLUPTUOUS TERRORS
2
120 HORROR & EXPLOITATION FILM POSTERS FROM ITALY

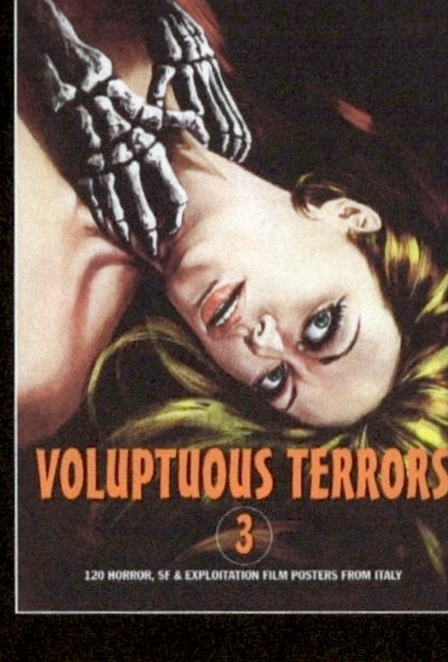
VOLUPTUOUS TERRORS
3
120 HORROR, SF & EXPLOITATION FILM POSTERS FROM ITALY

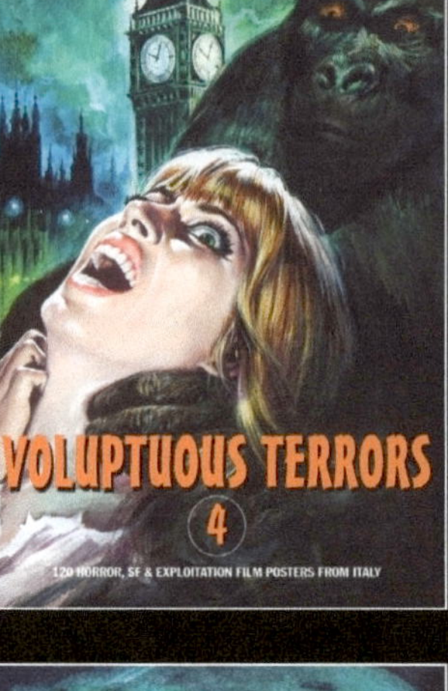
VOLUPTUOUS TERRORS
4
120 HORROR, SF & EXPLOITATION FILM POSTERS FROM ITALY

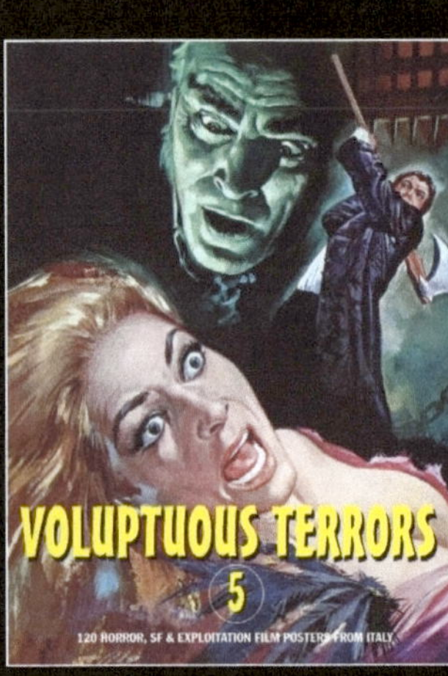
VOLUPTUOUS TERRORS
5
120 HORROR, SF & EXPLOITATION FILM POSTERS FROM ITALY

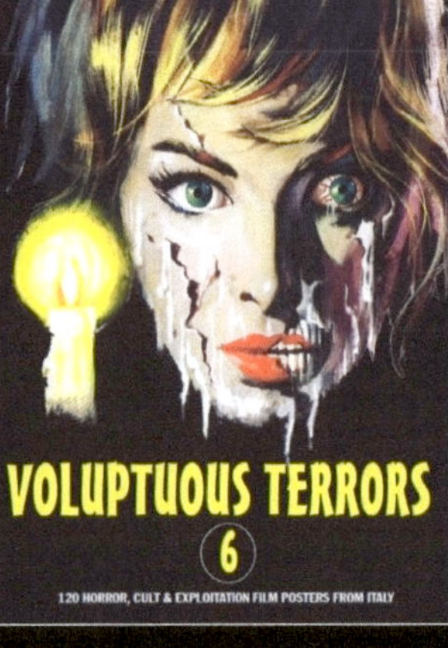
VOLUPTUOUS TERRORS
6
120 HORROR, CULT & EXPLOITATION FILM POSTERS FROM ITALY

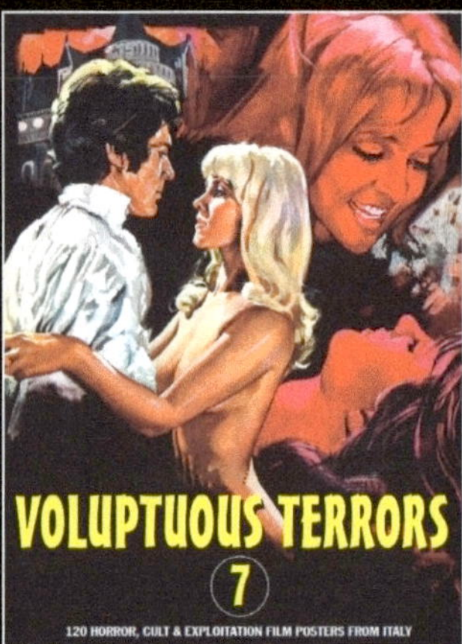
VOLUPTUOUS TERRORS
7
120 HORROR, CULT & EXPLOITATION FILM POSTERS FROM ITALY

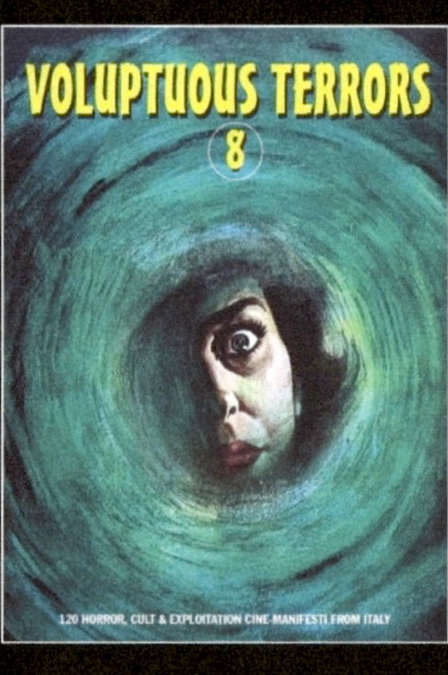
VOLUPTUOUS TERRORS
8
120 HORROR, CULT & EXPLOITATION CINE MANIFESTI FROM ITALY

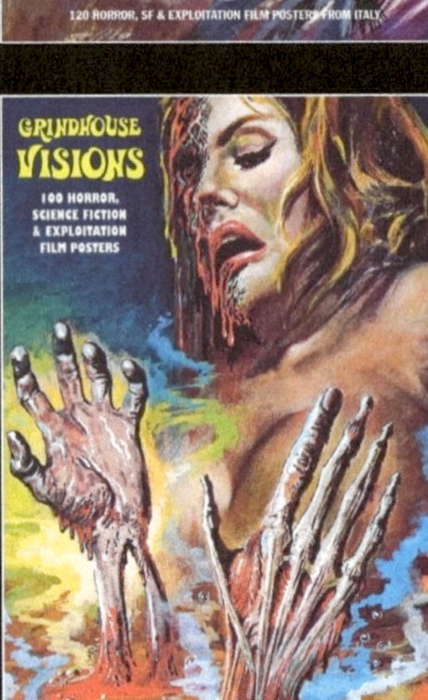
GRINDHOUSE VISIONS
100 HORROR, SCIENCE FICTION & EXPLOITATION FILM POSTERS

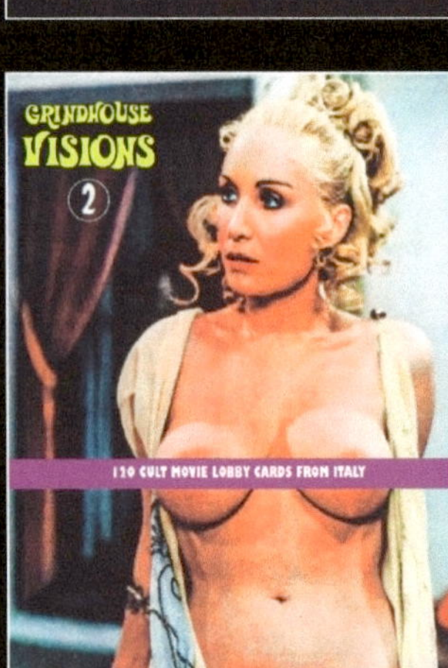
GRINDHOUSE VISIONS
2
110 CULT MOVIE LOBBY CARDS FROM ITALY

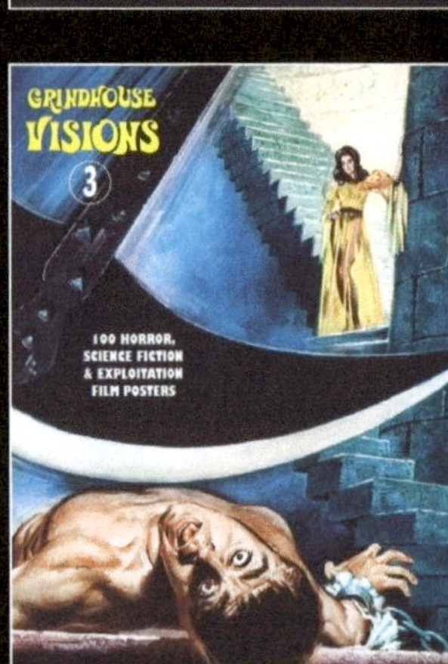
GRINDHOUSE VISIONS
3
100 HORROR, SCIENCE FICTION & EXPLOITATION FILM POSTERS

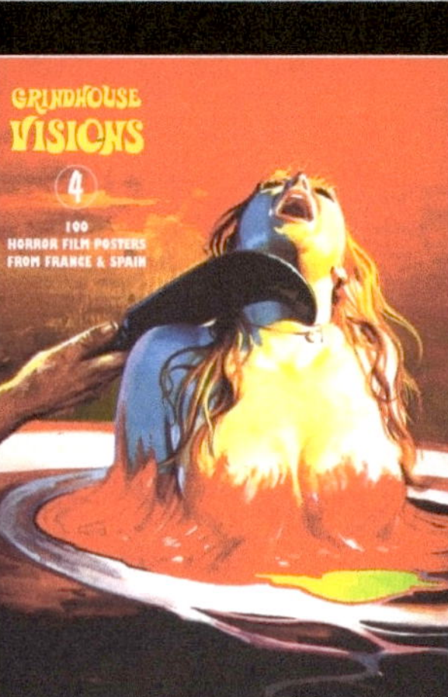
GRINDHOUSE VISIONS
4
100 HORROR FILM POSTERS FROM FRANCE & SPAIN

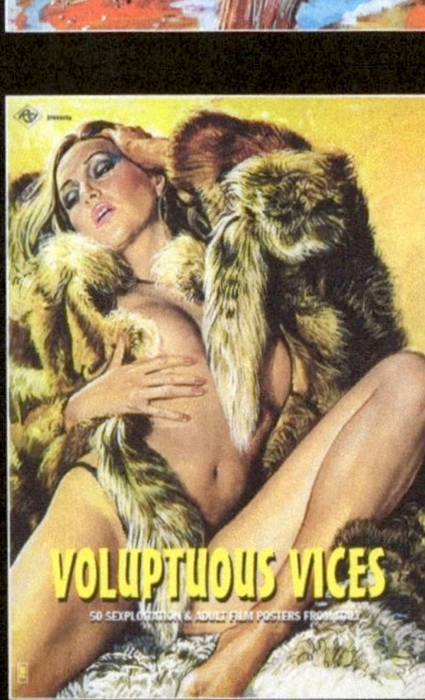
VOLUPTUOUS VICES
50 SEXPLOITATION & ADULT FILM POSTERS FROM ITALY

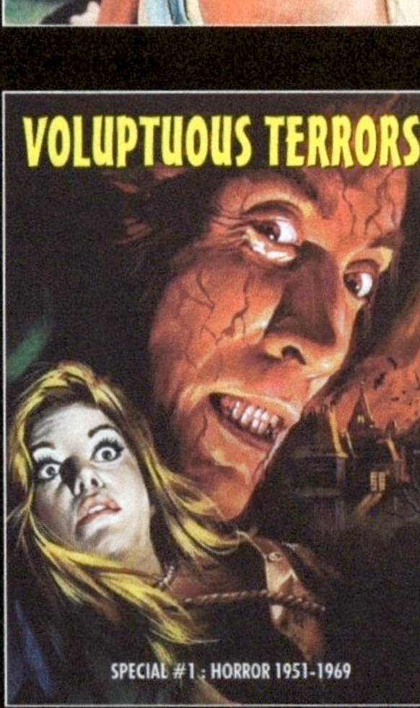
VOLUPTUOUS TERRORS
SPECIAL #1 : HORROR 1951-1969

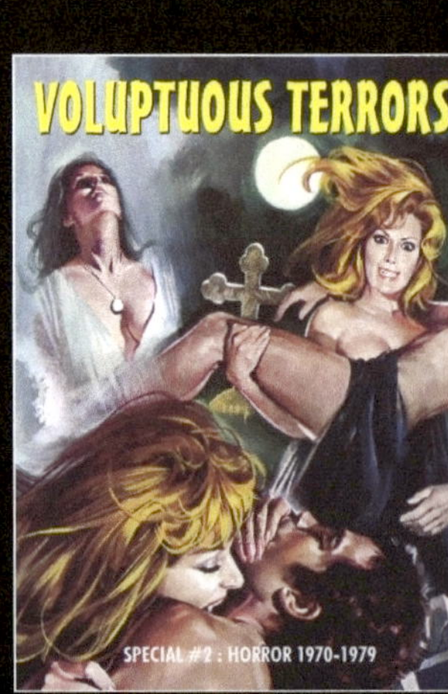
VOLUPTUOUS TERRORS
SPECIAL #2 : HORROR 1970-1979

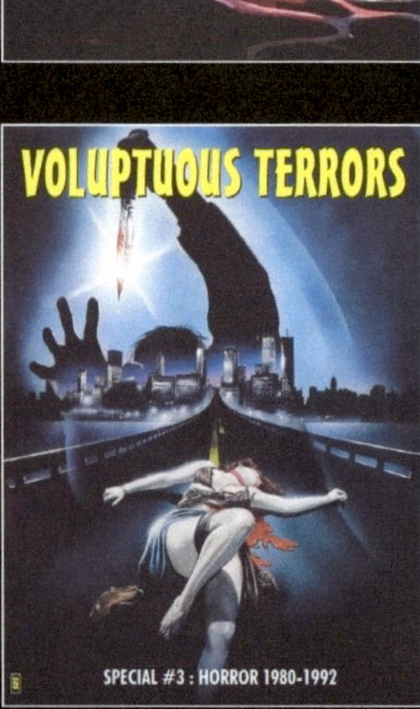
VOLUPTUOUS TERRORS
SPECIAL #3 : HORROR 1980-1992

www.ingramcontent.com/pod-product-compliance
Lightning Source LLC
Chambersburg PA
CBHW042110030726
47599CB00002B/164